Contents

Carolyn G. Heilbrun
Feminist in a Tenured Position

Carolyn G. Heilbrun

Feminist in a Tenured Position

SUSAN KRESS

UNIVERSITY OF VIRGINIA PRESS
Charlottesville and London

Acknowledgments for copyrighted material appear on pages ix and x.

University of Virginia Press
© 1997 by Susan Kress
Epilogue © 2005 by Susan Kress
All rights reserved
Printed in the United States of America on acid-free paper

1 3 5 7 9 8 6 4 2

First paperback edition published 2005
ISBN 0-8139-2536-3 (paper)

The Library of Congress has cataloged the hardcover edition as follows:

Library of Congress Cataloging-in-Publication Data

Kress, Susan, 1944–
    Carolyn G. Heilbrun, feminist in a tenured position / Susan Kress.
        p.   cm. — (Feminist issues)
    Includes bibliographical references (p.   ) and index.
    ISBN 0-8139-1751-4 (cloth: alk. paper)
    1. Heilbrun, Carolyn G., 1926– —Biography.   2. Women authors, American—
20th century—Biography.   3. Feminism and literature—United States—History—20th
century.   4. Women and literature—United States—History—20th century.   5. Criticism—United States—History—20th century.   6. Feminists—United States—Biography.
I. Title.   II. Series: Feminist issues (Charlottesville, Va.)
    PS3558.E4526Z75   1997
    813'.54—dc21
    [B]   97-8827
                                                                                              CIP

Frontispiece: *Departure*, Ruth Weisberg, 1988, lithograph

For my daughter Emma Carolyn
and in memory of her grandmother
Debbie Rose, 1920–1980

Acknowledgments

I have incurred many debts in the process of writing this book; at last there is a place to record them.

I want to thank those who agreed to talk to me about Carolyn Heilbrun: Wellesley alumnae Carol Logan Barnes, Helen Mary Ignatius Dlouhy, Sylvia Crane Eisenlohr, Nancy Posmantur Golden, Ann Hartman, Nan Weiser Ignatius, and Rose Wind Stone; Heilbrun's friends from Columbia graduate school days, Tom Driver and Robert Pack; colleagues from the Modern Language Association, Joel Conarroe, Phyllis Franklin, and English Showalter; Columbia graduate students past and present, Alicia Carroll, Susan Fraiman, Jonathan Gill, Beth Harrison, Susan Heath, Susan Nerheim, Victoria Rosner, Miranda Sherwin, and Margaret Vandenburg; team-teaching colleagues Nancy K. Miller and Judith Resnik; Columbia colleagues Joan Ferrante, Jean Franco, Robert Hanning, Betty Jemmott, David Kastan, and Steven Marcus; and professional colleagues Barbara Christian, Rachel Blau DuPlessis, Susan Stanford Friedman, Sandra M. Gilbert, Susan Gubar, and Catharine Stimpson. All took time from busy schedules to speak with me and patiently answer follow-up questions; many dipped into old files to confirm dates, find references or letters, recall class notes or the minutes of ancient committee meetings; and several sent me articles or pointed me in the direction of new sources.

I owe a special debt to Carolyn Heilbrun herself, who generously agreed to speak with me on a number of occasions, sent me manuscripts, résumés, and copies of her books, and was never too busy to respond to a question. She has graciously granted permission for me to quote from our interviews, her letters, unpublished manuscripts, speeches, and published works. Heilbrun first saw my manuscript only when it was ready for delivery to the publisher, at which point she recommended correction of a handful of factual errors.

I have profited from the assistance of a number of librarians and archivists. At Wellesley College, Wilma Slaight, Director of College Archives, prepared so carefully for my Wellesley visit that I was able to make the most productive use of my time; Jean Berry, Archives Assistant, tirelessly checked and rechecked references for me. Thanks are also due to the staff of Columbia's Columbiana Collection, Hollee Haswell, Rhea Pliakas, and Paul Palmer; to Jean Ashton and Bernard Crystal of Columbia's Rare Book and Manuscript Library; to Leslie Bernstein, Editor of *Columbia Magazine;* to R. Keith Walton, Secretary of Columbia University; and to Tom Mathewson and Susan Cahn of Columbia's Senate Office. I gratefully acknowledge the permission I have received to reprint photographs and to quote from various documents in the Wellesley and Columbia collections. From Wellesley College I have permission to quote from the *Annual Reports Number of the Wellesley College Bulletin* (1943, 1944, 1945, 1947), the *Catalogue Number of the Wellesley College Bulletin* (1943), *Legenda, WE of Wellesley, Wellesley,* the *Wellesley Alumnae Census* (1963), the *Wellesley College News,* and *Wellesley Magazine.* The Trustees of Columbia University in the City of New York have kindly granted permission for me to quote from *Columbia, Columbia Alumni News,* the *Columbia Daily Spectator, Columbia University Bulletin of Information* (1953, 1954), *Columbia University Forum, Focus, Jester,* and *Quarto.* Finally, I am indebted to the staff of the Skidmore College library, particularly Marilyn Sheffer and Tammy Rabideau at the Inter-Library Loan Desk, who handled my persistent requests for books and articles with cheerful good grace.

A number of colleagues and friends read this book in early or later drafts. To the following, who offered corrections, advice, discussion, and support, I am deeply grateful: Sheila Berger, Jeff Berman, Terry Diggory, Judith Fetterley, Charlotte Goodman, Sarah Goodwin, Frances Hoffmann, Phyllis Roth, Joan Schulz, Meg Wolitzer, and Joanna Zangrando. Other friends whose encouragement I have relied on include Carolyn Anderson, Judi Barlow, Ralph Ciancio, Gloria DeSole, Mary Ellen Fischer, Catherine Golden, Wilma Hall, Patricia-Ann Lee, Erwin Levine, Mary Lynn, Graeme Newman, Joan Newman, Martha Rozett, and Isabelle Williams. For her help in tracking down elusive books and articles, transcribing interviews, and keeping me sane, I am in debt to Johanna Zalkind, my research assistant for 1995–96.

At Skidmore College, especially in the English Department, I am lucky to work among congenial and stimulating colleagues, whose intellectual energy has inspired and instructed me. Thanks to the generosity of enlightened administrators such as Dean Phyllis Roth, and Associate Deans Dave Burrows and Tad Kuroda, I have received a series of grants to support my research.

Acknowledgments

A book like this inevitably draws on the accomplishments of many other scholars and writers. I have recorded specific debts in my notes for this book; but I am also aware of a more general indebtedness to that community of feminist scholars whose insights have changed the terms of my thought and the arrangements of my life.

Nancy Essig, Director of the University Press of Virginia, has guided my efforts with patience and intelligence; her enthusiasm for this project has kept me going in many a moment of dejection. Special thanks are due Managing Editor Deborah Oliver for her many valuable and detailed comments on the manuscript. To the other staff members of the University Press of Virginia, I also wish to record my appreciation.

My daughter Emma was much on my mind as I wrote this book; this was a story I wanted to tell for her. The book is dedicated both to her and to my mother. My sisters, Linda Ratcliffe and Joanne Hussey, and my life-long friend, Maureen Leman, have cheered and sustained me from across the ocean. To Jack Kress, my husband and partner, I owe the deepest debt of thanks. He has read drafts, argued points, and offered wise counsel—always with unwavering support for me and for the work I have chosen.

Introduction

> There are four ways to write a woman's life: the woman
> herself may tell it, in what she chooses to call an auto-
> biography; she may tell it in what she chooses to call
> fiction; a biographer, woman or man, may write the
> woman's life in what is called a biography; or the
> woman may write her own life in advance of living it,
> unconsciously, and without recognizing or naming the
> process.
>
> — CAROLYN G. HEILBRUN, *Writing a Woman's Life*

A young girl, Carolyn Gold, is standing before the biography section
of the St. Agnes branch of the New York Public Library. She
knows which volume she will choose next, for she has been reading the
books in strict alphabetical order; much later, she would repeatedly recall the intensity of this experience: "In my dreams to this day, I stand
before the biography shelves at St. Agnes, denying myself an attractive
book in R because I had reached only G."[1] It is worth pausing for a
moment over this dream of a younger self. The dream is American, of
course, with the shade of Benjamin Franklin hovering over the student
bent on self-improvement through discipline and self-denial. But, unlike
many such dreams, the goal is to enrich the imagination, not the pocket.
Moreover, it is not the dream we have conventionally tagged as female,
for there is no sign of a lurking prince, a ball dress, or a nicely decorated
palace with the mortgage all paid off. Instead, we are in a library named
for a virgin saint (whose rise to sainthood began with the rejection of a
bridegroom), and the dream is about shelf upon lovely shelf of books,
about dedication to the life of the mind, and about reading of the exemplary lives conjured up by other minds. For our student has a sharply
defined purpose: to read biographies, not history or fiction; and a large
ambition: to read them all, or all that are available to her. She does not

read at random, drawn by titles, names, or bright book covers, but according to a simple yet rigorous system, approaching her task with a singular determination.

All her life Heilbrun would be absorbed—one might even say obsessed—with questions of identity, especially with questions of female identity. In due course, she would study the available patterns for women's lives, investigate the ways those patterns were constructed, and propose that other patterns be devised. But for the girl who would grow up to write *Reinventing Womanhood* and *Writing a Woman's Life,* the question of identity was also a personal one. Conflicted (though perhaps not yet consciously so) about her class, her Jewish background, her assigned destiny as a woman, she needed, perhaps, to read every biography to see what lives were available to be lived, what self-inventions could be tried on, tried out.

An older Carolyn Heilbrun would unfold her selves like Russian dolls, or Chinese boxes, emerging mysteriously one from inside another. Thus Carolyn Heilbrun would triple herself to produce Amanda Cross, who would, in turn, produce Kate Fansler. Later still, Amanda Cross would create another voice in Fansler's niece, Leighton Fansler. Why did Heilbrun invent these new selves? What did they enable, what inhibit? Did they signify escape from self or exploration of the self's full possibilities? In the pages that follow, I explore the complex relations among these selves, noting the ways they grow, change, resist change, manage conflicts, write new plots, and contribute to the currents of an age in which women's ideas about their lives were being transformed.

Heilbrun's feminism first drew me to her work. In 1981, I read her Cross novel *Death in a Tenured Position,* and since I had recently achieved a tenured position myself, I now had the opportunity to think about many issues that the book raised. For the meeting of the Modern Language Association held in New York City that year, I wrote a paper on *Death in a Tenured Position,* focusing on what I perceived to be the tension at the heart of that book: whether a feminist woman could work within the (academic) establishment and whether her allegiance was due primarily to men or to women. Could a moderate line be taken? If so— or if not—what were the nature and quality of those allegiances to be? Throughout the 1970s, feminists were debating these issues; it was clear that feminists like me, with wedding rings and children, were finding it easier to survive professionally than those whose primary attachments were to women. I found my own anxiety about this mirrored in Kate Fansler and, perhaps, in Heilbrun, too.

What fascinated me at that time about Heilbrun was the fact that, although she was certainly a feminist, she was grappling with conspicuous conflicts. She had developed a voice of assurance and authority, but issues did not necessarily have easy answers for her and she was struggling for clarity. Later, I began to read other works by Heilbrun— essays, critical books, the earlier detective novels. A passage near the beginning of her book *Reinventing Womanhood* struck me with particular force: "I felt that, unlike so many of the women I had read of and known personally, I had been born a feminist and never wavered from that position. I do not mean, of course, that I expressed feminist views in the dreary masculinist years after World War II. But I never denied the pain to myself, nor lied about my anger."[2] This is no doubt true in large part, but it was not wholly satisfactory as a description of the person whose work I had been reading. From the retrospective vantage point of 1979, when *Reinventing Womanhood* was published, Heilbrun might have been able to look back upon a career that seemed to embrace feminism from the beginning—for, yes, indeed, she has been concerned about women's issues throughout her professional life. Yet to one reading Heilbrun's work in chronological order, essentially retaking the journey with her, the lines of her development are far more complex. Indeed, Heilbrun is interesting precisely because her journey toward feminism has been complicated, because she did not embrace radical views until she had struggled with them and sometimes not then, and because, as critic and as novelist, she has left such a fascinatingly detailed account of her intellectual evolution. Reading Carolyn Heilbrun is reading the narrative—not always straightforward, often elliptical, frequently shaped by conflict—of her evolution from traditional academic to courageously outspoken feminist.

Moreover, it is of particular interest to me that Heilbrun's writing life, spanning more than forty years, repeatedly brings into focus the public chronicle of this latest wave of feminism and embodies many of its debates and transformations. As we move through the fourth decade of the most recent women's movement, feminists tend toward the retrospective. A new generation has come of age, a generation that does not necessarily know either the story of the personal and political battles that have been fought or the historical context for the positions that have developed. Those of us born in the 1940s and 1950s want to take stock of the directions taken, the quality of the journey, and the prospects for the future. Carolyn Heilbrun, born in 1926 and growing up in the deadening years of women's "forfeited" selves, so graphically described by Betty Friedan in *The Feminine Mystique*,[3] beginning her professional writing career in 1957—four years after the English translation of Simone de Beauvoir's *The Second Sex* reached the bookstores—is one of the very few women of her generation to shape and be shaped by the feminist movement. She has spent most of her life within the walls of the academy, and arguably, the distinctive story of the academy over the last thirty years has been the interwoven and overlapping narratives of feminism. Heilbrun herself has consistently paid tribute to the ways she was supported and sustained by the contemporary women's movement, and yet it seems clear to me from reading her early work that she was, at least initially, temperamentally averse to political groups, and the women's movement was no exception. Her interest was in individual women, particularly distinguished women, and only subsequently was she drawn to the idea of a political movement. Of course, the fact that she embraced such a movement at all is extraordinary in one of her generation. My own mother, born six years earlier than Heilbrun, died, alas, without ever understanding her own sadness, and her story, with significant variations, mirrors that of many of the women I know or know of who were born in the 1920s and 1930s. And so one of the many puzzles that intrigued me is what, against probability and even, perhaps, inclination, drew Heilbrun to feminism after she was comfortably established as a professor at Columbia University.

Heilbrun has indeed become a prominent figure in the academy. Author of such influential (and controversial) books as *Toward a Recognition of Androgyny, Reinventing Womanhood, Writing a Woman's Life,* and *The Education of a Woman: The Life of Gloria Steinem,* she has served as president of the Modern Language Association and, before her dramatic resignation in 1992, held the prestigious Avalon Chair in the Humanities at Columbia University. Beginning with the publication of *Toward a Recognition of Androgyny,* Heilbrun wanted to make a contribution to the study of women that would unite theory and practice and also appeal to a large audience. Unlike the work of most academic critics in her field, hers is not narrowly defined as literary; even in her scholarly writing, she endeavors to cross barriers, to invade other disciplines, to avoid entanglements in the thickets of theory, and to keep her focus, above all, on women's lives, a life-long project she might first have begun to glimpse in the St. Agnes library, even though those biographies were mostly about men. But few feminist scholars have triumphed over their academic backgrounds to achieve national prominence (Kate Millett is an early and notable exception), and both *Toward a Recognition of Androgyny* and *Reinventing Womanhood,* after a flurry of attention and even controversy, seemed destined to be relegated by feminists to the margins of feminist discourse. In fact, Heilbrun's wish to appeal to a wider audience and to write the sort of clear, unmistakable prose for which English professors used to strive might even have diminished her influence within the academy. Nevertheless, as we shall see, those books constitute important documents in the contemporary debates about which feminist discourses would prevail; moreover, the ideas they set forth were often more innovative and influential than was acknowledged at the time. During the 1980s, Heilbrun's influence increased significantly, with *Writing a Woman's Life* earning a stint on best-seller lists across the country; by 1990, the publication of a selection of her essays in *Hamlet's Mother and Other Women* elevated Heilbrun to a position of considerable eminence.

As Amanda Cross, Heilbrun has appealed to a growing popular audience; indeed, the Cross novels enjoy something like a cult following. Their great triumph has been the creation of the central character: witty, urbane, feminist Kate Fansler, professor at a prestigious New York City university. If there are obvious similarities between Fansler and Heilbrun, there are also striking differences: Heilbrun is Jewish, Fansler an upper-class WASP; Heilbrun is both wife and mother, whereas Fansler, though married by the end of the third Cross novel, happily resists the temptation of children. Especially noteworthy has been the way in which Cross has constructed situations that take place not in hermetically sealed environments but that are open to the larger events and movements of history. The Vietnam War, the student protests of the 1960s, the women's movement, and Watergate all form the changing contexts against which Fansler plays out private conflicts, investigates problematic issues, and becomes increasingly politically engaged.

Meanwhile Heilbrun herself was also growing and changing. The pattern of her evolution is not necessarily typical or representative. As a white, heterosexual professor at a major university, she is undoubtedly privileged; nevertheless, the trajectory of her career, in its bold outlines, reflects the conflicts and tensions of many emerging feminists of this time. The particulars of her story are compelling: against the background of the gathering forces of the women's movement, Heilbrun, daughter of a Jewish immigrant, struggled to enter the world of letters and reconcile the claims of politics and profession even as she wrestled with her identity as Jew, as woman, as mother. In this book, I speak of her literary relationships to Virginia Woolf (whose inspiration pervades Heilbrun's work); to Dorothy L. Sayers (whose artful mysteries she emulated and whose biography she keenly wanted to write); and of her troubled and complex relationship with Lionel Trilling (who was her teacher and model for scholarly excellence but who could not acknowledge her even after she graduated from student to colleague). Like Trilling, Heilbrun aspired to become a critic of the culture and struggled to forge a voice and establish a space from which to speak. To some degree, Heilbrun's detective fiction, with its rich opportunities for inventing other selves, offered her ways to cope with her anger and to survive conflict. Indeed, the dead bodies she produces—and the villains she brands—provide a provocative subtext for her intellectual evolution. Above all, that evolution is informed by an increasingly complicated quest for self-realization. The paradoxical relationship between her conscious goal (an autonomous female self) and her conscious—and subconscious—self-splitting strategies makes for an exemplary story and places Heilbrun at the center of current theoretical debates about the nature of self.

Heilbrun has managed many roles, tried many experiments in female possibility. Indeed, she has tested self-contradiction in intriguing ways; one side of her seems always to be interrogating another, the critical intelligence always in play. She made the decision early to stay within the academy, publishing prodigiously and rising from rank to rank, and, at the same time, she pursued a parallel career as a writer of popular detective stories. I shall be interested in the fluctuating relationship between critic and fiction writer, in what one teaches the other, in the territory each charts out, and in the separate and connected stories each tells. Within the academy, Heilbrun survived and succeeded, yet mustered the courage to become increasingly provocative and radical, challenging the very establishment that had accepted her. She gained power in the profession, especially in the Modern Language Association, but not within her own institution. I trace her vexed relationship with Columbia up to her abrupt departure in 1992 and the ways her story might have more than personal reverberations. Ultimately, I am concerned with the costs of the kind of feminist life she has staked out for herself and with the nature of her contributions to the feminist conversation.

Taking Carolyn Heilbrun as my central character in this story provides the opportunity to observe changes within academic feminism and the women's movement from the point of view of the centered position Heilbrun often takes. I also place Heilbrun, from time to time, in the context of other feminists of her generation—especially Betty Friedan and Adrienne Rich—whose lives both parallel and challenge hers in important ways. Isolation has marked Heilbrun's life and, to some degree, her thought; she often chooses a solitary path, walks a little out of step, resists the rhythm of the group.

I am not writing a biography, the story of a life; rather, this is an intellectual biography, the story of a life's work. I do not deal with Heilbrun's personal life as daughter, wife, and mother, except insofar as she herself comments on these experiences in public utterances; rather, I shall be studying the emergence of a public self, the making of a cultural critic, the formation of a public intellectual. Although I certainly note some important facts in Carolyn Heilbrun's life, I read that life primarily through the various kinds of self-presentation I have observed in her work and through the political, social, and intellectual contexts in which she has developed: Wellesley in the 1940s, Columbia in the 1950s, the Modern Language Association in the 1970s and 1980s, and the women's movement in the 1960s and beyond. In Amanda Cross's tenth book, *The Players Come Again,* Kate Fansler is urged to write the biography of Gabrielle Foxx, a woman who, like Nora Joyce, was married to one of the great modernist writers. In the course of her research, Fansler comes upon an unpublished novel written by Gabrielle and ultimately decides not to write the biography but to edit and publish the novel instead. When her publisher presses her to do both the edition of the novel and the biography, she replies: "Whatever Gabrielle really was and thought, wherever she had her being apart from her obvious role as Emmanuel's wife, is in her novel. Scholars and biographers will be reconstructing her life from that novel for years to come."[4] In other words, the writing itself is of paramount importance and whatever is important is in the writing; Heilbrun (as Cross through Fansler) provides the authority for reading the intellectual life through the work.

Certainly, for Carolyn Heilbrun, work seems to be the central fact of her life. Throughout her life she has insisted that women must have access to meaningful work, and she has also, beginning with her early portrait of the prolific translator, Constance Garnett, in *The Garnett Family*, consistently praised productivity and accomplishment. Heilbrun has left a trail of clues to her own intellectual and psychological evolution in her essays, her critical books, and her fiction. Her story is to be found in and between and behind the lines of what she has written; in what she has said and, sometimes, in what she has left unsaid.

Given this approach, my narrative is necessarily personal. The way in which I choose to read Heilbrun, the issues and aspects I choose to emphasize, will inevitably reflect my own concerns, and I had better declare them at the beginning. Even though I am of a different generation, I came to feminism during much the same period that Heilbrun did, give or take a few years. This book is shaped by the fact that I am a white woman, a feminist, a Jew, a teacher, an immigrant from England; married for over twenty-five years, I am the mother of a daughter. Reading and writing about Carolyn Heilbrun is a way to recover some of the most significant experiences of my own life and those of many of my friends and colleagues, as well as the distinctive richness of a particular period in our history. Given the complexity of events and characters, the story I tell is necessarily partial, one among the many to be told.

Seeking to understand Carolyn Heilbrun, I have studied her face in photographs. Characteristically, she has avoided public exposure for many years, choosing to remain hidden. An unseen Carolyn Heilbrun could not, perhaps, be pinned down, identified; an unseen Carolyn Heilbrun could be whatever she or her reader imagined. She has said that she could not, in the early days, reveal herself as Amanda Cross, and she recoiled later from an identification between her and the ideally beautiful Kate Fansler. Thus, even as Carolyn Heilbrun, she has preferred book jackets without photographs, and only very recently has fame forced her reluctantly into view. Just a handful of photographs are publicly available: a few in the Wellesley and Columbia archives, and a few accompanying the articles reporting her 1992 resignation from Columbia. The Carolyn Heilbrun of the 1990s is captured in the photograph chosen for the back cover of her biography of Gloria Steinem. Heilbrun's pose is photographically conventional, head slightly tilted, chin on hand, the knuckles pressing up against gravity. She looks like a benign grandmother, the figure comfortably thickened, the hair that was short and dark in the Wellesley yearbook photographs now washed with gray, the smile warm but wary. Behind the plain spectacles, she has the eyes of a blackbird: bright, sharp, intent, the gaze directed straight at the viewer.

Unlike the face, the voice has always demanded recognition. Heilbrun began early to develop distinctive tones: witty, assertive, even authoritative. She quickly found a public style, a presence. At times, anger erupts, the woman behind the scholar; at times, this double voice resolves itself as the woman shapes the scholar's perceptions. In later years, just when we might expect a mellowing, a rounding of the edges, she forges a rhetoric of risk. During the course of this book, following the intellectual journey of Carolyn Gold Heilbrun, I pursue the defining characteristics of this voice, its changing tones, expressions, and modulations, its delineations of a protean self, its revelations of the woman, the critic, the teacher, the citizen, and the feminist.

In January 1992, when I was already well into the writing of this book, Carolyn Heilbrun granted me an interview, the first of several. In her important work on the complexity of the biographer-interviewer's role, Janet Malcolm has made it impossible not to reflect on the tangled motives that characterize such encounters, where both participants are seeking to create their own stories. Playing back the tapes of my conversations with Heilbrun, I hear myself trying to charm, yet I know I could not afford to be charmed; I hear Heilbrun trying to be responsive and yet guard her privacy, to tell her story, but only as much as she chooses. "You are writing an intellectual biography," she would remind me, whenever I strayed into more personal territory. Often, in these talks, I would proudly produce some pet theory that I had nourished in my study, only to have her pierce it with a deadly sentence. Once, after I had visited her, she wrote to thank me for a small birthday gift I had given her. We had spoken on several occasions of the fact that she liked gifts but had not received many as a child. This was interesting news about financially comfortable parents for whom Heilbrun was an only child, and I wondered about the later significance of this early lack of attention. She, presumably, was not sure what particular fancies I might have in mind, but in her letter she cautioned me with her usual wit not "to seize madly upon" this snippet of information. The sense of fun revealed here permeated our conversations; on the tapes, the talk often erupts in laughter. We are both wary but we like each other. We talk, on occasion, of the possibility of friendship—but is friendship possible when what ought to be private will have, of its very nature, a public dimension?

I realize that I cannot altogether avoid seizing madly upon things, that it is part of my job, in fact, to seize what I can, while also recognizing that people do seem to slide out from under the neat constructions we have made to explain them and keep them tidy. For conflict shapes the theme of this book, both in the larger feminist movement and in the model of Heilbrun's own development. In Heilbrun, conflict often drives intellectual change; but sometimes the tension holds, and sometimes the battle leaves a groove, worn by pain, that cannot be smoothed over. And so I hope, at least, that while telling my story about Carolyn Heilbrun's intellectual development, I have allowed the contradictions, the rough edges, a certain obstinate untidiness.

1

"Thy People, My People"

Because we are engaged in a day-by-day process of self-invention—not discovery, for what we search for does not exist until we find it—both the past and the future are raw material, shaped and reshaped by each individual.

— MARY CATHERINE BATESON, *Composing a Life*

Why . . . does this question of Jewish identity float so impalpably, so ungraspably around me, a cloud I can't quite see the outlines of, which feels to me to be without definition?

— ADRIENNE RICH, "Split at the Root: An Essay on Jewish Identity"

Being a woman and a Jew were in no way of comparable importance in my life. The first was infinitely more pervasive; not only because it was impossible to deny or change, but also because I recognized the condition of femaleness to be for me that which Yeats described as the greatest obstacle to achievement one might confront without despair.

— CAROLYN G. HEILBRUN, *Reinventing Womanhood*

To say that Carolyn Gold was born on 13 January 1926 is not only to give official biography a dutiful nod but also to establish the historical context for her early years, a time in which the world might well have seemed to be spinning toward catastrophe. She was born just eight years after the devastation known as the Great War; the Great Depression would strike before she entered kindergarten; and, during her final years of high school, U.S. troops would enter World War II. The childhood she constructs in the memoir included in her critical book, *Reinventing Womanhood* (1979), reveals her as curiously isolated and culturally detached: her parents were Jewish but dissociated themselves from Judaism; she was an only child, and the family had little to do with her father's relatives. She describes her father as a brilliant, self-made man who, coming from Europe at a young age, learned accounting at night school and, by the age of thirty, made a fortune that he lost in the Depression and subsequently remade. Her mother, made passive by wealth and lack of occupation, seems to have been a more shadowy and certainly less effective presence for Heilbrun.[1]

Born in East Orange, New Jersey, Carolyn Gold moved, at the age of six, with her family to New York City. The apartment building where she grew up, 275 Central Park West, is located directly across from Central Park, between 87th and 88th Streets; heavy wrought-iron doors guard the entrance and open into a dimly lit, dark-paneled lobby, decorated with gilt mirrors and, these days, with leather and velvet furniture. After Heilbrun's marriage and her graduation from Wellesley, she would live for a few years at 340 Riverside Drive, opposite another beautiful park, but in the mid-1960s would take up residence at the Kenilworth, on Central Park West, where she still lives. The foyer of the Kenilworth gives the impression of serious luxury: marble in the entranceway, sconces, high ceilings much ornamented with leaves and scrolls, and a tasteful oriental rug. Carolyn Heilbrun, though deeply committed to intellectual changes of scene, has thus spent most of her life on the same few New York City blocks within easy commuting distance of Columbia University, where she was graduate student and then teacher for over forty years. It is important to think of her as a woman with the financial advantages to make choice possible, one who has chosen to remain in the city even as most members of her generation have been lured to the suburbs. Attracted to metropolitan culture and variety and drawn, too, by the possibilities for urban isolation and anonymity, Heilbrun cannot imagine living anywhere but in New York City: she enjoys the vitality and diversity of the people, she loves to walk the city streets and travel by public transportation. She and her husband, James, spend weekends at their country house in the Berkshires. "But," says Heilbrun, "we only go away in order to come back." For the city offers solitude, too, opportunities for withdrawal and contemplation, the freedom to explore or keep close. The contemporary painter Heilbrun most admires is Edward Hopper, the artist of urban loneliness.[2]

By the time of Carolyn Gold's graduation from the private Birch Wathen School, World War II was dragging into its fourth long year. She had applied to Smith and Wellesley and, accepted by both, chose Wellesley because of its proximity to Boston.[3] Wartime fuel rationing prompted Wellesley to alter its academic calendar in 1942, and, the same arrangement persisting the following year, Wellesley opened its doors to students in late August 1943, in the still-warm days of summer.[4] As she was preparing that month for her future at Wellesley, Heilbrun could scarcely have missed the newspaper headlines insistently blaring news of the war, reporting food shortages, and calling for women to train for war jobs. Even though the 1 August *New York Times Magazine* ran a spread titled "Campus Hits," clothes that the well-dressed college woman would want to pack in her footlocker, the rest of the paper for that day was dominated by the fall of Mussolini.[5] Throughout the month, the tone of war reports was guardedly optimistic; the allies were gaining ground and, by 26 August, Roosevelt addressed the Canadian Parliament at Ottawa, giving "the Nazis stern warning that 'surrender would pay them better now than later.'"[6]

Even Wellesley featured in this war news, and Heilbrun was aware of the item reported in the *Times* of 20 August, noting that Wellesley would surrender two of its dormitories to house a branch of the Naval Supply Corps from Harvard.[7] In spite of such intrusions, Wellesley in 1943 must have seemed idyllically secluded from the war slaughter dramatized in daily news bulletins. The spacious green grounds, the lake, the elegant buildings spoke of privilege, taste, and exclusivity; the grey stones and Gothic arches deliberately referred to the traditions of a civilized Europe.

Yet the image Wellesley wished to project in those years was not one of splendid and sheltered isolation from world affairs. The "Historical Sketch," printed in the college bulletin for 1943, sets the inspirational tone by quoting Henry Fowle Durant, the founder, who announced in grand style to the first students of 1875, "I believe that God . . . is calling to womanhood to come up higher, to prepare herself for great conflicts, for vast reforms in social life, for noblest usefulness."[8] Durant, a converted evangelical Christian, had established the college on a staunch belief in women's worth: "We revolt against the slavery in which women are held by the customs of society—the broken health, the aimless lives, the subordinate position, the helpless dependence, the dishonesties and shams of so-called education."[9] In accordance with his convictions, Durant hired only women as teachers, offering further training to some when he could not find the number of qualified women he needed, and he installed the first woman as president of a college.[10] Indeed, unlike such women's colleges as Bryn Mawr, Smith, and Vassar, Wellesley has boasted an unbroken tradition of women presidents.[11]

Given this powerful legacy, it is not surprising that the author of the 1943 "Historical Sketch," writing at a time of national crisis, denies that Wellesley is an "'ivory tower' to which people withdraw from contact with world needs" and urges that Wellesley students perform vital war work, both at college and during vacation.[12] The example of service was set by the several faculty members (from the departments of astronomy, botany, economics, and political science) absent on war service[13] and especially by Wellesley's president, Mildred H. McAfee, who took a leave from Wellesley in order to direct the WAVES (Women Accepted for Volunteer Emergency Service), the women's auxiliary of the U.S. Navy. Her words in the president's report for 30 October 1945 are a call to continued action even after the war: "My experience as Director of the Women's Reserve ... has made me surer than ever that American women have vast responsibilities for the future of their nation and of the united world. Wellesley College will maintain its tradition and fulfill its promise if it recognizes these obligations of citizenship and prepares each generation of students to assume them gladly, intelligently."[14] Wellesley women were not supposed to sit and refine their minds in aesthetic surroundings while they waited to inherit the world they trusted their brothers to win for them. An editorial in the *Wellesley College News* for September 1943 roused "each Wellesley student [to] accept her kinship with these soldiers and do her best on the campus as they do their best on the battlefield."[15] The students were encouraged to "prepare for essential war work in industry or government, or for service in the period of reconstruction"; to respond to shortages for teachers and trained social and physical scientists; to fill the ranks of domestic workers at the college who were now employed in defense operations; to take extracurricular courses in such topics as military map making, to train as nurses' aides, and to attend lectures sponsored by the college's Committee on War Activities.[16]

Reading these documents of the times might suggest that the war loomed menacingly in the minds of Wellesley students. I spoke with several Wellesley alumnae from the classes of 1946 and 1947 (Heilbrun graduated in 1947) to get their impressions of wartime Wellesley.[17] Most remember the bad food and gasoline shortages, but only one or two recall feeling patriotic or concerned about the war. One did point out its democratizing effects: before the war, scholarship students would wait on tables and perform other similar tasks; with the regular college domestic staff called away to war work, all the students had to pitch in.[18] But generally, for those on the home front, especially those without relatives on the war front, history, as always, chalked up its events somewhere in the background while life bustled forward with its inevitable dailiness. Heilbrun herself remembers being "protected" from the war and not fully aware of the horrors until peace was declared and *Life* magazine published the first shocking photographs of dead American soldiers.

After the war was over, articles in the Wellesley magazine, *WE of Wellesley,* and the *Wellesley College News* urged women to take leading roles in the United Nations and to run for political office.[19] Wellesley students were instructed in different ways and voices and in a variety of different publications that they had important obligations to their country and their society. It made a difference, of course, that from its inception Wellesley was primarily a society of women, offering models of leadership and action from within its own ranks. In 1943, all the administrators, with the exception of two financial officers and the Superintendent of Buildings and Grounds, were women.[20] Wellesley's *Book of Official Statistics* for the years of Heilbrun's residence at the college reveals that the percentage of male faculty members was at 17.8 percent in 1943 and peaked at 20 percent in 1947. When Heilbrun entered Wellesley in 1943, the English literature and English composition departments (the two departments were combined in 1947), where Heilbrun would do most of her undergraduate work, consisted of nineteen women and three men (none of the men was a full professor).[21]

The professors were not the only interesting women in the Wellesley world. Some students might have been aware of the presence on campus of Margaret Mead, who, in the summer of 1944, was appointed director of the Wellesley School of Community Affairs "to work on questions of intercultural relations within the American community." Official calendars for Heilbrun's undergraduate years indicate that students might have attended (though Heilbrun herself did not) a poetry festival featuring Muriel Rukeyser on 24 March 1944 or the lectures given by Simone de Beauvoir, who spoke not of "the second sex" but of "Initiation à l'existentialisme," and "Tendances du roman français contemporain" on 16 and 17 April 1947.[22] A postscript to Beauvoir's Wellesley visit is the discovery that the enthusiastic review of *The Second Sex* ("a truly magnificent book"), published in the *New York Times Book Review* on 22 February 1953, was written by the Harvard sociologist Clyde Kluckhohn. Florence Rockwood Kluckhohn, his wife, taught in the sociology department at Wellesley and was described in glowing terms as a committed mentor and early feminist by those alumnae I interviewed who had majored in sociology.[23]

In spite of the presence of achieving women at Wellesley, and in spite of the rhetoric about action and responsibility, many Wellesley women were, like Heilbrun, not aware of that message. One editorial in the *Wellesley College News* deplored the "Wellesley apathy, of which we hear such constant and scathing criticism." Another expressed dismay that "out of 338 girls who graduated in June 1943 only 156 reported that they were employed as of September" and insisted that marriage was "no excuse" for not making a contribution. Yet another editorial, referring to an article in a Boston newspaper which claimed that women's colleges had "failed to fulfill their purpose" of educating and training leaders, since only two of these very colleges had selected women presidents, reluctantly conceded that many women did "squander four years aimlessly getting through college" without any larger goal or ambition.[24]

The Wellesley women I spoke with did not recognize this apathy as typical of the Wellesley students they knew. Helen Mary (Miggs) Ignatius Dlouhy recollected the "high-spirited" attitude of her peers and chose the word "intense" to capture her sense of the Wellesley atmosphere. Two of the women, who had majored in sociology, separately described themselves as activists; both had also participated in a project to examine housing conditions in Boston's North End. However, when I asked all these women what Wellesley had inspired them to do with their lives after graduation, their responses were mixed: one said the

Wellesley message was "to make things better"; another declared that the Wellesley graduate aspired to the "highest standards" no matter what she did; and one or two definitely wanted a career. But all, except the one who chose not to marry, gave up their careers at least temporarily while their children were young, and most acknowledged that marriage was assumed to be a primary goal. Said Nan Weiser Ignatius, married to the brother of Miggs Ignatius Dlouhy, "When the guys came home, having made the sacrifice, having put their lives on the line— without even analyzing it, we felt we owed them something." Another alumna summed it up ruefully, "Marriage? That was it. Oh gosh, that was it." [25]

Distractions from high purpose were easily available to Wellesley women. Boston and Harvard were a short car ride away, and it was no secret that many Wellesley women aspired to both a Wellesley bachelor of arts and a Harvard bachelor. [26] In October 1943, then, the arrival on campus of a branch of the Naval Supply Corps from Harvard caused a predictable stir. A *Wellesley College News* editorial cautioned Wellesley students to remember that their duty during this national crisis was to serious pursuits, to their books and courses—and not to the pursuit of "dates." [27]

Indeed, some issues of the newspaper convey the sense of schizophrenia many of the women must have felt. [28] For if the newspaper's editorials adopted a solemn, even hectoring tone about the necessity for women's public and professional ambition, other pages made room for the regular appearance of "Class Notes," the tallies of those engaged and married. On the one hand, some of the lectures published in the bulletins for the years 1943–47 addressed women as potential professionals: "The Role of Women in Italy," "Women in Newspaper Work," "Women in Politics," "Women in Aviation," "The Post-War Status of Women." On the other hand, the Marriage Lecture Committee, emphasizing that most Wellesley graduates saw their destiny as wives and mothers, sponsored such lectures as "The Physiological Aspects of Marriage," "Obstetrics," and "Marriage on a Budget."

Members of the faculty seemed to be under no illusion as to the eventual destiny of their students. In a revealing essay on the uses graduates might make of a major in English composition after college, Edith Christina Johnson, professor of English composition, quotes with satisfaction a letter from a former student who helped her husband-the-doctor write a paper later praised with "gratitude and incredulity" (presumably to the husband's credit) for its "excellent presentation." [29] Elizabeth Manwaring, another member of the English Department, captured the self-division afflicting so many graduates when she wrote that she had persuaded two excellent former students to return to their novels: "That is the trouble—some of my very best students let their talents lie buried in other concerns, such as diapers." [30]

Although Wellesley students were taught primarily by women, the curriculum instructed them largely about the achievements of men. Students entering college today, trying to make sense of the so-called culture wars, would be astonished to learn that the English courses listed in the Wellesley college catalog for 1943, Heilbrun's entering year, mention no African-American writers and only two women, Jane Austen and Mrs. Inchbald. College catalogs are not, of course, a precise measure of what is taught in particular courses; still, we can safely assume that women writers were given little attention. Given the times, Heilbrun and her classmates did not consciously register this omission as anything untoward. "We never learned anything about women," Heilbrun says now, though she recalls reading Dorothy Sayers and Virginia Woolf while snugly tucked away in the library, aware that such texts could not be included in a respectable college curriculum. And even if the women who stood at the head of the class were models of professional excellence, with doctoral degrees and other impressive academic credentials, "none of the students wanted to imitate them," recalls Heilbrun. They were "sexless"; they had "failed" because "they did not have a man." Florence Howe, another feminist critic of Heilbrun's generation, describes her women teachers at Hunter College in similar terms: "While I admired them, I did not want to be like them. They were spinsters; even a Dean I loved at Hunter was a spinster. I could not connect them with the women I read of in fiction; or the women men wrote poems about. Nor could I connect them with my mother or other mothers I knew. They were some strange form of being: neither male nor female. Or so I thought in my ignorance." [31]

In *No Man's Land,* Sandra M. Gilbert and Susan Gubar reflect that, during World War I, women began to assume more power as they took the places of the men who had gone to war. [32] Noting the fear women's newly released strength and independence produced in men, Gilbert and Gubar also describe the concomitant anxiety unleashed in women who climbed out of their conventional roles. In the similar social situation provoked by World War II, the anxiety of Wellesley women concerning their intellectual success is revealed in an article about Phi Beta Kappa students in February 1945: "The most spectacular of the Phi Betes is Joy Cohen Levy. She is spectacular because she is married."[33] The words are edged with defensive irony, but the message is plain: it was safe to have brains if one also had a man. A short piece of fiction, "The Story of Susan Chandler," written by a Wellesley student and published in *WE of Wellesley,* points to the terrors of being unmarried. Reminiscent of Edith Wharton's Lily Bart in *The House of Mirth,* Susan Chandler is a woman of twenty-seven who used to have her pick of suitors; now, younger belles are winning male attention and she is anxious to settle (in both senses of that word). At the end of the story, she capitulates with a cliché to a former, still faithful, admirer: "About that little white cottage, Bill—the one with the picket fence—."[34]

Sometimes the uneasiness took the form of jokes, such as one in a spoof issue of the *Wellesley College News:* "At the request of college government, which is thinking of making Wellesley a school exclusively for engaged and married students, we have made a survey of reasons why not one member of the news staff has become engaged since last year."[35] The same mood is struck in a proposed Wellesley cheer for the class of 1948: "1948 Wellesley rah! 1-9-4-8 Wellesley! Dateless '48! Mateless '48! 1948 Wellesley!"[36] Then a breezy article in *WE of Wellesley* for Christmas 1946 expresses relief that the wartime habit of blue jeans has been replaced by more feminine fashions: "The carefree wardays are over forevermore. Brother Jack and friend John are home, and do not like to see women walking around in *their* clothes."[37] Finally, there was the Wellesley tradition of the junior show, a musical comedy written and directed each year by the junior class. Members of the class of 1947 (including Miggs Ignatius Dlouhy and Nan Weiser Ignatius) performed, on 17 November 1945, the provocatively titled "The Body Politic." It would take a women's revolution to provide the terms for an adequate analysis of the ironies of this show which, even in 1945, relied on humor to disguise profound discomfort with the relation between a woman's desirability and her competition for power. Here is the summary provided in the 1947 *Legenda,* the college yearbook: "It was all about Leslie Carlton, an alumna from the class of 1947, who ran for the presidency of the U.S. Was opposed by Bill Smith, was eventually intrigued by Bill Smith, was eventually married to Bill Smith, was eventually installed in the White House as the power behind Pres. Smith. [Ed. note: Never underestimate the power of a member of the class of 1947.]"[38] Prevailing attitudes toward First Lady Hillary Rodham Clinton, Wellesley class of 1969, suggest that only some things have changed in the more than fifty years since 1945.

There is plenty of evidence, then, that while Wellesley overtly urged its young women toward public opportunities, other, perhaps more insistent, social pressures were also exerting their force. Indeed, Carolyn Heilbrun heard only one charge—that women should marry, produce children, and make any public contribution by means of volunteerism. Her view of the Wellesley ethos is captured by the old joke that Wellesley's motto, *Non Ministrari sed Ministrare* (to minister, not to be ministered unto) should in fact be translated as "not to be ministers but to be ministers' wives." Unlike a few of the other Wellesley graduates I spoke with, Heilbrun remembers none of the encouragement to professional achievement noted above. Betty Friedan, graduating in 1942 from Smith, the women's college Heilbrun decided not to attend, had a more positive experience: "the wide horizons of the world and the life of the mind had been opened to me." Smith, according to Friedan, not only offered abstract delights to the mind but also inspired active contributions: "I was taken seriously as a person and inculcated with an ineradicable sense of responsibility for the human destiny, and my own power to affect it." She recalls that "forty per cent of [her] college class at Smith had career plans," although options were already closing in.[39] Adrienne Rich, in 1947 entering another of the seven sisters, Radcliffe, reports: "I never saw a single woman on a lecture platform, or in front of a class, except when a woman graduate student gave a paper on a special topic." She and Heilbrun learned a similar lesson: "our real goal was to marry—if possible, a Harvard graduate."[40] To be sure, in the years 1943–47, Carolyn Heilbrun was not aware of being offended by this message; nevertheless, she was unhappy at Wellesley, where she passed a "bleak four years"; her disaffection is revealed by the fact that, after her graduation, she did not return to Wellesley for thirty-five years.

She was a member of a large freshman class, 478 strong; in spite of the war, applications for a place in the class of 1947 had been more numerous than ever. Her fellow undergraduates came mostly from New York, Massachusetts, New Jersey, and Pennsylvania, but Wellesley had also admitted students from Montana, Maine, Oregon, Texas, as well as from Brazil, India, and Iran.[41] Yet Heilbrun felt out of place. Comfortable in the big city, she found Wellesley "too countrified and a little prissy." She was "miserable," seeking solace in books and in visits to the movies four times a week.[42] Nowhere does she mention a friend or friends. When asked about companionship, she recalls that she went to Wellesley knowing two women, but she was essentially isolated: "I certainly made no friends there." Heilbrun's sense of difference from most Wellesley students is disclosed by her recollection that, when Roosevelt died in 1945, "nobody really cared except me." Wellesley women were "all Republicans." Still, she never thought of leaving Wellesley: "To my parents, to be able to go to Wellesley just seemed the fulfillment of a dream about America. It didn't occur to me to disappoint them."

To gain another perspective on the public Heilbrun at Wellesley, I spoke with four of her classmates. They all remembered her very well, though none of them had what one called a "personal" memory. She was "quiet," "a loner," and none was sure who her friends might have been. All agreed that she had the reputation of being brilliant. "She was an outstanding member of our class," recalled Miggs Ignatius Dlouhy, and most of her classmates were "just in awe of her"; Dlouhy herself was deeply impressed with Heilbrun and, as editor-in-chief of the yearbook, she created a new yearbook position, literary editor, for her. Heilbrun was so bright that she was "intimidating," recollected Nan Weiser Ignatius.[43] Indeed, her peers voted her "Most Brilliant" of her class, and the 1947 yearbook includes a picture of her (sandwiched between "Most Versatile" and "Most Beautiful") sitting on an imposing wooden throne, dressed in plaid skirt, buttoned cardigan, and loafers, holding her glasses in her lap.[44] Heilbrun remembers leaving those glasses off much of the time, as women did in the days before contact lenses; she suspects that her inability to see properly might well have contributed to her classmates' sense of her aloofness.

Heilbrun did well academically her first year, earning a place on the honors list.[45] Her name does not appear on the various lists of academic excellence for her sophomore year, but in her junior year she was selected as one of eighteen Durant Scholars (the highest Wellesley honor a student could attain) and graduated as a Wellesley Scholar (the equivalent of high honors) and as a member of Phi Beta Kappa. Perhaps Heilbrun's reputation for brilliance was the source of her loneliness and alienation, but all her classmates recalled another way in which she was different: she was married. On Tuesday, 20 February of her sophomore year (1945), a month after her nineteenth birthday, Carolyn Gold married James Heilbrun, Harvard class of 1946, just before he was posted overseas. There was no question of her leaving Wellesley before taking the degree: "he came back [from the Pacific] for my final year and we lived on the third floor of the Congregational Church parsonage in Newton Center while he took an M.A. at Harvard."[46]

During these years, marriage of Wellesley women while they were still at college was still rare, though not absolutely forbidden, as it had been before the war. My unofficial count of married names in the Wellesley *Official Directory* for 1946–47 reveals that at least seventeen members (including Heilbrun) of Heilbrun's class were married by the time of graduation; this number does not, of course, include those who left college to marry before their graduation. The class of 1947 consisted of 478 students in 1943 and had dwindled to 378 by the time of graduation. A comprehensive survey run by the college in 1963 reveals that of the 284 graduates of Wellesley's class of 1947 who responded, 91.2 percent married at some point (only four of those surveyed married before they were twenty, as Heilbrun had); and 86.3 percent had at least one child. A more significant statistic may be that, by 1963, only thirty-one had earned graduate degrees; of these, Heilbrun was one of only seven to earn a doctorate.[47] For women of her generation, including the bright women who went to Wellesley, earning a doctorate was clearly an extraordinary accomplishment.

Even with James Heilbrun posted overseas during her junior year, Heilbrun still did not seek out female companionship at Wellesley; those of us familiar with undergraduate life recall that usually, by this time, circles of friends have been established, and outsiders can rarely break in. A pattern is set. Much later, in the early 1980s, Heilbrun encountered one of her Wellesley classmates who had left before taking her degree to get married: Sybil Hart Kooper. She and Kooper, a lawyer, became and stayed close friends until Kooper's death from breast cancer, but they had not known each other at Wellesley. One classmate of Heilbrun's, Ann Hartman, retired dean of the School of Social Work at Smith College, is surprised that Heilbrun, now a noted feminist, had no friendships with women while at Wellesley. Nevertheless, Hartman identifies with Heilbrun's sense of alienation, recalling that "Wellesley was not an easy place to find a spot if you were different"; Hartman, who describes herself as an "eccentric" child of a politically liberal, single-parent family, was also slow to adjust to Wellesley, and did not find "[her] friends and [her] niche" until her junior year. Meeting Heilbrun over forty years later in 1990, when Heilbrun delivered an address at Smith, Hartman remembers Heilbrun's wholesale dismissal of the class of 1947 as not being "interesting." Hartman confesses to puzzlement and dismay that such an attitude had lingered even as late as 1990.[48] Referring to the brief autobiographies contributed by the class of 1947 to their 45th reunion book in 1992, Hartman praises the accomplishments of her classmates. Over three hundred of the surviving class members submitted responses for the book, among their number psychologists and teachers, lawyers and librarians, social workers and the occasional medical doctor. Most of these, presumably inspired by the women's movement, took up, or returned to, a profession after their children no longer needed constant care; by 1992, twenty-two members of the class had earned doctorates and ninety-six master's degrees. Still, on an informal survey printed in the 45th reunion book, only half of the respondents would describe themselves as feminists. Almost all of the Wellesley women I interviewed shied away from that term, too, fearing its power to brand them as "negative" or "man-hating."

In 1982, Heilbrun would publicly call Wellesley to account for its failure to provide feminist leadership. Invited back to Wellesley for a panel discussion entitled "Studying Women: What Difference Does it Make?" she returned to her alma mater for the first time since graduation. She took the opportunity to offend, referring to Wellesley as a "sheltered school for young ladies 'training to marry Harvard men,'" contending that her own accomplishments were earned despite a "total lack of support from Wellesley College" and criticizing Wellesley for failing to make women's studies a priority (an attack she would elaborate in her "Wellesley" novel of 1984, *Sweet Death, Kind Death*). Condemning Wellesley's attempts to socialize women into conventional, ladylike molds, Heilbrun is reported as saying that "*all* women have an 'inner core of rage' and . . . Wellesley does not allow its students to express it."[49] Nora Ephron, Wellesley class of 1962, returning to Wellesley for her tenth reunion in 1972, ten years before Heilbrun's visit, made similar charges: "How marvelous it would have been to go to a women's college that encouraged impoliteness, that rewarded aggression, that encouraged argument." Ephron dismissed as "pointless" Wellesley's decision to remain a college for women: "Why remain a school for women unless you are prepared to deal with the problems women have in today's society?"[50] However, most of the alumnae I spoke with found Heilbrun's 1982 attack stinging, and one or two pointed out that Heilbrun, after all, *had* married the Harvard man and was therefore not entitled to the moral high ground she had claimed. Ann Hartman, on the other hand, remarked that Wellesley had never paid the kind of attention to Heilbrun that one would have expected, noting that Wellesley, unlike Smith, had not even awarded her an honorary degree.[51] But others wondered if Heilbrun's own lack of appreciation for Wellesley had played a part in that neglect, pointing out that she was one of only two members of the class to be honored with a Wellesley Alumnae Achievement Award.[52]

In her senior year, Heilbrun became more visibly involved in the life of the college as a writer; somehow, she managed an excellent academic record, a marriage, and also found time to be literary editor of the yearbook and drama critic for the *Wellesley College News*. Her witty, acerbic reviews appear with regularity ("But *Happy Birthday,* unlike most rather bad plays, has Miss Helen Hayes to do for it what Atlas does for the world"), and it looks as if Heilbrun is in training for a career in journalism.[53] She had taken vacation jobs with the *New York Post* and a magazine called *Common Sense* and could look to journalism as one of those fields that the war had opened to women. Nora Ephron had accused Wellesley of not preparing students to form judgments and opinions, but here, again, Heilbrun was an exception.[54] Her drama reviews are defined by their clear convictions: she didn't like *Barefoot Boy with Cheek,* which set out "to amuse the audience with some of the most tasteless and senseless smut that has passed the footlights recently in Boston," and she most definitely did like *Call Me Mister,* which had "whatever it is that makes a show click from beginning to end."[55] Her style is already uncluttered by deference or prevarication.

Heilbrun's literary endeavors made college more bearable; she took nine literature courses, covering all the major periods with the exception of the eighteenth century. She remembers loving her Chaucer course, offered by Ella Keats Whiting, who subsequently became dean; and she was enthralled by the Shakespeare course offered by Katherine Balderston, a specialist in the age of Johnson who had performed the noteworthy feat of producing a scholarly work on a woman, Hester Thrale, Johnson's close friend.[56] Heilbrun's major, English composition, was considered one of the most intellectually demanding majors at Wellesley; Heilbrun took seven composition courses, concentrating on the essay, the magazine article, and the short story. For one of her major projects, she dramatized Joseph Conrad's *Victory*.

Heilbrun recounts that she had been encouraged to write by two faculty members: Charles Kerby-Miller and Mary Curran.[57] Given Heilbrun's own later development, it is worth noting that Charles Kerby-Miller would collaborate in writing *Candidate for Murder,* a detective novel, and that Mary Curran would publish a critical study of *Dubliners* by James Joyce.[58] Their influence thus may have extended beyond Heilbrun's undergraduate days, since Heilbrun would become a mystery writer as Amanda Cross; moreover, her second mystery, *The James Joyce Murder,* was based on *Dubliners*. Nevertheless, Mary Eleanor Prentiss taught the class that enabled Heilbrun to make her public literary debut and earn the greatest triumph of her undergraduate career.

Out of 371 stories submitted by college students to the college competition run by *The Atlantic Monthly* in 1946, Heilbrun's "Thy People, My People" won first prize. On 15 June 1946, the school newspaper announced that "Cacky" (Heilbrun's nickname) was "amazed" at winning and attributed "her secret of success" to marriage. "'Everybody seems to think that marriage and college are mutually antagonistic,' said Cacky, 'and it's NOT true!'"[59] To be sure, this statement offers an ironic counterpoint to her remarks years later that Wellesley women "didn't have, as far as I could see, a thought about anything except getting engaged";[60] but it also bespeaks a passionate argument for a woman's right to have a life beyond her marriage, for the notion that marriage even made such ambitions possible. Heilbrun has said on numerous occasions that James Heilbrun actively encouraged her academic and literary endeavors; indeed, the probability that her emotional needs were officially settled by the fact of her marriage might have enabled her to focus without distraction on her intellectual work. Nevertheless, the words about the combination of college and marriage, the publicly expressed appreciation of her husband, suggest an anxiety familiar to women juggling domestic life and intellectual ambition.

It is surely a sign of that postwar period that thirteen of the fourteen prizewinners announced by the *Atlantic Monthly* in June 1946 were women and that most of the teachers were also women. In the *Wellesley College News* article, Heilbrun reports that her story would appear in a supplement to the *Atlantic Monthly*. That supplement, apparently distributed to colleges but not to regular subscribers of the magazine, has not survived in library holdings or in the magazine's own archives;[61] however, I discovered Heilbrun's story in the autumn 1946 issue of Wellesley's literary magazine *WE of Wellesley*. The story was an unusual choice for the *Atlantic Monthly* to have honored: 1946 was a time for pious public challenges to anti-Semitism, not for the kind of tortuous ambivalence Heilbrun's story expresses.[62]

"Thy People, My People" tells the story of eighth-grade Stella Unger's relationship with her grandfather, who, carrying a small bag of candy, meets her daily on her walk home from school. For Stella, his favorite grandchild, her grandfather is the central figure in her life: "As long as Stella could remember, Grandpa had been the person who mattered most. Papa worked all day and was tired at night, and it seemed to Stella that there had always been younger children to take up Mama's time."[63] Her grandfather plays pinochle with her every night and mends the dresses she tears climbing for apples, without betraying her escapades to her mother. Nevertheless, Stella feels ambivalent about his, and her, Jewishness: "In her innermost self she knew she loved him terribly, and so she suffered that peculiar, insidious pain known only to those who have come to hate what they love. For every time that Stella claimed Grandpa, and walked off with him from the school yard, she as much as yelled to the onlooking children: I am a Jew, and proud of the fact" (23).[64] Grandpa is unmistakably marked as Jewish by his beard and hat; indeed, the illustration provided in the Wellesley magazine portrays him as a stereotypically orthodox Jew, with long beard and black clothes. Drawn as a prehensile claw, his hand clutches what looks like a cloth bag of coins, though we know from the story that it should be the paper bag of candy he daily brings for Stella (23). Stella, on the other hand, looks like a Gentile, according to the narrator; even though her schoolmates know she is Jewish, her blond hair and blue eyes enable her not to impress or impose that fact upon them; enable her, in other words, to pass.

On the day the story takes place, Stella's anguish about her Jewish identity comes to a crisis. She decides to avoid her grandfather who, as usual, is waiting for her outside the school gates. She walks right past him, ignoring his calls to her, swept up, yet not fully included, in the gaggle of friends whom she so desperately wants to resemble.

This story picks up tensions in Heilbrun's own attitude toward Judaism. In *Reinventing Womanhood*, Heilbrun says that both her parents cut themselves off from their Jewish roots. Her father's immigration story is familiar: his two older sisters (Fannie and Mollie) came to America as teenagers and earned the money to pay the passages of their mother and two younger siblings; their father was dead. Living in cramped quarters, the family struggled to survive in the new country. After he grew up and left home, Heilbrun's father provided financial support for his mother and for his youngest sister when necessary.[65] So much is conventional. What is not conventional, and perhaps even extraordinary, given the ways immigrant families tend to cling together in an alien country, is Heilbrun's statement: "I never knew my father's family. The strangeness of this did not occur to me until many years later. My father, in fact, deliberately chose to separate me from the conditions and influences from which he had already separated himself." Many children enjoy listening to tales of their parents' childhood; Heilbrun, who nevertheless loved to read stories of other lives in the St. Agnes Library, differs: "I realize now that I never really wanted to know about my father's childhood, just as he never wished, until after my mother's death, to talk about it, because it was something we both conceived of as past, overcome, left behind."[66]

Heilbrun reveals that, later in his life, her father had a breakdown after the "head of [his] firm was struck down . . . by a heart attack." Psychoanalysis enabled him to accept that he was reliving a false sense of guilt for the death of his own father; apparently, superstitious and cruel villagers had held the four-year-old responsible for his father's death.[67] Heilbrun does not acknowledge here that, while he was certainly innocent of killing his father in the old country, he had effectively suppressed all trace of his family in the new country. Yet, as Adrienne Rich points out, in telling the painful story of her own Jewish father who had denied his Jewish identity throughout his life, she was left "high and dry, split at the root, gasping for clarity, for air." Rich rejects the possibility that the past can be overcome: "Because what isn't named is often more permeating than what is, I believe that my father's Jewishness profoundly shaped my own identity and our family existence."[68]

Heilbrun's mother, the eldest of seven children and six daughters, also rejected her Jewish background, according to Heilbrun: "My grandmother welcomed her Jewish relatives, whose manners and faith appalled my mother even as a small child. All about her, the gentile children seemed gayer, happier, less burdened with guilt and fear. Blond like them, she wanted to be one of them." Later, passing as a Gentile, Heilbrun's mother took a job in a bank that did not hire Jews; later still, she unsuccessfully urged her husband to change his name.[69]

Heilbrun herself gladly attended school on Jewish holidays ("My favorite days in the year were the Jewish holidays when I, and the gentile children, were in school, the student body much diminished in number") and worshipped with her parents at the "Divine Science" Church of the Healing Christ, keeping the latter habit secret, sensing "there was something not quite 'right' about it." Nevertheless, her Orthodox Jewish (maternal) grandmother "was for me the chief loving force in my early childhood." That grandmother died in 1936, hit by a car; ten years later, Heilbrun would write "Thy People, My People."[70]

Given these circumstances, adolescent rebellion might well have manifested itself in Heilbrun's case as a return to Judaism. Not so. "Had I been offered three wishes," the older Heilbrun recalls, "one of them, I now guess, would have been not to be Jewish." Heilbrun does not recall encountering "egregious anti-Semitism," and perhaps it is necessary for those who deny their Judaism also to deny experiencing anti-Semitism in order to avoid noticing the similarity between the two attitudes. Nevertheless, she did write to Emmet Fox, pastor of her church, for advice as to whether she should admit that she was Jewish on her college application forms. On one page in *Reinventing Womanhood,* Heilbrun says she did not deny her Judaism: "What I denied was the power [Jewishness and femaleness] had to limit my *self*-development"; two paragraphs later, however, she admits: "Probably because of my parents' attitude toward Jewishness, being Jewish was for me altogether unreal. I practiced what I have since learned to call denial."[71] The ambivalence expressed here suggests Heilbrun's discomfort with her identity—both with being Jewish as well as with her parents' choice to follow unconventional forms of worship. The young Heilbrun, an only child, was intensely isolated—burdened with secrecy, cut off from family roots, and detached from any tradition. Nonetheless, her experience would also produce a sturdy intellectual independence; for the older Heilbrun would frequently replay similar scenarios by choosing isolated positions or finding herself caught between opposed ideologies, traditions, or conventions.

Writing *Reinventing Womanhood* in her early fifties, Heilbrun was, in the initial chapters, attempting to understand and describe her development as a feminist. Intending to revise our notions of womanhood, she urged the development of the "whole" woman, a topic explored more fully in a later chapter. But her subtext was what might be called the healing of her own self, and part of that project was an excavation and reinterpretation, perhaps reinvention, of her personal history. It is instructive that one of the first items of unfinished business is her identity as a Jew and the relation of her Judaism to her feminism. In the act of looking back, of revision, that she performs in *Reinventing Womanhood,* Heilbrun finds a way to reclaim her Judaism. The status of outsider that Judaism conferred upon her allowed her to develop the strength she needed to become a feminist: "I began to understand that having been a Jew, however unobserved that identification was, however fiercely I had denied the adamant anti-Semitism all around me as I grew up—still, having been a Jew had made me an outsider. It had permitted me to be a feminist." The point is that, even though Heilbrun denied her Judaism, it was, as far as the outside world was concerned, undeniable; moreover, from this vantage point, Heilbrun can see her negative attitude toward Judaism as a positive aspect of her nascent feminism: "My mother was not alone in her break away from Jewishness, her sense that Jewishness was exactly what held the Jewish mother confined in her 'sustaining' role. I am certain that it was my grandmother's orthodoxy, her acceptance of her role as server, that, in my mother's eyes, imprisoned her and her daughters."[72] These retrospective views are persuasive, and we see them sharply dramatized in "Thy People, My People."

Nevertheless, in her candid revelations about this period of her life, Heilbrun acknowledges that this neat (and simultaneous) reclamation and repudiation of Jewish identity may not be the whole story. Jews were not only to be condemned for their attitudes toward women but for their appearance and class: Jews who looked like Jews could not be tolerated. In "Thy People, My People," Stella deplores her grandfather's appearance; in *Reinventing Womanhood,* Heilbrun notes that if her mother "saw Hassidic Jews on the streets of New York, she would insist on analyzing for me how horrible they looked, how utterly unattractive were their clothes and manners." We are told that Heilbrun's mother "determined . . . to cut herself off from everything Jewish and 'common,' her favorite word of condemnation."[73] To be Jewish, especially if one came from eastern Europe and looked a certain way, was also probably to be lower class. Adrienne Rich, from a different geographic position, makes the same point: "With enough excellence, you could presumably make it stop mattering that you were Jewish; you could become the *only* Jew in the gentile world, a Jew so 'civilized,' so far from 'common,' so attractively combining southern gentility with European cultural values that no one would ever confuse you with the raw, 'pushy' Jews of New York, the 'loud, hysterical' refugees from eastern Europe, the 'overdressed' Jews of the urban South."[74] Heilbrun's parents obviously strove to improve their social class. They moved to Central Park West and enrolled Heilbrun in a private school where "the tone was distinctly high Episcopalian." And they sent her to prestigious Wellesley College. Although the older Heilbrun described herself, with some relish, as having been "scraped off the Lower East Side,"[75] the pressures on the young Heilbrun to look and act as if she had a certain pedigree were considerable. These pressures were doubtless increased when she went to Wellesley.

Wellesley in the 1940s was an almost entirely white, middle-class society. Cheryl Wolfe, an African American interviewed for Brett Harvey's oral history, *The Fifties,* graduated from Wellesley in 1948. She recalls: "They said there were no quotas, but there were never more than three black students the whole time I was there. . . . I should say that all three of us were also light-skinned. I don't know if this was a conscious thing on Wellesley's part or just what they were comfortable with."[76] In 1944, an editorial in the *Wellesley College News* deplored the action of an alumnae club in the Midwest that "refused admittance" to a Negro alumna.[77] The magazine, *WE of Wellesley,* for April/May 1945 contains two revealing stories. One story, "Brief Encounter," by Joanne Emerson, denounces American racism among the U.S. armed forces in Italy; the other, "The Changing Years" by Josephine Batchelder, reinforces class prejudice with an amazing lack of self-consciousness. The protagonist of "The Changing Years" is attracted to one Al Morini, in spite of her parents' disapproval. She later finds that Mr. Morini cannot be trusted and confirms her parents' values by learning to appreciate the eminently eligible Courtlandt Hillard Smith III, a Harvard man who is going into the Air Corps. Class obviously mattered at Wellesley. The student publications were studded with advertisements advising Wellesley women where to buy their flowers, select their chic clothes, and store their furs. In 1946, the college was sufficiently concerned about "the possibility of Wellesley's becoming a one-class college" to institute a new financial aid policy that would ensure greater economic diversity among the students.[78] A few of the alumnae I interviewed assured me that one did not necessarily have to be affluent to attend Wellesley, and more than one described the student body as a "mix," but Ann Hartman, a scholarship student, does remember feeling "outclassed." A revealing remark comes from Miggs Ignatius Dlouhy: "We never talked about politics and money."[79]

In this context, it is worth noting that an older Heilbrun would invent Kate Fansler as an upper-class WASP. In an interview even as late as 1989, Heilbrun, describing Fansler's origins in fantasy, says, "She had to be a WASP. She is richer than I was and WASP-ier, but in many ways it was the world I knew."[80] Assuming the interviewer has transcribed accurately, the slip about her own assumed WASP identity is telling. Further, in choosing her pseudonym, Amanda Cross, Heilbrun would have been hard pressed to find a name that more effectively renounced her Jewish origins. Put another way, no one who reads Amanda Cross's novels would suspect their author was a Jew "scraped off the Lower East Side."

One final observation should be made about Heilbrun's discussion of her Judaism in *Reinventing Womanhood*. From the perspective of 1979, she suggests that her youthful attitude toward Judaism was settled and that she did not give the matter much thought. Following the persuasive example of her parents, she had dismissed it from her life. Then, at the beginning of *Reinventing Womanhood,* she describes being unexpectedly reminded of Judaism in connection with Wellesley. She reports that in meeting classmates from Wellesley in preparation for a thirtieth-year reunion, "it became clear that Wellesley had always been, in the nicest way, anti-Semitic. I was told, truthfully or not, that some of its former administrators had been notorious for this attitude." Heilbrun had thought that Wellesley "ignored" her because she was a feminist; now she learned she might have been slighted because she was a Jew.[81] Yet, to what degree is that middle-aged surprise a product of willed forgetfulness? It was apparently no secret that Wellesley did not welcome Jews. Cheryl Wolfe pointed out that "being Jewish kept you out, too, incidentally. There was always a fixed number of Jewish girls there, it never changed, although, again, they said there were no quotas."[82] When asked about anti-Semitism at Wellesley, three of the alumnae I interviewed shared Heilbrun's view and declared they did not remember any prejudice at Wellesley; others acknowledged its existence, and one recounted an experience of being urged to go to a mixer with the assurance that there would be "no Jews there."[83] Three of the alumnae were Jewish, but not practicing; even so, they told me that their closest friends at Wellesley had been Jewish. Of Carolyn Heilbrun I was told, "Everyone knew she was Jewish."

In a dramatic series of articles and letters in the Wellesley alumnae magazine (fall 1985 and winter 1986), Wellesley graduates attacked Wellesley's ingrained "institutional bias against Jews": Wellesley routinely admitted only 10 to 12 percent of Jewish applicants when comparable colleges were accepting 25 percent; further, Jewish students who were admitted learned that Wellesley would make no allowances for the diets and sabbath observances of practicing Jews.[84] Given the blatant nature of Wellesley's discrimination against Jews, it is surprising now that Heilbrun and some of her classmates took such little note of it. True, Heilbrun was, as she says, "a secret outsider,"[85] but people can sometimes see all the more clearly from their hiding places. Yet it is difficult to thread one's way back into the assumptions of an earlier time, especially when those assumptions are often not only unspoken but unacknowledged. What seems obvious now in retrospect might have been very far from obvious then.

In order to place Heilbrun's attitudes and those of her parents in a larger context, we need to take a longer perspective. My own experience as a Jew tells me that the long history of anti-Semitism makes Jews especially prone to the temptations of assimilation, dissimulation, and denial. Few among us have resisted the impulse to merge or accommodate at one time or another. I remember the delight I experienced donning the uniform for my new English high school; long afterward, I realized that I relished the uniform, unlike most of my peers, because it enabled me to pass, to seem like all the others. Florence Howe recounts a similar experience: "From the day I entered kindergarten in the mid-thirties and heard another child chastised for speaking a Yiddish word, I willingly dismissed my heritage. . . . I became truly American."[86] Nevertheless, for most secular Jews, however deeply implicated in ambivalence, there is a distinction between the private self, defined as Jewish, and the public persona. The construction of Heilbrun's private and public identity, the public self invading the private, the private self erasing what was, as she later recounts, nevertheless indelible, is much more complicated.

One might imagine that to declare oneself a Jew after World War II was a matter of pride, but news of the Holocaust only sent the more open expressions of anti-Semitism of the 1920s and 1930s underground,[87] even as Jews were reminded once again that it was dangerous to be Jewish. Whether or not Heilbrun remembered encountering specific incidents of anti-Semitism during her Wellesley years, the *Wellesley College News* reported anti-Semitic outbreaks in Boston and covered a seminar at the nearby Andover Newton Theological School focusing on the problem of anti-Semitism.[88] In 1945, Bess Myerson encountered open anti-Semitism after being chosen as the first Jewish Miss America;[89] in 1947, the film that excited significant attention at all levels of society and garnered a share of Oscars was *Gentleman's Agreement,* an exposure of anti-Semitism in American life.

If Jews expected a more enlightened attitude from the academy, they were to be disappointed. Adrienne Rich recalls her father's hopes for academic advancement at Johns Hopkins: "The appointment was delayed for years, no Jew ever having held a professional chair in that medical school."[90] Intolerance of Jews was especially powerful in English departments. Irving Howe recounts the anguish of Ludwig Lewisohn as he tried to find an academic position in the 1920s; and the story of Lionel Trilling's difficulty in becoming the first Jew tenured in the English department at Columbia in 1939 is well known.[91] During this period, members of the group that would come to be known as the New York Intellectuals, many of whom were Jewish and among whom Trilling was a dominant presence, were struggling both with their relation to what was increasingly seen as an anti-Semitic culture and with their own ambivalent feelings about their Jewish identity.[92] Trilling had written a story when he was twenty (Heilbrun was also twenty when she wrote "Thy People, My People") called "Impediments," about the struggle of a young man with a Jewish alter ego; the Jew is defeated.[93] In Illinois, far from New York intellectual life, we find Betty Friedan, growing up as one of a small minority of Jews in Peoria, the only one of her high school class not pledged to a sorority. In Boston, Adrienne Rich, marrying a Jew, finds that neither her Jewish father nor her Gentile mother will attend the wedding.[94] Yet even acknowledging the strong parallel traditions of anti-Semitism and Jewish self-hatred, we should note the exceptional histories of denial and deletion of Jewish identity in both the Rich and Heilbrun families.

Little wonder, then, that the question of identity seemed to be, on the mind of the twenty-year-old Heilbrun. Knowing these significant details of her family life, we may venture to suggest that "Thy People, My People" was a very personal story. Heilbrun even appropriates Unger, the maiden name of James Heilbrun's mother, for her protagonist's family name. Yet if her protagonist successfully hides her self-division from her peers, Heilbrun's narrator certainly reveals hers. Ambivalence is revealed in the divided thoughts of Stella, who both loves her grandfather and despises what he is, and in the divided attitude of the narrator, who both understands and condemns Stella. But when Stella deliberately ignores her grandfather, the ambivalence is no longer concealed; when Heilbrun publishes her story, her secret, too, is out in the open. The story would have been risky for its author in 1946, and it is possible that Heilbrun, working on this story for an English course, never expected it to make a public move out of the classroom. Nevertheless, that she wrote it at all suggests that the "secret outsider" was under pressure to explore her feelings about identity. It is worth noting that she would not deal publicly again with her feelings about Judaism for another three decades, until the writing of *Reinventing Womanhood*, and that she would refer to this revealing story publicly only twice, and never to its theme.[95]

But the story suggests that Heilbrun was reflecting not only on Jewish identity but on her identity as a woman. Buried beneath this story of a Jewish girl's self-division and self-hatred is yet another story that corroborates Heilbrun's later sense that a young girl's development might be limited by Judaism and that also points more generally to the constraints placed on women by society. Given the times, Heilbrun herself may not have been fully conscious of this theme of female identity (which is subordinated to the idea of Jewish identity) when she wrote the story, but there are clues to it throughout. Stella is an eighth grader, thus probably about thirteen; if she were a boy, she would at thirteen have had a bar mitzvah, the symbolic initiation into the world of men. As a girl, however, she is still a child, still treated to small bags of candy and exposed to the possible humiliation of an escort home. Stella is a tomboy, the first of a long line of Heilbrun protagonists who rebel against their restricted female roles. When she goes to her grandfather with "a torn dress she did not want Mama to see, he would mend it for her so cleverly that even Mama's sharp eyes did not detect the mischief" (24). But he also reminds her of her place: "*Ach, mein schafchen,* don't you know that little girls should not climb trees? You think perhaps you are a monkey?" The narrator adds, "At times like this there was kindness in the old man's voice, and a severity which grew, not out of anger, but from his love for her" (24). It is such kindness, such love, that keeps little girls like Stella in their places, and Stella knows that her grandfather approves of that place even though he will conspire with her to hide her trespasses from Mama.

Stella explains to him: "But there were apples up the tree, Grandpa, big ones, and green like I like them." Stella wants the apples that are green, tart to the taste, perhaps not quite ripe, probably out of reach. "And she would smile that smile which always brought a twinkle and sometimes the glisten of tears to those bright blue eyes." The grandfather wants to keep her a child: "If you want apples, you come to me. I buy you all you want, and more" (24–25). The mode of seduction for this Eve would not be the lure of forbidden knowledge but the temptation to sit in passivity while the apples are bought and delivered. But then, no one-dimensional patriarch, the grandfather has ambivalence and complexity, too: "'You climb trees again like this, and I tell your Mama.' But Stella knew he would never tell Mama, and that if she came in with her dress torn twenty times, he would fix it, and always with the same words" (25).

The title of the story is taken from the biblical book of Ruth. As a Wellesley student required to take a course in the Bible, Heilbrun could rely on her audience to recognize some of the most well-known words from the Old Testament: "Intreat me not to leave thee, *or* to return from following after thee: for whither thou goest, I will go; and where thou lodgest, I will lodge: thy people *shall be* my people, and thy God, my God" (Ruth 1:16). Heilbrun's use of the title is ironic, of course: for while the alien Ruth gives up her identity as a Moabite and embraces Naomi's people and Naomi's religion, Stella just as firmly rejects her grandfather's people, her grandfather's religion, choosing, instead, allegiance to the secular world of her school friends.

Such a choice commits Stella to concealment. At one point, Stella reflects on the ritual of disguise associated with the game of pinochle that she regularly plays with her grandfather: "In pinochle one always pretended to have a wonderful hand. Grandpa had taught her that from the very beginning, and she understood somehow, that he meant it to apply not just to pinochle, but to life" (24). Indeed, the art of dissembling enters other parts of her life. She and her grandfather dissemble when he mends her dresses without her mother's knowledge; she dissembles when she pretends not to see her grandfather upon leaving school; she dissembles when she pretends she is no different from her schoolmates. After Stella has walked away from her grandfather, she wonders whether he will still come to visit in the evening, whether he will still play pinochle (the game of pretense) with her. If he does, "to Mama and the others there would be no difference, but Stella would know it, and Grandpa would. With the conviction of those who have made a vital decision, Stella knew that something had changed for always, and would never, never be the same again" (25). This reflection in the final lines of the story suggests that young Stella knows well the painful disjunction between the actor and the mask. Yet she also knows that dissembling enables her to wear the masks of blond non-Jew, of good little girl; such masks enable her to find an uneasy place in a world from which she obviously feels displaced and estranged: "And so Stella had been accepted by her Gentile friends, and had made a place for herself in a world where to be a Jew is to have to work for what others get just by the asking" (23). This last sentence speaks to something essential: what needs to be hidden, discarded, lost, or pushed underground in order to survive in the public world—in short, what is at stake in the formation of a public identity.

In 1946, when she wrote this story, Heilbrun was twenty years old, a time of life when self-questioning is surely conventional. Yet, the circumstances of Heilbrun's life, as they have been portrayed here, suggest that Heilbrun's self interrogations would be especially intense and, as we now know, would lead to a lifelong examination of selfhood. In this light, it is not surprising that the young girl in the St. Agnes Library was consuming biographies with such passion. What is also clear from this story is that one of Heilbrun's ways of dealing with painful conflicts is to work them out in fiction through the means of a fictional persona; thus in time would Amanda Cross give birth to Kate Fansler and take up the themes of self-exploration first sounded in 1946.

The older Heilbrun regards the quality of being a Jewish outsider as relevant to her later feminism; perhaps the wish to assimilate is just as relevant. The traditional models for rebellious outsiders have been male—both in life and in literature. For women, on the other hand, one unacknowledged mode of rebellion is to strive to become an insider. The fear of the hatred of others, the fear of rejection from desirable public opportunities, the fear of exclusion from privileged social circles are powerful motives to repudiate Jewish roots and to assimilate, especially if one already has valid questions about religious faith and practice. Feminists typically scorn assimilation because it implies blending in, blurring edges, becoming compliant, similar, and therefore invisible. Adrienne Rich, alert to the dangers of self-deception, secrets, and passivity, recalls her anger that "I had never been taught about resistance, only about passing."[96]

But there is another way to look at "passing." Let us assume that the desire to assimilate can prompt an ambitious woman to a first step on a path to worldly success and significant achievement, an expression of rebellion against an assigned woman's place. Perhaps, hidden somewhere here, there is a hint to explain why so many Jews became passionate feminists and leaders of the feminist movement.[97] Jewish women, necessarily conscious of the strategic advantages of role-playing to assimilate themselves to the contours of an inhospitable society, might imagine playing still other roles, might imagine themselves participating in public or professional life, might imagine themselves valuing accomplishment as much as their fathers or brothers, might even imagine themselves taking on the roles of those men. Here, to be sure, we come up hard against one of the limitations of assimilation, for it may well be that such women, including Heilbrun, could imagine different roles for themselves but not, however, fundamental changes in those roles or in society itself. They could imagine reform, not revolution. The revolution would come later.

The narrator of "Thy People, My People" recognized the pain of assimilation, both understanding and condemning the young girl who forsakes her grandfather to join her friends; pain is Stella's lot. Meanwhile, the writer who created that narrator and character was not well practiced in assimilation. Although she denied her Judaism, she had not committed to the "staunchly blond"[98] ranks of her Wellesley peers: at Wellesley, she had no circle of friends, made no particular effort to be accepted or approved. "I was an only child. I was always lonely. I was always alone" is a refrain punctuating Heilbrun's recollections of the days before the women's movement. But her loneliness, her lack of affiliation with any group, and her intelligence laid the foundation for a gritty independence of thought. That such independence exacted a price is underlined by the contradictions that emerge from the Wellesley period of Heilbrun's life: the conflicts embodied in the woman who would become a feminist but who lacked female friends; in the Jew who had written off Judaism and dismissed it from her life—but yet wrote of passing; in the young woman who married at nineteen but saw her peers as the ones with nothing on their minds except marriage; in the woman who detached herself from Wellesley but still wanted institutional recognition.

In 1947, to the Wellesley graduate, it was not yet clear that assimilation as a woman might be a wholly different matter from assimilation as a Jew. For the moment, the idea (if not the practice) of assimilation represented freedom, a declaration that the self was not bound by its own origins; it was a means to a more fluid sense of identity, to a greater array of life's possibilities. Not accepting what she was, not, perhaps, knowing who she was, enabled Carolyn Heilbrun to imagine what she might be.

2

The Unwilling Mentor

This idea of a conceived and executed life is a very old
one. . . . And cognate with the idea of making a life, a
nicely proportioned one, with a beginning, a middle,
and an end, was the idea of making a self, a good self.

— LIONEL TRILLING, "The Uncertain Future
of the Humanistic Educational Ideal"

As I was going up the stair
I met a man who wasn't there.

— HUGHES MEARNS, "The Psychoed"

It's not an accident that college clinics are filled with
healthy young men who are having potency problems. . . . But how is this not going to happen if women
make men out to be those beastly creatures who treat
them as sexual objects? I mean, what is more charming
than to have a man want you as his sexual object?

— DIANA TRILLING, interviewed in
Columbia Daily Spectator, 1977

Let us begin in 1950 with a tale of academic life published in *Quarto,*
a literary magazine produced by the students of Columbia's School
of General Studies, the only school at Columbia University then admitting both men and women undergraduates. The magazine regularly
printed stories written by or about women, many of which make chilling
reading, focusing on lonely, dispirited women, women without men,
grotesques somewhat in the manner of Sherwood Anderson.[1] One in
particular, "Summer Session," stands out, telling the sad, familiar tale
of a graduate student who adores her witty, clever, charismatic teacher.
Lonely, approaching forty, prone to hearing "voices," she fantasizes
elaborate conversations with him and an eventual romance. In order to

meet him, she plans to ask a question, "a wonderful question, scholarly, subtle, profound." Too soon the course is over; she approaches him to ask the question, but it sticks in her throat and, unable to name the true object of desire, she can only say, ineffectually, that she "loved" the course.[2]

Much of this story belongs to cliché. In one such formula, the eager student worships her intellectually accomplished professor; in another, the professor seduces his physically appealing student. Had the story appeared in *Redbook* or *McCall's*, the protagonist would have been younger, more attractive—and wedding bells the consummation devoutly to be contrived. As it is, this story's protagonist is far from fetching; odd, older, intellectual, she is crazy, destined to be thwarted in her attempts to fulfill the only destiny conceivable for a clever woman: marriage to a cleverer man. But in the 1950s few could imagine another script; few would dare to make a story of a woman's wish for intellectual attainment, intellectual recognition. The available academic plots had no place for the woman as *quester* (to use Heilbrun's language), only as romantic addendum, whether scorned or desired. As for the esteemed male professor, there was no walk-on role for him as guide, paraclete, as mentor even, whose primary purpose in the script was to nourish the aspirations of our woman-student-as-hero. We come, then, to the question: what were the roles and relationships possible at Columbia in the 1950s for Lionel Trilling, professor of English and comparative literature, and for Carolyn Heilbrun, graduate student?

For those growing up in the 1960s, challenging public institutions and testing private inhibitions, the 1950s represented everything that needed to be resisted. Those were the cold war years, the years of espionage and counterespionage, the years of black lists, brinkmanship, and Joseph McCarthy. In 1950, Alger Hiss, a seeming "paragon of the establishment," was toppled from his comfortable life by Whittaker Chambers and sent to prison for lying about his alleged communist affiliations;[3] by 1953, the Rosenbergs were dead, executed for treason. The penalties for not knowing your place, for being un-American, unmanly, or unwomanly, were severe. Not surprisingly, the mood of the times was fearful, drearily conformist. Its essence was distilled in three classic works of the era—William H. Whyte's *The Organization Man*, David Riesman's *The Lonely Crowd,* and C. Wright Mills's *White Collar*—analyses of the ways in which alienated individuals were being swallowed up by bloated bureaucracies and fragmented in the clutch of giant corporations. Lionel Trilling, who would publish in 1955 his own contribution to this matter of the embattled individual, *The Opposing Self,* declared himself "far more enthusiastic about the work being produced these days by social scientists than by writers of fiction."[4] Fiction needed forceful selves to drive the imagination; these works of sociology told us that our selves were no longer our own.

Several recent books have offered reappraisals of the period that resist the pessimistic conclusions presented in the important sociological analyses of the time. Allan Bloom, in his controversial *The Closing of the American Mind,* one of the most startling best-sellers of the 1980s, recalls a golden age in the academy when the canon was fixed, standards were clear, and authority unquestioned. Dan Wakefield, in his memoir, *New York in the Fifties,* challenges the notion that the 1950s were "a time of quiet acquiescence to the status quo,"[5] pointing to the excitement of life in Greenwich Village, intellectual adventures with those who were (or would become) some of the most important thinkers of the day, and engagement in social struggles that predated the more violent expressions of the 1960s. Less given to sentimentality than these two, David Halberstam's capacious *The Fifties* offers a broad overview of the decade, with portraits of important figures (from Eisenhower and Nixon to Levitt and Sanger) who shaped the times. Susan Douglas, beginning her excellent study of women in the media, *Where the Girls Are,* in the 1950s, finds redeeming signs of female spunk in such television characters as Lucy of *I Love Lucy,* Alice Kramden of *The Honeymooners,* and Gracie Allen of *The Burns and Allen Show,* thus assuring her readers that the 1950s were not altogether flat for feminism.[6]

These writers appropriately remind us that the 1950s were more complicated, more nuanced, perhaps even more honorable, than is generally supposed. Civil rights activists could point to the landmark decision in *Brown* v. *Board of Education of Topeka* in 1954 and, in 1955, to the bus boycott in Montgomery following the refusal of Rosa Parks to move to the back of the bus. Signs of resistance and rebellious individualism could also be discerned in some of the popular idols of the period: Elvis Presley, James Dean, the iconoclastic Marlon Brando. And the Beats sent up their long howl of protest against a life of social and sexual blandness dictated by a "square" official culture.

Yet, whether one extols the virtues of stability as Bloom does or uncovers pockets of insurrection as Wakefield does, neither of these exercises in nostalgia provides much comfort for women. If Bloom craves a return to his beloved 1950s, few women would wish to share that journey with him. The portraits provided by David Riesman and C. Wright Mills of "white-collar girls" and "salesgirls" (classified by Mills under such types as "the Elbower," "the Charmer," "the Social Pretender") are grim indeed; and one is scarcely consoled by the fact that most of these women were only marking time until marriage whisked them to the suburbs, where they could realize a destiny as "a prisoner at home with the small children, the telephone, and the radio or television."[7] In spite of Susan Douglas's efforts to find feisty women in the popular culture of the 1950s, women of those years were without a ready form for whatever resistance they might have felt. That the modes of rebellion were essentially male does not diminish those achievements. Women, having been displaced from wartime work by returning veterans, found themselves moved back into their old places as homemakers and, increasingly, moved out into the isolation of the suburbs. Where could women look to find their fantasies mirrored: in the airbrushed photographs of *Playboy*? In the newly founded Disneyland? They could comb the pages of women's magazines such as *Redbook* and *Ladies' Home Journal* or emulate the kitchens of June Cleaver or Harriet Nelson. But could adolescent girls, dreaming of a destiny, imagine themselves as Elvis or as Jack Kerouac? Or even as companions of those men? Surely, one of the trademarks of such rebels was the dismissive treatment they accorded the women in their lives, women who represented for them the very claims of a society they wished to resist.

In the next decade or so, feminists would develop such an analysis, but for now, women could eke out little solace in the fact reported by Dan Wakefield that women were always part of the Bohemian scene.[8] For the parts they played were scarcely tempting. Take the "accidental" death of William Burroughs's wife, shot in the head during a party game when he missed the glass balanced on her head in a "William Tell act." Or ponder the routine pastime of Gary Snyder and Allen Ginsberg who, with a young girl, performed "an Oriental form of sex based on the mystical formula: 'Om, the thunderbolt in the void.' They were the 'thunderbolt,' and she, of course, was the 'void.'"[9] Nor could strong women look for themselves in Tennessee Williams's *A Streetcar Named Desire* or in Samuel Beckett's *Waiting for Godot,* a play that opened in

New York in 1956 and that captured for many the essential meaning-lessness of a post-Holocaust, post-Hiroshima world. Simone de Beauvoir's *The Second Sex,* originally published in 1949 and published in translation in the United States in 1953, initially cast only a few ripples in intellectual circles. Indeed, women's aspirations of the time were perhaps best captured in the fairy-tale transformation of Grace Kelly into Princess Grace on the occasion of her 1956 marriage to Prince Rainier of Monaco.

There were exceptions, but the blueprint for appropriate behavior was clear. Adrienne Rich sets it forth: "these were the fifties, and in reaction to the earlier wave of feminism, middle-class women were making careers of domestic perfection, working to send their husbands through professional schools, then retiring to raise large families." In *The Feminine Mystique,* Betty Friedan reports that possibilities for women, which had expanded during and just after World War II, contracted again in the late 1940s and throughout the 1950s. Reading "issue after issue of the three major women's magazines" in the late 1950s, she was unable to find "a single heroine who had a career, a commitment to any work, art, profession, or mission in the world, other than 'Occupation: housewife.'"[10] In short, "normal" women were expected to marry and produce children. If women did dare build a career, then they usually did not marry and were regarded with varying degrees of pity and condescension by the rest of society. Very few women in those years were so bold as to attempt both marriage and a career; very few men were able to withstand the potential intrafamily competition of another wage-earner who would implicitly direct public criticism at their inability to provide for the family.

Carolyn Heilbrun, however, was one of the bold ones: it did not seem to occur to her that she would not have a career. After graduation from Wellesley, she became an editorial assistant at Houghton Mifflin; when a new editor fired her, she went to the Jewish Theological Seminary to run a radio program. Her distaste for the attitudes expressed toward women by the Conservative Jews of that institution, recorded in *Reinventing Womanhood,* prompted her to resign.[11] Meanwhile, routine neighborhood walks past Columbia University helped crystallize a decision to continue the study of literature. With, as she recalls, the active encouragement of her husband, Heilbrun applied for admission to Columbia University as a master's degree student. She planned to complete her degree and then apply to medical school: her ambition, she says, had always been to become a doctor.

To enter Columbia University, as Heilbrun did in 1949, was to enter at the height of its power a great university that had a formidable influence on the culture and politics of the time. As Susanne Klingenstein points out, "New York City, with its Olympus of Columbia University, was the intellectual and cultural center." The faculty could boast such eminent figures as Lionel Trilling, Mark Van Doren, and C. Wright Mills; moreover, the president of Columbia University, Dwight D. Eisenhower, ascended in 1952 to the presidency of the country, drawing the institution into national politics. When Grayson Kirk was inaugurated as Columbia's new president in 1953, his speech made clear that Columbia had nothing short of a national mission: "The days are gone when academic life could pursue its course with little or no concern about the outside world." Kirk, of course, was talking about the Cold War, and he took pains to declare that academic freedom did not extend to communists "who have sworn allegiance to beliefs which are the antithesis of all that we stand for."[12]

Columbia College's newspaper, the *Columbia Daily Spectator,* for this period, yields some sense of the concerns of undergraduates. They agonized about the draft for the Korean War, feared a diminishing job market, and demanded bomb shelters on the Columbia site. They vigorously challenged the justification for the loyalty oath, debated the wisdom of inviting known communists (such as Howard Fast) to speak on the campus, and published repeated accusations of discrimination against Negroes (including charges that Henry Steele Commager's book, *Growth of the American Republic,* written with Samuel E. Morison, was racist). Beyond the fears about security—both national and personal—the most powerful themes emerging from the pages of the newspaper have to do with who and what should and should not be welcomed in the institution: Should the history of Negroes be included in the curriculum?[13] Were communists welcome to express their views? In what ways should the institution respond to the plight of the poor?

These debates about exclusion and inclusion remind us that the university saw its proper business as setting standards and making distinctions; indeed, we might observe that Columbia University was an expert in distinction-making, for it was not one institution but many, each with its own clearly defined place in the hierarchy. The three components of the system that would affect Heilbrun directly consisted of Columbia College, the school for male undergraduates; the Graduate Faculty of Philosophy, which admitted men and women for graduate study; and the School of General Studies, a place where adult students could return for undergraduate degrees earned by more unorthodox timetables. Steven Marcus, Columbia faculty member since 1957, explained that, with respect to the study of English, a central department theoretically oversaw the faculty teaching literature in all three schools; but, in practice, the three divisions operated more or less autonomously.[14] Columbia College was the jewel in the crown; graduate students were generally perceived to be of more variable quality than the bright male undergraduates; as for the School of General Studies, debates persisted as to whether it should exist at all, whether its bachelor's degree tainted the integrity of that offered by the College.[15] Although some faculty taught in all three schools, others were restricted. The most eminent faculty, men of letters such as the elegant, erudite Lionel Trilling and the cultured Mark Van Doren, preferred to teach in the College. The graduate school housed the more old-fashioned historical scholars. The also-rans and the women faculty, always very few in number, were typically relegated to the School of General Studies. Only notable and rare exceptions, such as the redoubtable seventeenth-century scholar, Marjorie Hope Nicolson, were able to cross the line into the College. A place of rigidly hierarchical compartments and categories, Columbia's divided English department scarcely represented one's ideal of the humane and liberal academy.

Heilbrun received her doctorate from Columbia University in 1959, left to become an instructor at Brooklyn College for a year, and then returned to teach at Columbia in 1960, taking her place, of course, in the School of General Studies. Steven Marcus recalls that movement from one school to another came about through invitation, based on the perceived quality of a faculty member's work. It was not until the late 1960s that Heilbrun was invited to cross over into the graduate faculty. By the early 1970s, the department was effectively centralized, but not before, as I was told by a number of present-day Columbia faculty, the history of divisiveness had already done its damage.

Columbia might have had more divisions than most universities, but it was surely not alone in its inhospitality to women in the 1950s and 1960s. Columbia College was, of course, only for male undergraduates (the women attended Barnard College); there were few female graduate students, fewer female professors, and no one seemed to have any sense that this situation was in any way discriminatory. Conspicuously absent from the political debates in the pages of the *Spectator* and elsewhere were questions about the place of women—whether in society or in the institution. A women's club for graduate students had been founded for the specific purpose of gathering women together "for comfort and support: comfort in the form of social activities, and support in determining their position in regard to their work and its recognition";[16] by the time Heilbrun arrived at Columbia, the club offered social teas, limited scholarship money for needy applicants, and opportunities for charitable acts, but no sustained professional support.[17] In any case, Heilbrun, married and not seeking such social interactions at school, did not join the club. The place of women is deftly summed up by the renowned physicist I. I. Rabi, who delivered an address entitled "Science and the University" at the commencement of 1954 (during which John Foster Dulles received an honorary degree). In arguing that the scientist is broadly educated and the humanist is not (Rabi's anticipation of the "two cultures" debate that C. P. Snow would make famous at the end of the decade), Rabi offers this throwaway line: "If any [problem in the scientist's connection with the humanities] existed, Mrs. Scientist would make up for the difficulty."[18] A liberally educated wife could presumably perform all sorts of domestic miracles, including that of humanizing Mr. Scientist.

The tone and nuances of the time are captured in *Jester of Columbia,* a satirical magazine put out by the students of the College—and, in particular, in the "We Hate Women" issue of March 1950, the spring after Carolyn Heilbrun joined the university as a graduate student. Not vicious, certainly not witty, the magazine sets forth a dismal Thurber-esque vision of the "cold war" between males and females. The issue features a puzzle page with a bikini-clad pinup for a dartboard, lame Freudian jokes about women with teeth who frighten their dates, and half-hearted surveys and contests on "Why I Hate, Detest, and Abhor Women." Even so, a review in the *Columbia Daily Spectator* for 27 April 1950, found the March *Jester* "a more decent one—literarily speaking—than what has preceded it this year."[19] This was the kind of atmosphere women encountered at Columbia in the grim 1950s.

In Heilbrun's graduate classes at Columbia, there were few women.

She remembers in particular a woman from Switzerland, but they never became friends. She did, however, have two male friends, Tom Driver and Robert Pack, both of whom also went on to conspicuous success as academics. Tom Driver remembers that they formed a trio; in Oscar Campbell's Shakespeare seminar, they "played to each other," all participating vigorously in the seminar discussions. Robert Pack recalls Heilbrun from those years as "brilliant and vivacious," a woman who was "a great source of intellectual stimulation and excitement." In class, she was "always very articulate and poised," with a "confident sense of herself." When Pack showed Heilbrun his poems and essays, he found her "a wonderful critic and reader." Neither Pack nor Driver remembers reading her essays; Pack thinks "she had not really come out as a writer" at that point. Presumably, as she had at Wellesley, Heilbrun was keeping her own counsel. Both Pack and Driver recall this period as an exciting time, one of vital conversations about literature, politics, and philosophy. The friendship extended to the social hours, too, when the spouses of all three were included. According to Pack, they met for drinks, played word games, and even went bowling.[20]

Robert Pack's sense of Heilbrun as "a joyous person," who "enjoyed her friends, enjoyed the study of literature, enjoyed her classes," cannot accommodate her subsequent changes in literary and political direction. Indeed, Pack confesses surprise at the turn her life and writings have since taken: she never struck him then as "an ideological person," and he would not have anticipated her subsequent disaffection with Columbia. The biography he would have expected her to complete in 1995 was not Gloria Steinem's but George Eliot's. In the mid-1960s, Pack moved to Vermont to take up a post at Middlebury College; he attributes his present distance from Heilbrun to geography and regrets they are no longer in touch; she sees the distance between them as defined by a difference of politics. Heilbrun and Tom Driver have, on the other hand, remained good friends.

Tom Driver corroborates, in a more measured way, Pack's memories of that time. But Heilbrun herself looks back to the 1950s as a time of despondency. In writing about the "Poetics and Gender" colloquium held at Columbia in the mid-1980s, she summons up an earlier self deprived of such discussions: "yet my new, graduate-school self in 1950, permitted . . . to attend [this] colloquium in 1985, would have been . . . convinced of angelic powers."[21] What to make of these different memories? What did Driver and Pack fail to perceive? Did Heilbrun allow subsequent experiences at Columbia to cast too long a shadow backwards? To be sure, their sense of possibility, of options opening outward, had to be different from hers. They could look about them to a world that welcomed and cheered their achievements; she could scarcely do the same. So she juggled the masks of clever student and 1950s wife, hiding whatever tensions needed to be hid, without necessarily being conscious of the sleight of hand. A close woman friend might have discerned her struggle, but she had no such friend. Still, her friendships with Driver and Pack meant that Heilbrun was not as isolated at Columbia as she had been at Wellesley.

Like other women students of the time, Heilbrun felt little regarded by her professors. She wrote her master's thesis under the inattentive eye of William York Tindall and began her doctoral dissertation with him, too. But then, she reports, "he couldn't be bothered," and she transferred to Jerome Buckley, who later moved to Harvard. Her doctoral orals "did not go well"; she was stumped by a question on the medieval period and disconcerted by the fact that no one from Columbia's comparative literature faculty stayed for the full session—except for the supportive Susanne Howe Nobbe, the only tenured woman in the department aside from Marjorie Hope Nicolson. The dissertation defense was more successful, with Buckley leaping to her aid when she was attacked for daring to suggest that the epic was no longer a viable genre. Tom Driver, close to completing his own dissertation, remembers Nicolson, then the formidable chair of the department, announcing that she would help him find a job if he were willing to leave New York, where academic positions were in short supply; Robert Pack, recommended for a Fulbright by Jacques Barzun and Lionel Trilling, recollects, while still in Italy on his fellowship, getting a letter from the chair at Barnard College, asking if he were interested in a job. Heilbrun recalls receiving no such offers of assistance. It is fair to say that her qualifications were not so dazzling as Pack's; by that time, Pack had one book of poetry published, another under contract, and a critical book on Wallace Stevens under contract, too. However, as Driver corroborates, her credentials were every bit as strong as his. Heilbrun did find a post at Brooklyn College and then, despite her sense that she was unappreciated, must have made some positive impression, because she was subsequently hired by Columbia in 1960, albeit in the School of General Studies. That her dissertation was quickly snapped up for publication by Macmillan as *The Garnett Family*, at a time when dissertations were not commonly published, might have influenced Columbia's decision. But all Heilbrun recalls is the resounding lack of impact her presence had: she recalls approaching Quentin Anderson (then administrative head of the College English Department) at a social event after she had been teaching at Columbia for some time, but he did not know who she was. And certainly, she was convinced, Lionel Trilling, whom she esteemed above all the rest, "didn't know [she] existed."

By the time Carolyn Heilbrun was admitted to Columbia as a graduate student in the early 1950s, sitting in, as she says, on all of Trilling's classes "not limited to College boys,"[22] Lionel Trilling had not only built a local reputation as a brilliant, eloquent teacher and distinguished member of the New York intellectual milieu, but also established a national critical presence. In their series for two book clubs, the Readers' Subscription and the Mid-Century,[23] Jacques Barzun and Lionel Trilling (with the assistance of W. H. Auden) influenced the tastes and reading habits of intelligent readers (such as Heilbrun herself) eager for cultural instruction. Publishing in the *Nation, Kenyon Review,* and *Partisan Review,* Lionel Trilling was not merely a narrowly focused literary critic who wrote on such figures as Arnold, Forster, James, Hawthorne, Wordsworth, Keats, and Austen, but a wide-ranging critic of the culture—a penetrating analyst of the power of mind, the relationship of self and culture, the intersections of literature, psychology, politics, culture, and society. Of his many influential works, the best known are *The Liberal Imagination, The Opposing Self, Beyond Culture, Sincerity and Authenticity,* and the novel, *The Middle of the Journey.*

Those who recall the teacher Lionel Trilling in memoirs invariably describe him as elegant, donnish, aristocratic.[24] His manner in front of a class was famous. Impeccably dressed in a three-piece suit, always smoking a cigarette, Trilling would deliver the day's wisdom. Dan Wakefield reports that he was "accessible and supportive of his students, especially the aspiring writers," and that was certainly true in his relationship to Allen Ginsberg, whom he helped in more than one extracurricular circumstance.[25] For some, he was a father figure, a phenomenon noted, too, by Diana Trilling.[26] Nevertheless, Dan Wakefield faithfully records the words of Marion Magid, who remembers Columbia's treatment of Barnard's undergraduate women students in the 1950s: "We weren't allowed to take the famous Columbia courses—in retrospect, it's the only thing I feel resentful about. You never questioned that Trilling was for the boys and you were a girl, so you had to make do."[27] And Lyndall Gordon, though writing about the 1960s, reports on the graduate student's experience once entrance to a Trilling class had been achieved: "All through that semester we listened to Trilling in nervous abjection. We slumped on our elbows. No one ever spoke. His lofty manner seemed to preclude the possibility that we could say anything worth hearing by a man of his eminence." She would make an even more sweeping indictment: "No woman of my generation failed to leave that department unscarred by abjection. It was the legacy of men of famed intelligence, like the critic Lionel Trilling, who spoke, like Jehovah, through a cloud of smoke as he puffed his cigarette at the ceiling of Philosophy Hall." Having moved to Oxford in the 1970s, she confides to a friend, "At Columbia you could be a mistress, a mother, or a freak—but not a colleague."[28]

Lionel Trilling evoked complex responses. Photographs reveal a handsome man, features delicately carved; as time goes on, his receding hairline exposes a powerful domed forehead. Everything, from the carefully knotted ties to the lines etched in his face, intimates a man of refined sensibility, of personal fastidiousness, of imposing intellect. None of the photographs I have seen reveals a smile. Trilling's face is always somber, melancholy, the face of a man struggling with weighty inner burdens. Many Trilling observers note the ink-dark circles around his eyes, earned, as Dan Wakefield, for one, surmises, from hour upon hour of reading and steady contemplation;[29] sometimes, indeed, his face, with its dark eye stains, has the look of a tragic mask.

That Lionel Trilling paid a price for this public persona, the mask of the aristocratic gentleman scholar, is presumably, after the publication of Diana Trilling's memoir, no longer in doubt.[30] Lionel Trilling was born in New York City in 1905 to middle-class Jews. His father, sent to the United States from Bialystock while still a boy, became a tailor and later a furrier; his mother, born in London of parents who emigrated from Russia and then moved to the United States, encouraged his literary aspirations. Trilling attended Columbia as an undergraduate and subsequently earned his doctorate there. After brief stints as a lecturer at the University of Wisconsin and at Hunter College, he returned to Columbia, where he became the first Jew to be tenured in his department. The story has been told by Diana Trilling: Trilling was informed in 1936 that "'as a Jew, a Marxist, and a Freudian,' he was not happy in his Columbia job and that his appointment would not be renewed." Instead of accepting this dismissal, Trilling confronted members of his department and assured them of his worth, an assurance he had himself hitherto lacked, according to Diana Trilling's account and to Trilling's own notes from the time. Indeed, Diana Trilling's reading of the situation is that Columbia disdained him not so much because he was a Jew as because he lacked "force." Henceforth, Diana Trilling tells us, he gained a new authority: "The fact that . . . he was able to reverse the decision of his department and be reinstated profoundly altered his sense of himself. From this time forward he spoke and wrote differently, bore himself differently, and truly became a different man. He produced a different impression on others. The career by which we now know him dates from the moment in which he refused to be dismissed from Columbia and was able to persuade his senior colleagues to value him as he wished to be valued."[31]

Diana Trilling's perspective is revealing. Clearly, she herself disparaged Trilling's "powerlessness," the way his "manner . . . invited denigration." She admired the "extraordinary feat of self-renovation" Trilling achieved through his anger at his Columbia colleagues. (We should remember this anger because it will be instrumental in Heilbrun's intellectual evolution, too.) But Trilling's reinvention of himself (to use the term Heilbrun would make famous) and his adoption of a mask of manly authority and invulnerability were also a source of irritation to Diana Trilling. She reports that "the social relevance and moral intensity which in our American mid-century gave criticism its newly important role in society made Lionel himself into a kind of moral exemplar for his students." Trilling "unconsciously . . . conspired" in creating this impression of himself and was (especially before students) "at pains not to reveal the human fallibilities which had sent him into analysis." Diana Trilling resented this image of faultless superiority and wonders what Trilling would have done, in an autobiography, with the secret of his lengthy psychoanalysis.[32] What must concern us here is the psychic cost of being this Lionel Trilling and the expectations (especially from students) that his public persona provoked.

"At all stages of education there are teachers who become symbolical figures for their students—they have it in common with analysts that certain of their students vest their phantasies in them," writes Diana Trilling; she was, of course, naming this phenomenon as it related to Lionel Trilling.[33] In *Reinventing Womanhood*, Carolyn Heilbrun explains at some length her personal experience of Lionel Trilling. Although Heilbrun's book was published in 1979, four years after the death of Lionel Trilling, and when Heilbrun herself was fifty-three, her wounds are still raw. The deepest cut, unwitting though it may have been on his part, was simply that she did not exist for him. Heilbrun remarks, "William Gibson has said that in every lucky life there is one teacher who places his finger upon our soul. For me that teacher was Trilling. The irony here—an irony characteristic of women's lives—is that the touch was accidental; Trilling neither intended nor acknowledged it. Most women for whom male teachers become mentors turn to them with a devotion either daughterly or loverlike. I was neither attractive nor submissive enough to have made either role possible, and Trilling had no sense of my discipleship." Several paragraphs later, she recalls the situation after she had joined him as a member of the Columbia faculty: "During all the years we were colleagues he never once talked to me, except in the most routine way of politeness. I used to fantasize that we would one day engage in dialogue—this ponderous phrase exactly explains what I aspired to—and his death, ending all hope for that, released me strangely, not only to frank disagreement with his disciples, my colleagues, but to a realization that the dialogue did not require his presence, could not, indeed, have encompassed it."[34] But the word *dialogue*, with its air of quaint formality, is not quite precise. For if Heilbrun engaged in (written) conversation with Trilling, if he was always a member of the audience Heilbrun imagined for herself, if he was named as influence or adversary in numerous of her books and articles, and if she was deeply in his intellectual debt, she figured for him not at all. It is no surprise that not a single reference to her can be found in any of his works. On the other hand, Heilbrun's one-sided relationship with the "symbolical figure" of Lionel Trilling takes many forms: at times, praise amounting almost to adulation; then anger, which, though slow to show itself, gradually deepens; finally, the transformation of some of Trilling's key ideas for feminist purposes. She writes to Trilling, at Trilling, after Trilling, with Trilling in mind.

What, then, did Lionel Trilling mean to Carolyn Heilbrun? Why did he feature so dramatically in her intellectual life? One might say that, in many respects, he was what she was; in addition, however, he was what she wanted to be. Like Heilbrun, he was a Jew and, again like Heilbrun, a Jew who was both carefully assimilated into New York life and yet alienated from it. If Heilbrun gently derides Trilling's aristocratic pretensions and his gestures toward elegant assimilation, she herself created a protagonist for her detective novels who bears all the marks of aristocratic privilege. And then, to play that Freudian fugue again, in spite of the fact that she says she was not submissive enough to be daughterly, he, born in 1905, was the intellectual father that she, born in 1926, might have had; he modeled the pattern of accomplishment she sought to emulate; he was "the most powerful and honored presence" during her years at Columbia;[35] he was, in fact, not just a teacher, not just a critic, not just a writer of fiction, but a public intellectual, who had the power to shape minds. Himself an outsider, he might have shown the immigrant's daughter the way in—and thus the way out.

Trilling offered many lessons to his eager graduate student. Above all, he laid out what Heilbrun was later to call a "Trilling universe" of "moral choices,"[36] a notion that politics and literature were inextricably entwined, a belief that literature had consequences, that it affected, shaped, challenged real experience. Literature was not simply a matter of tropes held in artful tension; it objectified the drama of the moral life, disciplined the sensibility, exacted a serious, strenuous study of ideas. Many of these ideas, informed by Freud, and to a lesser extent by Marx, were expressed in the immensely influential *Liberal Imagination* (1950), which sold a hundred thousand copies.[37] In his famous essay, "Freud and Literature" (first published in 1940, revised in 1947, and later included in *The Liberal Imagination*), remarking the debt of criticism to the "Freudian system," Trilling offers a striking insight into the complexity of literary texts; he says we now "read the work of literature with a lively sense of its latent and ambiguous meanings, as if it were, as indeed it is, a being no less alive and contradictory than the man who created it." This remarkably modern view of a text is reinforced later in the essay when he claims that "changes in historical context and in personal mood change the meaning of a work and indicate to us that artistic understanding is not a question of fact but of value." Very early on Trilling exposes the limitations of New Criticism, arguing that "the historical context of a work . . . [and] anything we may learn about the artist himself may be enriching and legitimate."[38] In another essay, "The

Sense of the Past," first published in 1942 and also included in *The Liberal Imagination*, Trilling asks, "What is the real poem? Is it the poem we now perceive? Is it the poem the author consciously intended? Is it the poem the author intended and his first readers read? Well it is all these things. . . . But in addition the poem is the poem as it has existed in history . . . as it is a thing which submits itself to one kind of perception in one age and another kind of perception in another age. . . . This makes it a thing we can never wholly understand."[39] Trilling not only points here to the essential elusiveness of art but also lays the groundwork for the kind of political inquiry into the nature of literary value, the relation of art to the assumptions of its time, the relation of reader to text, that feminists would pursue (albeit without Trilling's approval) a quarter century later. Indeed, it is something of a joke to recall that, when members of Columbia's English Department attempted to dismiss him from his post, Trilling was attacked for being "too sociological" in his approach to literature;[40] that charge would certainly become familiar to feminists in due course.

Lionel Trilling not only taught Carolyn Heilbrun how to approach literature, he also (unknowingly) bequeathed to her his lifelong concern with the autonomous self and the embattled relation of that self to culture. Mark Krupnick's presentation of Lionel Trilling in his book, *Lionel Trilling and the Fate of Cultural Criticism*, explains, in part, what drew Heilbrun to Trilling. Krupnick depicts Trilling as a wide-ranging cultural critic who "mediated between the university and the general culture." This critic of the culture, often self-divided, changes, as his conception of the culture changes, and as the culture itself changes over the decades; he is always repositioning himself. Toward the end of his career, he becomes increasingly conservative. His "overall project in criticism required that he invent a cultural identity for himself"; and the self that engages him, in true American tradition, is a "solitary self inventing itself and going forth to meet its destiny." That self, fearful of losing its boundaries, defines itself most forcefully in resistance to the culture, as an opposing self.[41] I pick up the strands of this account in my story of Carolyn Heilbrun, both to show her affinities to Trilling and her radical departures from his model; but it bears saying here that, despite personal crises, intellectual doubts and difficulties, the self Lionel Trilling presented to his students was seamless, a model of integrity and independence, a self seemingly so confident of its own edges that it could time after time take the unsafe and disputed middle ground in complicated intellectual and political circumstances.

Could Lionel Trilling's cultural identity be emulated by a woman? Could a woman become a critic of the culture, finding a locus from which to speak a vision that would resonate beyond the walls of the academy? Such a notion would have been alien indeed to Trilling. And so we return to women's complaints about Trilling; those complaints were, of course, also about the other eminent men who disdained women at Columbia, but Trilling was a special target, just as he was for radical students during the riots of the 1960s, because those who saw themselves in the fight for a society ruled by principles of justice wanted the champion of humanism in their corner. But where women were concerned, there was a gap, a chasm, even. For the most part, in his criticism as in his fiction, Trilling simply could not imagine women as centers of consciousness, as moral agents.

This chapter began with a tale of academic life told from the point of view of a woman student; let me set alongside it a story by Trilling narrated from the point of view of a young, idealistic male professor. In "The Lesson and the Secret," Vincent Hammell is teaching a class of rich, society matrons "Techniques of Creative Writing." Like "Summer Session," the short story from *Quarto*, this story focuses on a central question; but, in this case, the students do not wish to astonish the professor by the depths of their comprehension. Instead, they want the key to a secret, the secret not of making stories but of selling them. Several of the students express their contempt for a professor who cannot help them succeed in this, but the real secret of this story is the contempt of the instructor for his female students, for their moral obtuseness, for their inability to rise above crass materialism. In the course of the lesson, Hammell reads them a story of two young girls who visit a priest and, while he is called away, secretly tread the homemade wine he is preparing in a tin bathtub, "the drops of red wine splashing up to their thighs." Thus, as Hammell watches his middle-aged students' self-conscious adjustment of "skirts over knees," he reminds them of the only lesson women can embody: literally, the sensuous, earthly, material pleasures of the body.[42] This lesson Trilling would drive home in his portrayal of Emily Caldwell in *The Middle of the Journey*, and in the ringing denouncement of Mrs. Alving from Ibsen's *Ghosts,* who is blamed for Captain Alving's fateful dalliances because she was "prudish" and thus "kill[ed] the joy of living" in her husband.[43]

Given his position, Trilling could presumably have been Heilbrun's mentor; indeed, he was her mentor, but, since he had no conscious knowledge of the fact, his mentorship was, as Heilbrun would put it, "unwilling."[44] Much later, in her presidential address to the Modern Language Association, Heilbrun would quote a passage from Alice Jardine's brilliant essay, "Death Sentences: Writing Couples and Ideology": "For there would appear to exist a seeming historical necessity for the heterosexual woman who wants to create, to write—and be read—to couple herself in fact *or fantasy* [emphasis added], albeit if only temporarily with a man who also writes or wrote, a famous man in her life or in her writing—if not the *necessity,* then the *desire* to do so, under the illusion that it will be easier that way."[45] Heilbrun invokes Jardine's theory to point out that "for many of us, one of the men we trained with became . . . part of . . . 'the writing couple,'" and to suggest that we may now (in 1984) be at the stage where we can imagine different writing couples, perhaps even women mentoring women.[46] But Jardine's paradigmatic couple is Simone de Beauvoir and Jean Paul Sartre, and her model, the heterosexual one, proposes a famous and powerful male who can open doors for a talented female. Such a model might have seemed the only possible one for an ambitious woman of the 1950s, and Mary McCarthy's union with Edmund Wilson is representative. Yet, given the nature of the available model, such a relationship was doubtless impossible for Lionel Trilling and Carolyn Heilbrun, even had he thought her worthy of his notice. While it was perfectly acceptable for male professors to mentor men, mentoring women was highly risky, opening any self-respecting mentor to suspicions of untoward goings-on. When the only available models for relations between male and female are sexual or romantic, the heterosexual male, careful of his reputation, must needs mentor only his wife or his lover. A case in point: Heilbrun recalls asking William York Tindall, her supervisor, for a date to go over her master's essay. "A date?" he asked, looking flustered for a moment, no doubt thinking she was asking for the only possible "date" that could occur between a man and a woman. Surely, it would have been difficult for a male professor of this time *not* to fail his female students and colleagues.

Certainly, at Columbia, those female colleagues were few indeed.

Could they be mentors? Marjorie Hope Nicolson was "not particularly supportive of women,"[47] and that left Susanne Howe Nobbe. Heilbrun has spoken eloquently of Nobbe, "who stood alone as a model of female scholar and support" in Heilbrun's early years at Columbia. Heilbrun "loved" Nobbe, but according to Heilbrun, Nobbe was "suffering" herself and simply did not exert the kind of power in the academy and in the world that Trilling did; in spite of a substantial scholarly record, Nobbe could not get promoted to the rank of full professor. Trilling was the mentor Heilbrun wanted. When I reminded Heilbrun of the passage from Jardine quoted in the previous paragraph, she declared that the paradigm about writing couples could not be applied to her and Trilling because he was unaware of her presence. "But," I pressed, did it apply "in your mind?" Her response: "Definitely." To be sure, in the case of this fantasy couple, there could be little in the way of reciprocity. Indeed, it would doubtless have come as a great surprise to Trilling to find himself thus coupled; and such a coupling certainly did not make things (in Jardine's words) "easier" for Heilbrun.

The story of Lionel Trilling, professor and critic of the culture, and Carolyn Heilbrun, graduate student, is significant because it is both particular and representative. That both had complex lives and responsibilities is evident. Lionel Trilling, as Diana Trilling relates, as a young man took on the financial burden of supporting his parents—and he struggled with the physical and psychological problems of his wife. A powerful figure at Columbia University, he helped forge the cultural, literary, and political discourses of his time. Carolyn Heilbrun was merely a graduate student. Married, and by 1955 a mother, she was likely to get her degree and disappear into suburbia. Instead, she stayed at Columbia, relinquishing her dream of a medical degree for a doctorate in literature. Earning that degree took her eight years—too long, as she thought—but she was unsure of her goals, unsure of her ambition. She attended seminars, spoke up, wrote papers, and completed her essay for the master of arts and her dissertation for the doctorate. She would have liked some notice, some acknowledgement. But, "Nobody at Columbia ever paid any attention," she would say.

Should anyone have noticed her? Did anyone notice the normal run of male graduate students? Surely it is just in the nature of things that graduate students are humiliated and ignored by eminent professors. On the other hand, we cannot forget that Trilling was a "symbolical figure," that he set up expectations. He was, after all, according to Heilbrun, "the clearest, best writer, the best thinker"; he knew, unlike the other denizens of academe, that "there was a world." He opened a door to the moral imagination; if *he* could not recognize women in their full humanity, who could?

And so we see these two figures, caught in the web of history, figures of their time and of their place. Was it possible for the one, Trilling, not to fail the other? Lionel Trilling is a "symbolic figure," but not quite in the way that Diana Trilling intended: he was the best the world of letters could then offer, yet even he could not invite women to join in the adventure of the intellectual and moral life. He did not exactly turn his face away from Carolyn Heilbrun because he could not even see where she was. Her demand to be seen, to be recognized and acknowledged, is important; for it distinguishes her from those who suffered similar neglect. She would not be acquiescent, a good quiet girl nicely minding the boundaries of the acceptable. That demand for acknowledgment would not become vocal for many years, but it was there—a seed.

As Heilbrun's own development unfolds in the following chapters, I point to the strength of Trilling's presence in her intellectual life, her dependence on, and liberation from, his thought. He will not be, of course, the only influence on her intellectual development, but he was the first, the most significant, and therefore singular. He appears, disguised as a character in Amanda Cross's detective stories and stands behind or against Carolyn Heilbrun's ambitions as a public intellectual. I contend, for example, that *Toward a Recognition of Androgyny* (though it is not explicitly acknowledged as such) was conceived as an argument against Trilling's view of women and that *Reinventing Womanhood* reconceives and reinvents the Trillingesque self for women.

The question arises whether the Heilbrun we know—one of the very few feminists of her generation—would have existed had Trilling acknowledged her, encouraged her, perhaps even welcomed her into the charmed circle of New York intellectuals. Certainly, working through her relationship with Trilling contributed to the making of her feminism. She spent her graduate student days "at [his] foot," "in [his] shadow,"[48] admired his ideas, appropriated his methods, transformed some of his themes, and attempted to make his texts responsive even when he himself refused to be. However, the most radical transformation Carolyn Heilbrun achieved was not of Trilling's ideas but of herself.

3

Split Selves: The Mother
and the Writer

In my twenties, I gave birth to three children within
four years: a radicalizing experience.

— ADRIENNE RICH, *Of Woman Born*

The first of these preconceptions is that maternity is
enough in all cases to crown a woman's life. It is nothing of the kind. There are a great many mothers who
are unhappy, embittered, unsatisfied.

— SIMONE DE BEAUVOIR, *The Second Sex*

A gifted and vital woman, recognizing the veracity of
her professional drives, cannot question too closely the
values of the society within which she succeeds. . . .
For safety, she must exalt her common female capacities for motherhood and marital service and suppress
any feelings of hostility or resentment. If she is successful in repressing them, her own journals, letters, and
conversations will not openly reveal any inner doubts
or tensions.

— CAROLYN G. HEILBRUN, review of
Dorothy Thompson: A Legend in Her Time,
by Marion K. Sanders

The late 1950s were a time of new beginnings for Carolyn Heilbrun.
In 1955, she gave birth to her first child and, in 1957, she gave
birth to herself as a professional writer, publishing her first essay, "The
Character of Hamlet's Mother." The obvious connection between these
two events, the experience of motherhood, belies the extent to which,

for most women in the 1950s, motherhood and professional accomplishment were mutually exclusive.

Carolyn and James Heilbrun married in 1945 but waited ten years to produce their first child. This delay is, in itself, an astonishing fact. Most women of the time saw marriage as their primary goal, and it did not occur to them that they could choose whether or when to have a child. Children followed as naturally on the heels of marriage as a period closed a declarative sentence; few dared substitute a question mark; fewer still dreamed of other options. Adrienne Rich published her first volume of poems before she graduated from Radcliffe. Married in 1953, she had a second book in press while she was pregnant with her first child in 1955. She gave birth to two more sons in 1957 and 1959: "By July of 1958 I was again pregnant. The new life of my third—and, as I determined, my last—child, was a kind of turning for me. I had learned that my body was not under my control; I had not intended to bear a third child." [1]

Perhaps Carolyn and James Heilbrun did not feel they could refuse to have children, but they did choose to wait ten years. In conversation, Carolyn Heilbrun has spoken of the enormous pressure for women to have children in the 1950s. "Motherhood is too seldom a choice," she said, speaking of her "conscious choice" to "have the one child," but then of later giving birth to twins. One wonders, of course, given the times, to what extent any decision to have a child could be freely made. However, Heilbrun did adamantly choose—against advice and against convention—to stay in New York City rather than move to the suburbs—and she also chose to continue, without a pause, her professional career. By the time Emily Heilbrun was born in 1955, Carolyn Heilbrun was twenty-nine years old and, having earned her master's degree at Columbia in 1951, was steadily closing in on the doctorate in English. In 1957, she gave birth to twins, Margaret and Robert. Now, with three children under the age of three, the pressures on Heilbrun to relinquish her ambitions for a career mounted. Struggling with the demands of a doctoral program is difficult under any circumstances, but especially so with complications added by the responsibility for three small children, by the more or less complete lack of support for such a choice, and by the absence of other women successfully coping with career and family whose example could be emulated.

In need of domestic help, Heilbrun hired a woman to take care of the children every day until five in the afternoon. "My salary paid hers," she said. It was well worth it. Heilbrun hated sitting in the park with the other mothers, hated conversations about diapers and recipes. In due course, she also hired someone to clean the house twice a week; indeed, this woman, now in her eighties, still does some housework for her. But even though her children were well cared for and she herself spent several hours a day with them, she did not escape the inevitable self-reproaches: "I had such guilt about working." None of this guilt finds its way into Heilbrun's work—either in this decade or the two following.

Both Betty Friedan and Adrienne Rich (like Heilbrun and Rich, Friedan also had three children) describe the anger, the self-division, the frustrations of motherhood. In *The Feminine Mystique,* Friedan quotes woman after woman suffering from the desperation, the exhaustion, and the rage of those who had accepted "a half-life, instead of a share in the whole of human destiny." Rich recalls moments of joy and pleasure in her children but does not flinch from the memories that made her feel, at times, monstrous: "I remember being uprooted from already meager sleep to answer a childish nightmare. . . . I remember going back to bed starkly awake, brittle with anger, knowing that my broken sleep would make next day a hell, that there would be more nightmares, more need for consolation, because out of my weariness I would rage at those children for no reason they could understand."[2]

On the personal anguish of motherhood, Heilbrun is surprisingly silent. Much later in her life, she expresses her relief that her children are now grown and independent, but she says little in print of her early engagement with them and especially little of any personal ambivalence.[3] Even in the autobiographical chapters of *Reinventing Womanhood,* she does not mention her own experiences of bearing and coping with young children, although she does raise theoretical questions about motherhood in other chapters. According to Rich, motherhood necessarily and inevitably shaped her feminist identity; indeed, motherhood would "radicalize" her.[4] In describing the influences on her own feminism in *Reinventing Womanhood,* Heilbrun mentions the example of her father's achievements, her status as a Jewish outsider, and her position as an only child—but not her experience as a mother. If there were conflicts about her decision to raise children and pursue a profession, Heilbrun does not mention them; if there were conflicts as a result of that choice, Heilbrun does not mention them, either. And yet it was an extraordinary choice to commit to a professional life, while still raising young children, even if one had the financial resources to make it possible.

Perhaps Heilbrun is silent on this matter because she did not suffer the anguish described by Rich. She did have a career, after all; she did not settle for the "half-life" so poignantly described by Betty Friedan. But more important: to write honestly about motherhood is to risk one's children's reading those words in due course. Little wonder that motherhood is the least examined aspect of women's lives. Nevertheless, if the silence of the Heilbrun of 1979 in *Reinventing Womanhood* seems strange, there were good reasons for the Heilbrun of the late 1950s to keep quiet about the difficulties of managing a family and a career. In order to blend into the professional landscape of the 1950s, Heilbrun had to be careful not to be dismissed as a woman and mother. Of course, the bind was double: to be a mother was not to be taken seriously by one's peers; yet not to be a mother was to be suspect as a woman. The only way to manage these oppositions (which were doubtless internalized as well) was to be a mother and yet ignore the conflicts that experience produced in one's professional life, to keep the problems of mothering sharply out of view and out of consideration. It is no surprise, then, that Kate Fansler, the protagonist of Heilbrun's detective stories, remains childless after a conveniently late marriage.

If it is true to say that Heilbrun ignores the *struggles* of mothering in print, there is nevertheless ample evidence that the experience of mothering was shaping her literary point of view, that, indeed, the mother in her was striving to be heard. In the mid-1950s, Heilbrun was engaged on her dissertation, a study of the Garnett family that would become her first book. Yet her first published article, appearing in 1957, had nothing to do with the Garnett family or even their literary period. Heilbrun traveled to another century to perform a rescue mission on a famous literary mother, Gertrude, mother of Hamlet. In an article whose title signals her unexpected focus, "The Character of Hamlet's Mother," she bravely takes on those weighty male critics who have dismissed Gertrude as "well-meaning but shallow and feminine, in the pejorative sense of the word: incapable of any sustained rational process, superficial and flighty."[5] Arguing for Gertrude's intelligence and clarity and for the possibility that a woman over forty might be sexual, Heilbrun performs the unusual critical act of seeing Gertrude not from Hamlet's perspective, as male critics had implicitly done, but from Gertrude's own point of view. In Heilbrun's hands, she is thus translated from a mother who fails to behave in the way that a good mother should (erasing her sexuality, nurturing her son, and certainly not standing in the way of his possible political ambitions by marrying a man who would usurp her son's claim to the crown) and becomes a woman, a subject, with her own needs, her own desires. In fact, in Heilbrun's version, Gertrude becomes a woman capable of tragic stature whose one weakness, lust, causes her to marry Claudius in haste and thus to set in motion the chain of destruction that composes the play.

This early essay is remarkable for the self-confidence of Heilbrun's tone and voice, her willingness to resist accepted views, and her sharp awareness of the ways in which Gertrude has been trapped by role and gender, not only within the play but by practiced readers of the play, too. In retrospect, one might indeed say that in "The Character of Hamlet's Mother," Heilbrun assumes one of the first tasks of the feminist critic, the rereading of female characters. The method is conventional scholarly debate, but the subject, the reading of female characters by female critics, or the rescue of female characters from negative stereotyping by male critics and writers, would subsequently become key to the important first stage of feminist literary theory. Particularly significant is the fact that Heilbrun chooses to write about a mother and to allow that mother a life. Delighted with her first publication, Heilbrun sent a copy to Lionel Trilling; he did respond, on a postcard, saying that he did not realize that Gertrude's character had been in dispute. The painful irony of that lack of realization was not lost on Carolyn Heilbrun.

This essay did not become part of the context in which later literary critics examined women characters. Perhaps it was not sufficiently theoretical or wide-ranging, and perhaps it did not fully spell out its implications. More significant, there was no context within which it could be read; in that sense, it would await, while simultaneously anticipating, more developed feminist theory. Still, it was a noteworthy achievement, an early exercise in combat, and it is worth emphasizing that this article was published in 1957, admittedly eight years after Beauvoir's *The Second Sex,* but well in advance of Friedan's *The Feminine Mystique* (1963), Mary Ellmann's *Thinking about Women* (1968), and Kate Millett's *Sexual Politics* (1970). Nevertheless, the rumblings that would give rise to this latest feminist movement were beginning to be discerned at this time. In 1957, the year Heilbrun's article was published, Betty Friedan, in preparation for the fifteenth-year reunion of her class at Smith College, sent questionnaires to alumnae, asking about their lives and the choices they had made. Their responses, detailing widespread discontent, led her to ponder "the problem that has no name" and offer her diagnosis in *The Feminine Mystique*. And while Heilbrun was writing a distanced, scholarly article about Hamlet's mother and Gertrude's rights to sexuality and to her own choices, Adrienne Rich was writing anguished entries in her diary about her personal experience of mothering.[6]

In 1961, with the turn of a new decade, Carolyn Heilbrun, in the sober disguise of a conventional literary critic, published her first book, based on her doctoral dissertation. *The Garnett Family* was, in effect, a group biography. In the tradition of literary historians, Heilbrun tells the story—not hitherto well known—of members of the English Garnett family, establishing their contributions to intellectual and public life in the nineteenth and twentieth centuries. Heilbrun takes the opportunity to bring to light as-yet-unpublished letters and provides a useful source book for scholars, though the loose organization of the secondary material does, at times, threaten to overwhelm the tidy edges.

What attracted Heilbrun to the Garnetts aside from the need to find a suitably unexplored dissertation subject? No doubt she was drawn by the notion that they were members of "the intellectual aristocracy, that peculiarly English phenomenon" that had a contemporary American counterpart in the New York intellectuals. None of the members of the Garnett family was a great original writer, but Heilbrun clearly admires all of them for their energy, their productivity, their investment in work, and the variety and scope of their occupations: one Garnett, for example was librarian, poet, biographer, essayist, and translator; another was a publisher's reader, reviewer, dramatist, editor, and memoirist. Perhaps, too, given the discontinuity of her own family and the ways each generation invented itself anew, Heilbrun might have been intrigued by the tradition and continuity of a family where one generation took up the work of a former.[7] Yet, with one notable exception, Heilbrun seems not to be fully engaged with the Garnett family, and the well-known English critic, Richard Hoggart, gave the work a stern review in the *New Statesman,* calling it "a slight book" that "lacks the texture its subject demands."[8]

Nonetheless, *The Garnett Family* reveals some fascinating data for the student of Heilbrun's feminist development. In the first place, Heilbrun might easily have construed her task as limited to the fathers and sons of the Garnett family. But Heilbrun includes, in what turns out to be the strongest chapter of the book, a study of Constance Garnett, distinguished translator from the Russian, who was married to Edward and mother of David Garnett. The vivid center of the chapter is an image of Constance Garnett (from a description by D. H. Lawrence) steadily, systematically producing page after page of her famous translations. No doubt, the author of "The Character of Hamlet's Mother," who had championed a mother's right to a life beyond mothering, respected Constance Garnett for her ability to combine the roles of mother and successful translator. Indeed, from Heilbrun's account, Constance Garnett emerges as a wife and mother for whom, despite these welcome obligations, "personal independence was her highest ideal for human life." Throughout *The Garnett Family*, Heilbrun is alert to the status and place of women. She admires Edward Garnett for his belief in "complete sexual equality" and his championship of the rights of women artists. She also approves Constance Garnett's advanced idea "that if women were brought up to expect to earn their own living and have love affairs, [prostitution] would disappear." But Heilbrun's sharpest observations concern education for women and show evidence of the spark, the assurance, and the tartness that would later become characteristic of her voice: "The female mind might be naturally weak—most men agreed that it was—but it was beginning to occur to some men that it might not be further weakened by the study of Latin and Greek." Having pointed out that Constance Garnett "belonged to the first generation of women that received an education comparable to a man's," Heilbrun notes, with delicious wit, that "she and a handful of others were to demonstrate in the decade following that education was not wasted on women, that it did not—and this was more generally feared—unsex them or drive the men forced to glimpse them near the University into God-knew-what fits of depravity."[9]

The theme of appropriate education for women haunted the young Heilbrun and emerged in a bold essay, written for the *Columbia Forum*, with the prescient title, "Educating Female People" (1962), in which Heilbrun turned her attention to the real world of the present. Inspired by a lunch with Erik Wensberg, editor of the *Forum*, Heilbrun agreed to write the article and delivered it in three weeks. Her sense that it might cause a flap is conveyed in her letter to Wensberg accompanying the essay: "Here is the article. You asked for it." [10] In this essay, Heilbrun joins the debate on "the woman question" and raises the very issue of wasted women's minds that Betty Friedan would address with such passionate intensity in *The Feminine Mystique*. Heilbrun's dramatic proposal, inspired by teaching "extraordinary" older women students at Columbia's School of General Studies, argues for deferred education for women, following marriage and childbirth, so that their careers might be uninterrupted: "If marriage and the full employment of the female mind are not to remain hopelessly at odds, it is not the quality of women's education, but the timing of it which must be fundamentally altered." Her twofold theme is one that will resonate throughout her work: How can women balance lives of accomplishment with the roles of wives and mothers? What models exist for female achievement? Moreover, she does not subscribe to tokenism. In discussing Dr. Mary Bunting, president of Radcliffe, she points out that Bunting's achievement proves not that every woman can emulate her but that many cannot. Indeed, Heilbrun's early feminism leads her to hope that "we shall have made the accomplished woman not the exception but the rule." Nevertheless, she assures her audience that the goal is not militant feminism but the balance of Bunting's agenda: "She [Bunting] was concerned neither with woman as feminist nor with woman as brood mare. She spoke of woman as the mother of children, thereby dispelling forever the shade of Susan B. Anthony, but she also spoke of woman as needing 'something awfully interesting that she wants to work on awfully hard.'" [11] If Heilbrun has internalized the argument that it was not "normal" for women (like Susan B. Anthony) to refuse motherhood, it is also undoubtedly the case that, for her, what has become known as the superwoman position was the desired one: the realization of the whole person in whom mind and marriage could be reconciled.

Heilbrun's proposal never suggests what women will do between high school and Prince Charming, and Heilbrun does not revive this particular idea again, but it did indeed cause a stir. The piece was picked up by the Associated Press, the *New York Post,* the Toledo *Blade,* and *Time,* among other newspapers and magazines, and earned Heilbrun some early notoriety for her first foray into activism. [12] A host of readers, including Midge Decter and Ellen Moers, wrote letters, not all of which could be printed in the *Forum;* a letter from a housewife in Kansas City, Missouri, is especially moving: "Your ideas so clearly echo the disorganized thoughts I have accumulated through the last seven years of child-rearing and house-ordering, years in which my hands have been busy and my mind starving, constantly, insistently craving for the knowledge I failed to obtain when it was available."[13]

Heilbrun's proposal had touched a nerve. Pointing to her early concern that women were being educated in a system that answered men's needs but not theirs, the essay also subtly signals the conflicts with which she herself may have been coping as a mother. Her thinking on the preparation of female people for becoming agents in the world would culminate in her 1979 *Reinventing Womanhood;* her sense that women's lives demanded a different pattern from men's would be developed in the 1989 *Writing a Woman's Life.*

In another article for the *Columbia Forum,* "I've Been Reading: A Course of Mistaken Identity," Heilbrun, once more thinking from the point of view of the mother and writing from her own experience of bearing twins, ponders the phenomenon of twins in our cultural tradition. Thus early, again (a revised version of this will appear in *Toward a Recognition of Androgyny*), she sounds a dominant theme of her life's work: "'Androgynous' is of course the key word; the double human experience of being male and female." Her response to the common misapprehension that boy/girl twins are "identical" is to suggest that it "arises from a deeper, more unconscious knowledge that when we speak of 'identity,' a whole human being, this is what we mean: boy-girl, man-woman, encompassing the possibility of all experience."[14]

Heilbrun received a warm response to this article from the new editor of the *Columbia Forum,* Peter Spackman ("I always want perfection but seldom get it"), and she requested that "special copies" be sent to certain of her Columbia colleagues, Robert Gorham Davis, William York Tindall, and Carl Woodring: "I know they would all get it anyway in the normal course of events, but this way they may actually notice it."[15] Heilbrun was eager to join Columbia's intellectual community, to communicate the excitement of the new work she was doing, but, according to her later recollection, her efforts went unrewarded. The department was large at that time, numbering close to seventy faculty members, and so tended to split into smaller groups. The difficulties of commuting in the city also tended to work against the possibility of community. Still, it is instructive to place against Heilbrun's experience a statement from Steven Marcus, quoted in James Gold's obituary notice for Lionel Trilling in the *Columbia Daily Spectator:* "Faculty members who were in the midst of an idea or in the process of putting one down on paper would 'see how it bounced off Trilling,' said Marcus. 'He was an important part of the audience.'"[16] But the "faculty members" referred to here were an exclusive group in which Heilbrun, for one, was not included. Heilbrun herself would say, three decades later, "I'm only now beginning to realize how desperately lonely I must have been."

Heilbrun's early essays, growing from her experiences as teacher and mother, question the different treatment of men and women in the educational system and beyond. She recognized, too, that under present conditions neither males nor females had access to identities as "whole" persons. Stylistically, Heilbrun seems to be seeking "wholeness" herself. These articles are a daring blend of the personal and the professional; she is a scholar, yes, but also a teacher and mother, whose experiences have shaped the kinds of subjects she has chosen to write about. In these significant writing choices, Heilbrun would anticipate the personal style adopted by later feminists and would express her early decision to write from knowledge that was not purely academic. The Heilbrun of the 1960s is finding her ideal literary expression in the loose and unrestricted form of the essay.[17] The tone is new and her voice is becoming distinctive: clear, witty, self-assured; her audience is not narrowly confined to scholars but includes a general readership of educated people.

By 1963, demonstrations in the South against racial segregation were increasing, leading to the landmark Civil Rights Act of 1964, and Betty Friedan had sounded the alert about other forms of discrimination in *The Feminine Mystique.* Carolyn Heilbrun did not review this book but was thinking about women along much the same lines as Betty Friedan. In 1965, she published the scholarly article "The Woman as Hero," which was later incorporated into *Toward a Recognition of Androgyny.*

This article raises questions about women in a more systematic way than Heilbrun has yet done and claims a new territory. Here, Heilbrun is not simply looking at one misunderstood character but theorizing about a whole group of women characters. In the process, she seems to be attempting something quite different in critical discourse. The article was first delivered as a speech but even so is notable for its lack of footnotes; young scholars—and especially young women scholars anxious to fulfill professional expectations—usually weight their work with scholarly apparatus. Liberally sprinkled with "I's" and including a reference to her seven-year-old son, Heilbrun's essay is marked by the rhythms of her singular voice, a voice unafraid of assertion, full of confidence in the deployment of her arguments. Although the subject matter, the wit, and much of the manner are entirely hers, the influence of Lionel Trilling is palpable in her assured expansiveness, in her tendency to prefer the illuminating generalization over the close reading of texts, and in the conviction that she is speaking at the place where literature and culture intersect. In ways that may not have been altogether apparent to her at that time, Heilbrun was also beginning to adapt Trilling's ideas about the self for her own purposes. Joining the debate about selfhood, she, however, was talking about the selves of women; for this particular endeavor, she had no models at hand.

In "The Woman as Hero," Heilbrun distinguishes between the hero and the heroine (whom she defines as "that female character who plays the largest, or most important role in the life of the hero, who is the chief sexual event in his life") and is the first critic, so far as I know, to appropriate for women the word *hero,* "the character who undergoes the central action, the character whom men, as well as women, may view as an actor in a destiny possible for them." Isolating a period of about fifty years around the turn of the century, Heilbrun writes of those singular women heroes invented by such male writers as James, Ibsen, Lawrence, Forster, and Shaw. That article, written well before a feminist theoretical framework had been established, is remarkable for its vital insights about women's lives, particularly the need for "a new concept of identity," the need to recognize "woman as a person before she is thought of as mistress, wife or mother." Indeed, Heilbrun writes with exhilaration of the autonomy and independence of these women in quest of their own identity, their own destiny. But, despite Heilbrun's confidence in her material, the way in which she declines the implications of her perceptions is striking; she wants "to avoid 'feminism' as an issue" and endorses what she sees as these writers' view of the woman hero as a "metaphor for modern man." "Ibsen," she says, "using his woman hero, was writing of the need of every human being to be himself freely and strongly." [18] These sentiments situate her firmly in what has become a liberal feminist tradition, one valuing individual female accomplishment, a tradition to be challenged by the work of radical and socialist-feminist theorists, which would emerge shortly thereafter.[19]

A similar advance-retreat is sounded in "The Bloomsbury Group," published in 1968 and also later included in *Toward a Recognition of Androgyny*. Heilbrun sets out to rescue the unconventional Bloomsbury Group from its numerous detractors, points out its resemblance to contemporary rebels, and isolates its special quality as androgyny, which enabled the group to consider men and women "equally valuable as human beings," to be pacifists in the face of a senseless war, and to create and respond to "new concepts of art."[20] Yet Heilbrun cautions—herself perhaps more than the reader—"I have avoided the word feminism, with its inevitable odor of militancy. Nothing could have been further from the quality I wish to identify as uniquely a part of Bloomsbury,"[21] and we note once again the double voice, the mind struggling against itself, against the evidence of its own clear judgments. Nevertheless, if these insights were not part of a systematically developed and supported feminist philosophy, we must recall what inner and outer pressures were then exerting themselves against such a philosophy, and what dangers lay in wait for one who dared articulate feminist politics. Although Heilbrun was then a tenured associate professor at Columbia, the likelihood of being ridiculed or professionally demolished by both male and female colleagues was still great.[22] Moreover, Heilbrun, like many of us, still had to unlearn a rigorous training that declared criticism should be disinterested and certainly not adulterated by political action. Apposite here is an observation Heilbrun would make more than a decade later in "Virginia Woolf in Her Fifties" (1981), noting that there were two obstacles in the way of Woolf's expression of "her sense of society's deprivation of women": "the first, outside herself, was the ridicule, misery, and anxiety the patriarchy holds in store for women who express their anger about the enforced destiny of women"; "the second . . . within herself" was "her own sense of the importance to literature of separating art and propaganda."[23] At this time, then, Carolyn Heilbrun, mirroring the tensions suffered by many academic women, was struggling with opposing needs: the need to be an accepted and respected member of the literary establishment and the need to articulate women's "deprivations."

For those tensions, however, Heilbrun found a unique solution. During the same period, unknown to her colleagues and peers, Heilbrun invented another self, Amanda Cross, the mystery writer. In *Twentieth-Century Crime and Mystery Writers*, Heilbrun explains: "I began writing the Amanda Cross novels in 1963 because I could not find any detective fiction that I enjoyed reading." Her predilection for "literary mysteries," "conversation," and "fiction in which women figure as more than decoration and appendages, domestic machinery, or sex objects" proclaimed her a devoted follower of Dorothy L. Sayers, whom she praised for her style and brilliant combination of "murder and manners."[24] If Lionel Trilling towered in Heilbrun's life as the model for intellectual scholarly endeavor, then Dorothy Sayers served as the model for a female fiction writer. Indeed, Heilbrun wrote a brilliant essay rediscovering Sayers and capturing her essential qualities in "Sayers, Lord Peter, and God," published in 1968. In *Writing a Woman's Life,* Heilbrun reveals, "It is impossible to overestimate the importance of [Sayers'] detective novels in my own life during what should have been, but was not, a time of hope."[25] There are even a number of similarities between the lives of Sayers and Heilbrun: both were only children encouraged to achieve; both were devoted to their work; both were novelists as well as scholars; both were noted for their wit and humor; both were charged with snobbery and elitism; both used the detective story as a vehicle for working out social (especially feminist) issues; finally, both in some sense led double lives, Sayers hiding the birth of her illegitimate son and then later keeping her husband out of sight, and Heilbrun also guarding her domestic privacy and inventing the persona of Amanda Cross.[26]

This brings us to the question of why Heilbrun adopted a pseudonym. More than other writers, perhaps, the mystery writer is likely to conceal identity under an alias; indeed, in her own *The James Joyce Murder,* Carolyn Heilbrun depicts an academic who goes to great lengths to mask his identity as a writer of thrillers. Now, presumably, there are good reasons for this. Carolyn Heilbrun has noted the expert efficiency of the academic establishment in drawing lines between popular culture and masterpieces.[27] Perhaps a young academic, careful of a professional reputation, would not want to be known as a writer of mysteries which, as we know, rub spines with Gothic and Sci-fi and do not get shelved under Literature in respectable bookstores.[28] But in *Writing a Woman's Life,* Heilbrun proposes another theory: in addition to the obvious need for professional respectability, the creation of an alias fulfilled her then unconscious need for "psychic space," for a "secrecy [that] gave me a sense of control over my destiny that nothing else in my life, in those pre-tenure, pre-women's-movement days, afforded."[29] There were, then, special reasons for a woman academic who was in conflict, as we have seen, to maintain disguise. An alias grants her a secret self not bound by the same rules, categories, and biases as her professional self, and she has the power to choose the precise moment when that disguise will be triumphantly discarded; moreover, as a writer of mystery stories, she holds sway over an imaginative world that demands moral action, a world where villains can be brought to task, injustice exposed. As for the protagonist, surely no fictional form offers its main character as much control as the detective mystery: the detective must take charge, must solve the crime. If the woman academic was, perforce, in a male-dominated institution, powerless, then the woman fictional detective, by the very demands of the form itself, had to be powerful.[30]

Yet initially, Heilbrun was interested in writing what she defined as comedies of manners, "those works of art refined by the extraordinary attention their characters pay to conversation and the subtleties of personal relationships; their energies are not expended on social revolution."[31] In effect, Heilbrun, as Cross, was committing herself to a genre that celebrated the social surface, and she had no conscious intention of cutting the social fabric. Indeed, the detective story is hardly a form which readily accommodates revolutionary ideas. It may grant its protagonist and writer control, but it allows that power at the cost of generic flexibility. First, the detective mystery poses a question, whodunit, if you like, or a mystery, and an assumption, borne out by the plot, that the mystery can be solved, the question answered. Since the detective story, in its conventional form, seeks to preserve the status quo, it presents a world which may be frighteningly chaotic for a while, but whose certainties are regularly restored at last. Moreover, the established method of arriving at solutions is through deduction, and while the deducer may be brilliant in assembling and ordering the pieces of the puzzle, the process, the logical linear method of concluding from the givens, much celebrated in the genre, must by its very nature be associated with social and intellectual orthodoxies.

When Carolyn Heilbrun alias Amanda Cross published *In the Last*

Analysis (1964), then, revolution did not yet seem to be on the agenda, though the fact that she had chosen a female amateur detective, rather than the more typical male, announced a new territory.[32] This book introduces Professor Kate Fansler, detective and central character of Amanda Cross's novels. We may speculate that Fansler is yet another possible self for Heilbrun, a self both like and unlike her creator; indeed, Heilbrun confirms this, too, in *Writing a Woman's Life:* "I sought to create an individual whose destiny offered more possibility than I could comfortably imagine for myself."[33] According to Heilbrun, Fansler is a fantasy figure, without parents, "without children, unmarried, unconstrained by the opinions of others, rich and beautiful."[34] This Kate could be free and independent, unhampered by domestic roles, oblivious to housework and the mysteries of cooking, and unconcerned by the judgments of colleagues. Yet, embedded in the powerful fantasy of an independent feminist knight on a quest that the older Heilbrun describes is another powerful (unacknowledged) fantasy expressing the need to be an exceptional woman assimilated into an influential ruling class. While Heilbrun spent a long period of time denying her Jewish background, Kate Fansler, in contrast, is a pedigreed insider, a bona fide WASP. Despite the fact that Fansler rejects many of the stuffier and more unappealing attitudes of her family (and thus, as in all good fantasies, can have her class and reject it, too), the class status of Kate is a vital ingredient in the fantasy. Moneyed elegance and inherited privilege would be essential parts of Kate's charm; ethnicity would not.

The older Heilbrun regrets that she endowed Kate Fansler with beauty, but she does not admit that such beauty was a necessary component of the fantasy. A sophisticated professor of literature at a prestigious New York City university and sister to three rich, much older brothers, Fansler is invariably the most accomplished and desirable woman in a world inhabited primarily by men. Perhaps, in Heilbrun's fantasy, Kate is the kind of woman that Lionel Trilling might have welcomed into his exclusive circle of New York intellectuals. In fact, Fansler would be approached by a Trilling figure in *Poetic Justice*. She is certainly the kind of woman of whom a later Heilbrun would say, "Exceptional women are the chief imprisoners of nonexceptional women, simultaneously proving that any woman could do it and assuring, in their uniqueness among men, that no other woman will."[35] Indeed, one of the more striking aspects of Kate Fansler is that allies and enemies alike acclaim her superior qualities and attainments; any serious flaws she may have are unacknowledged.

In spite of this general approbation, however, Kate Fansler remains, especially in the early novels, an isolated figure. Her parents dead, she is cut off from her brothers (she is, significantly, without a sister), and no close female friends share her solitude.[36] She does, however, have a male admirer, Reed Amhearst, and, in their relationship Heilbrun as Cross seems to be working out her notion of an ideal heterosexual union, a theme also developed by Heilbrun in her critical work.[37] Some readers apparently claimed that Amhearst too often rescued Fansler in the early novels, and Heilbrun has responded to that criticism in the later novels, even allowing Amhearst the weakness of a midlife crisis in *Sweet Death, Kind Death*.[38] If Amhearst changes during the course of the series, so, too, does Fansler, expressing a deepening anger at the injustices of her world and learning a more strenuous feminism.[39] Heilbrun as Cross said she wanted to write books which reflect a "moral universe," her tribute to Trilling, and this commitment becomes increasingly sure in each succeeding book.[40]

The first two novels, *In the Last Analysis* (1964) and *The James Joyce Murder* (1967), revolve around the work and ideas of two cultural figures, Sigmund Freud and James Joyce. Shortly after *In the Last Analysis* opens, a young graduate student from Kate Fansler's university is killed on a psychiatrist's couch. Clues are dropped in dreams, analysis is discussed, and Freud is defended. *The James Joyce Murder* takes its chapter headings from the titles of stories in James Joyce's collection, *Dubliners,* includes thematic material from Joyce (especially the Joycean "deadness" of some of the characters who are unable to feel or receive passion), and stages a murder relating to a missing Joyce manuscript. *In the Last Analysis* includes a pointed reference to Lionel Trilling, a clue to the powerful influence he exerted over Heilbrun's thinking. In this case, the murderer is incriminated in part because he quotes a famous theory of Trilling's dealing with a genre of novels about young men from the provinces. Fansler reasons that this theory (which will crop up again in Heilbrun's later work) could only have come from the graduate student who heard it in one of Fansler's own classes, and thus she establishes the relation between killer and victim. In this early book, the reference to Trilling appears as an unobtrusive compliment, perhaps even a sly hint as to Cross's real identity.[41]

Cross's manipulation of these male figures is remarkably clever and entertaining and may superficially disguise the degree to which her ideas, especially those about women, are shaped by these thinkers. On the one hand, she offers us a woman protagonist, "a knight who has set off to slay the dragon," an independent woman who refuses to marry the devoted Reed and prefers that they remain as "two circles . . . which touch each other."[42] On the other hand, Reed provides assistance in solving the mystery of *In the Last Analysis,* and solves the mystery entirely in *The James Joyce Murder,* even while acknowledging that he does so by thinking "like a professor of English." Moreover, Cross seems especially concerned that, even if Kate looks suspiciously like a feminist, she will not give up her feminine appeal; thus there is a good deal of emphasis on the fact that while Kate is unmarried she is certainly not celibate. She may be a professional woman, but she still desires men and wants to be desired by men, as is revealed in a telling moment in *The James Joyce Murder* when she offers her reasons for allowing her nephew to practice rifle shooting against her better judgment: "I've always loathed and detested guns. But I was afraid of impinging upon a masculine prerogative. . . . Let's face it, modern Freudian lingo has got us so frightened of appearing to be castrating women that we won't even take a gun away from a boy."[43] Perhaps a similar Freud-induced fear accounts for her skittish attitude toward homosexuality in this book, an attitude she later vehemently repudiated, going so far as to have the deprecating remarks deleted from subsequent printings at her own expense.[44]

In this context of Fansler's fundamental conventionality, we should note that Cross repeatedly assures us that Kate's arrangements are unconventional: in *In the Last Analysis,* her continuing (friendly) relationship with a former lover, the psychiatrist—and his wife; in *The James Joyce Murder,* her supervision of a summer household consisting entirely of men—two graduate students and one small nephew. In both books, it is taken for granted that policemen, rural inhabitants, and other lower middle-class types could not possibly understand or appreciate Kate's way of life.

Of all the women characters in these two early novels, Kate is the only one with both an intellectual and a sexual life. In *The James Joyce Murder,* this issue is dramatically focused as women from different generations ponder their relation to work and to men. The attempt to balance seeming contradictions in women's lives, a tendency that persists through much of Heilbrun's own intellectual development, may show the influence of Dorothy Sayers whose name is often invoked in these novels. Sayers also explored the ways in which women could reconcile the claims of profession and the claims of womanhood, especially in her novel of academic life, *Gaudy Night,* featuring Harriet Vane, mystery writer and amateur detective. In this context, it is worth noting that while the scholarly Heilbrun defends the lustful Gertrude in "The Character of Hamlet's Mother," Amanda Cross the detective writer kills off a lustful, middle-aged mother in *The James Joyce Murder.* In the detective novel, the mother is a villainous character mourned by none, a woman whose intense energy is marshaled for destructive purposes. Clearly, Heilbrun-Cross had some ambivalence about this figure: on the one hand, she was able to see behind the mother to the person with legitimate emotional, sexual, and intellectual needs; on the other hand, the woman whose only identity was that of mother and wife was liable to destroy herself and others with her own excess energy.

Heilbrun's struggle between her feminism and her professionalism is played out here as well as in her nonfiction works. In spite of some witty attacks on university bureaucracy (*In the Last Analysis*) and the ills of a system that values publication over teaching (*The James Joyce Murder*), Kate essentially identifies herself with professional and institutional values. This point is worth emphasizing because we shall watch that attachment slowly loosen. But in *In the Last Analysis,* she assumes her psychiatrist friend is innocent of murder because no "genuine" psychiatrist would do a dirty deed in his own office. Her faith in institutions amounts almost, at times, to naïveté: "You know, Reed, it would be a hell of a blow to psychiatry if they arrested Emmanuel. I mean, he's not a fly-by-night crank, or someone who had just taken up psychiatry. He's a member of, and therefore backed by, the most austere institute of psychiatry in the country. Even I, who argue with Emmanuel constantly, cannot believe that they would admit as a member, after the extended analysis they require, a man who could murder a patient on a couch. And I'm sure they didn't. Even if he weren't convicted, his arrest would be a hell of a blow."[45] Professional and institutional ideals are valued in both books (in the academic and psychoanalytic worlds), but we may also note that, in *In the Last Analysis,* although such a notion is not explicit and perhaps not even conscious in so early a book, the female victim is nevertheless destroyed by a (symbolic) constellation of the male professional world: a doctor (appropriately named Barrister, the English term for lawyer) and a Freudian psychoanalyst.

Given these contradictions and given Heilbrun's own propensity for doubling, we should not be surprised to find doubling a motif in these novels, too. *In the Last Analysis* presents a villain who has (for reasons, significantly perhaps, never made clear) violently snatched the identity of another and whose illegitimate doubling leads from one crime to another. In *The James Joyce Murder,* the doubling is more like Heilbrun's own. There, an academic whose professional publications are judged to be mediocre is also the secret author of a popular series featuring a James Bond-type character. The academic is not a very savory man, attempting seduction of a vulnerable woman on one occasion and also committing several misdemeanors in order to keep secret his identity as a purveyor of popular fiction. His inclusion in the novel is along the lines of an inside joke, and the anxiety associated with discovery is nowhere near the level of that in *In the Last Analysis,* where the villainous double is literally stripped to his skin to uncover his secret. Exposure as a professional imposter might have been the worst fate the young Heilbrun could imagine.

In these first two novels, Heilbrun has created her wonderfully witty and talented detective; demonstrated that character's feminist independence as well as her aristocratic femininity;[46] and proved her loyalty to friends, her hitherto unquestioned respect for institutions, and her commitment to her profession (she even considers the idea of becoming a university president). Yet she has shown Kate Fansler moving primarily in a world of psychological and literary ideas rather than in a world of social facts and forces.

The Carolyn Heilbrun of this time was a woman in conflict. She was still struggling to assimilate and had made an impressive debut as a professional scholar with *The Garnett Family.* But her self could not be entirely accommodated by the official academy, and so she wrote personal essays for a general readership and invented another self who could freely play in a space of fiction not held to the same strict standards as so-called serious literature. With the word *play,* I mean to emphasize the pleasure of creation but not to underestimate the urgency of a need that drove a woman who hates the dawn to get up at five every morning to work on a project that had nothing to do with either her domestic or professional life. If, as Heilbrun was to remark later, she had a "Gatsby sense of self-creation, acquired from [her] father," she had a large sense of what that self would, could be.[47] Writing, she tried on different writing selves. As witty journalist, she was becoming a regular book reviewer for the *New York Times;* as critic, she was experimenting with a new discourse and voice, reaching beyond the confines of academic prose; as secret fiction writer, she began "to write [her] own life on a level far below consciousness."[48]

Heilbrun's interest in women's issues, especially in women's education and in women characters who play out their fictional destinies in novels, emerged well before the cresting of what has become known as the second wave of the feminist movement. Yet, she stopped short of an explicit and unreserved feminist position; in an era of intense political activity, she was not interested in causes and political movements. Several reviews of those years, including those dealing with children's books, show her drawing back from political reforms and social problems.[49] She would not be angry ("anger against 'masculine tyranny,' like the anger of any oppressed group, approaches the fringes of hysteria and paranoia, and arouses similar states in those under attack").[50] Moreover, her academic training, her wish to succeed within the terms of the institution, militated against the frank expression of a feminist politics. Such a struggle was the pattern for numerous emerging feminists in the late 1960s and early 1970s; Heilbrun's example makes that pattern visible.

Many women, too—though not many of Heilbrun's generation—were struggling with their relation to motherhood. Heilbrun is extraordinary in the ways she allowed her experience of motherhood to shape her choice of writing subjects and her literary perceptions and to give a voice to a more-or-less silent and silenced figure; the point to make here is not how little Heilbrun says in the 1970s and 1980s about the problems of mothering children, but how much she writes about the needs of a mother in the benighted days of the 1950s and early 1960s when few others were exploring that material. She avoids dealing with the relationship of mothers and children, of course, because she chooses *not* to see mothers as mothers but to see them as people who can act in the world. Mothers, she was saying, in a variety of ways, matter. But she also evades openly confronting the problems challenging those who attempt to combine traditional women's domestic roles with more public professional ones. Only in the work of Amanda Cross do these anxieties emerge indirectly, in the welcome death of a mother, and in the motherless, childless state of Kate Fansler.

Heilbrun's tension was expressed, as we have seen, in the double voice characteristic of some of her articles, and in the splitting of her self into the scholar, the woman, Amanda Cross, and Kate Fansler—selves in turn shaped by conflict. The record left by many contemporary women writers suggests that, if a woman did have ambitions beyond the conventional, conflict was inescapable. Such a woman would hold herself together at tremendous personal cost, juggling domestic and artistic work, trying to fulfill all the obligations that were imposed upon her. And for all the women who survived such juggling acts, like Mary McCarthy, there were others who buckled under the strain, turning to oblique or direct forms of self-destruction. Sylvia Plath provides an image that captures the struggle; here is Esther Greenwood from *The Bell Jar* in the city hospital, clutching a ball of mercury from a thermometer she has deliberately broken: "I opened my fingers a crack, like a child with a secret, and smiled at the silver globe cupped in my palm. If I dropped it, it would break into a million little replicas of itself, and if I pushed them near each other, they would fuse, without a crack, into one whole again." Indeed, it is unsettling to note how many women writers of the time took as a theme their own self-division or the divided selves of their characters. Adrienne Rich, looking back on her poem "Aunt Jennifer's Tigers" (1951), is "startled because beneath the conscious craft are glimpses of the split I even then experienced between the girl who wrote poems, who defined herself in writing poems, and the girl who was to define herself by her relationships with men." Anne Sexton, suffering from mental illness, said "it is the split self . . . that is the mad woman" and believed that writing made her "whole."[51] Shirley Jackson wrote of a fictional woman with multiple-personality disorder in her novel *The Bird's Nest*. Little wonder that one of the most popular movies of the time was *The Three Faces of Eve,* another story of a woman with multiple personalities, a role for which Joanne Woodward received an Oscar.

One might say that Heilbrun did not allow herself to be divided; she took charge and divided herself. Indeed, far from restricting activity in Heilbrun's case, her invention of new selves proved a productive strategy for alleviating the "anxiety of *female* authorship." The authors of this phrase, Sandra Gilbert and Susan Gubar, would themselves find a certain freedom from anxiety, perhaps, by way of another (related) form of self-empowerment: the creation of a new, a double self though their collaboration.[52] Nevertheless, although the splits in identity proved fruitful and necessary for Heilbrun's survival,[53] they were also problematic for one whose scholarly self was narrowly confined and restrained from expressing her political perceptions. The solution Heilbrun would choose was the model of androgyny, a model that she had begun to think about at least as early as her journalistic piece on twins, but a model that was itself riven with unresolved conflict.

4

The Androgyny Model

[Henry James's] *The Bostonians* . . . is a story of the parental house divided against itself, of the keystone falling from the arch, of the sacred mothers refusing their commission and the sacred fathers endangered.

— LIONEL TRILLING, *"The Bostonians"*

Is there a way to write . . . without killing our mothers, the mother in us?

— ALICE JARDINE, "Death Sentences: Writing
Couples and Ideology"

Perhaps to think . . . of one sex as distinct from the other is an effort. It interferes with the unity of the mind.

— VIRGINIA WOOLF, *A Room of One's Own*

But deeper than the problem of the relation between the sexes is the problem of the reunification of the sexes in the self.

— CAROLYN G. HEILBRUN,
Toward a Recognition of Androgyny

Thirteen boxes of letters in the Columbia University Archive are labeled "The Columbia Crisis of 1968"; the label, the staggering number of boxes, and the frenzied tone of many of the letters remind us of how devastating the Columbia student uprising of 1968 had been for almost all members of the community. Protests against the escalating war in Vietnam had exploded on college campuses across the country, but Berkeley on the West Coast and Columbia, Heilbrun's institution, on the East, suffered the greatest disruptions. In her caustic assessment of the Columbia rebellion, "On the Steps of Low Library," Diana Trilling recalls that "The uprising had the declared intention of large social destructiveness, the largest. In an open letter to President Grayson Kirk on 22 April, Mark Rudd wrote: 'We will destroy your world, your corporation, your University.'"[1] In spite of their claims of protesting specific ills—the Vietnam War, the university's alliance with defense organizations, discrimination against black students, and the university's decision to build a gymnasium on ground adjoining neighboring Harlem, the students really seemed to be rebelling against, and indeed bent on destroying, the institution itself. Moreover, the unaccountable surprise in all this was the success of the revolutionary leaders in attracting hundreds of moderate students, and even faculty, to their cause.[2]

Inevitably, the rebellion forced most associated with the institution to examine it more closely. What did Columbia stand for and what was the relation of students, faculty members and administrators to it? Where did Heilbrun, who had been tenured in 1967 and was therefore a senior member of the institution, stand? Tom Driver, Heilbrun's longtime friend, told me the following story about Heilbrun's reaction to the April 1968 student rebellion. He was in Cambridge, England, at the time and received a letter from Heilbrun that he summarized from memory; obviously, the picture she conveyed to him in that letter was still vivid in his mind:

> She described walking across the Columbia campus and discovering the students inside Low Library, the police surrounding the building, and a group of faculty between the police and the entrance to the library—and wearing armbands. So those faculty were the buffer to protect the students against the police onslaught. And Carol says that she came walking across there and she suddenly saw this scene and realized, "Well, I have either got to walk on by or to go over there and put on an armband and stand with those others. And whichever I do, it's a decision." And then she said something like, "The next thing I knew I had on the armband and I was standing there."

Said Driver, "I would not have predicted that that would be her response. Public demonstration is not her style."[3]

Driver's story dramatizes a turning point for Heilbrun. On the one hand, she was deeply attached to the idea of the university, the institution, and deeply committed to the profession. On the other hand, she could not help but be aware of the university's shortcomings and of the ways she herself did not fit its mold. We do not know how many moments it took for Heilbrun to transform herself from an observer to a participant. Taking her place between the students and the police on the steps of Low Library, she stands for all those faculty, and especially those women faculty, who, for the first time, were publicly questioning their institutions.

In 1970, Carolyn Heilbrun (alias Amanda Cross) published *Poetic Justice*, a pivotal novel in Heilbrun's development, articulating an increasingly complicated relation to the institution. If the Kate Fansler of *In the Last Analysis* seemed to support institutionalized professions (while the seeds of subversion were comfortably buried), the Fansler of *Poetic Justice* questions her powerful attachment to the university but does not deny the accompanying ambivalence and anxiety. Set against the student upheavals of the late sixties, *Poetic Justice* is easily Cross's best and most complex novel to date.

Fansler's relation to her academic institution is set squarely in the foreground.[4] Alienated by some of the extreme tactics of the revolutionary students, Fansler nevertheless wants to take responsibility for the failures of her institution with respect to students. Consequently, she responds to pleas from a group of her colleagues to help save University College, a unit of the larger university that serves mature students and particularly women. The existence of University College, the one part of the institution that has retained the loyalty of its students, is threatened by a band of elitist standard-bearers, who declare that there can only be one first-class college in the university—and that must be the one for male undergraduates. Cross is writing very close to the facts here: University College represents Columbia's much-abused School of General Studies, and contemporary documents confirm that General Studies students did behave responsibly, holding their building, Lewisohn Hall, against the extremists and earning for that building the name of "Switzerland."[5]

Fansler's loyalty to the institution is still powerful in this novel, though she cannot, even by its end, explain the nature of her love or the nature of the institution's claim on her. Aware of its flaws and mistakes, its absent president and distracted faculty, she is nevertheless frightened that it might indeed be crushed under the pressure of events. In fact, at times it seems as if the victim in this murder mystery is not so much the dead Professor Cudlipp, one of the standard-bearers who himself is guilty of trying to "kill" University College, but the institution itself, which is often associated in the novel with the language of death and murder.[6]

Raising questions of prejudice about class and sex, Kate Fansler's examination of the structure of the university is associated with a rigorous self-examination, and the self in this novel is not so much private and self-enclosed but has a much richer social context. As in *Toward a Recognition of Androgyny,* which Heilbrun was writing at this time, Cross is absorbed by questions of balance—in individual personality, in human relationships, in the academy, and in the social world at large. Fansler admits that her "assurance" of who she is has been undermined by the disruptions of the institution, making plain how dependent she is upon the university for her identity. In this state of mind, the independent Fansler decides to marry her patient suitor, Reed, entering a marital alliance precisely because the institutional alliance threatens to dissolve. The reader may question, as she herself does, whether this decision is a symptom of her gaining or losing balance.[7]

Poetic Justice seemingly argues for both/and rather than either/or, and the notes of harmony and poise are sounded throughout the novel, in the quoted poetry of W. H. Auden, whom Kate appreciates for his "balancing act between frivolity and earnestness," and in the work of the humorously eccentric Peter Packer Pollinger, a scholar studying the obscure Scottish writer, William Sharp, who (androgynously) published also under the pseudonym Fiona Macleod.[8] But balance can produce a static effect, or rather, a seesaw motion signifying concession rather than progression. Kate Fansler apparently defeats the forces of reaction by saving University College, the one school of the institution with which an honorable alliance is possible. Nevertheless, her anxiety about the breakdown of the university is revealed by the ways in which, at various personal and institutional levels, she concedes to the fathers, to patriarchy: faced with the terrifying opportunity for change, with the old forms breaking down everywhere, Kate Fansler takes shelter in a university that will co-opt and contain rather than change fundamentally. As her radical colleague Hankster points out to her: "You really think, don't you, that we've seen the last of the troubles. That from now on, we just rebuild our university, better than before but not fundamentally different."[9] Finally, Kate chooses, out of acknowledged weakness, a marriage over independence and autonomy.[10]

Fansler is not Cross—or Heilbrun—of course, but the anxieties about the institution embodied in this novel surely mirrored Heilbrun's own. Moreover, there were other signs of social unrest and change that would occupy Heilbrun and other women at this time. Women had participated enthusiastically in the peace movement, and, earlier, in the civil rights movement and other radical reform efforts. But they found their own rights ignored or trivialized and, increasingly dissatisfied with the sexist treatment received from their male peers, they began organizing their own women's liberation groups.[11] The women's movement of this time drew its energy not so much from charismatic leaders and theorists but from the consciousness-raising groups spreading across the country at an astonishing rate. Within those groups, women probed their personal experiences, daring to speak of matters that had formerly been regarded as private. As Robin Morgan put it: "Women's liberation is the first radical movement to base its politics—in fact create its politics—out of concrete personal experiences. We've learned that those experiences are *not* our private hang-ups. They are shared by every woman, and are therefore political. The theory, then, comes out of human feeling, not out of textbook rhetoric."[12]

From these women's groups emerged a broad range of goals and an equally disparate set of strategies and tactics for achieving them. The National Organization for Women (NOW), founded in 1966, reached out to a broad cross section of women. NOW limited its agenda to maternity leave, abortion rights, day care centers, tax deductions for home and child care expenses, equal access to education and jobs, and the Equal Rights Amendment—abortion rights being the most controversial of these demands.[13] As NOW was increasingly associated with moderate, middle-class, married women, more militant feminists split off to form their own groups.

Radical groups such as the Feminists, the New York Radical Feminists, and the Redstockings, rallied by such leaders as Shulamith Firestone and Ti-Grace Atkinson, declared women an oppressed class, called for an end to marriage, urged reproduction by technology, challenged heterosexual norms, and advocated nonhierarchical modes of political organization and action. Even as feminists were struggling within and across groups about ends and means, the Redstocking Manifesto defiantly asserted a universal sisterhood:

> We identify with all women. We define our best interest as that of the poorest, most brutally exploited woman.
>
> We repudiate all economic, racial, educational or status privileges that divide us from other women. We are determined to recognize and eliminate any prejudices we may hold against other women.
>
> We are committed to achieving internal democracy. We will do whatever is necessary to ensure that every woman in our movement has an equal chance to participate, assume responsibility, and develop her political potential.[14]

Some NOW members feared that those on the radical edge would scare off mainstream women, especially since the media loved to project feminists as generically militant. For example, the press seized upon the story of Valerie Solanis, who shot (and almost killed) Andy Warhol, and eagerly reported that feminists acclaimed her action. Way out on the radical fringe, Solanis had drawn up the manifesto for SCUM (Society for Cutting Up Men): "Life in this society, being, at best, an utter bore and no aspect of society being at all relevant to women, there remains to civic-minded, responsible, thrill-seeking females only to overthrow the government, eliminate the money system, institute complete automation, and destroy the male sex."[15] Note the sweeping, unconditional language, the incongruous tripling of "civic-minded, responsible, thrill-seeking females" amounting to self-parody, the sense of fun, and the climactic surprise of the final phrase. Solanis did have supporters among radical women but for most feminists, she represented an extreme, her rhetoric channeling the release of anger through laughter.

Many voices pressed the case for revolution. Mary Daly castigated the sexism of the Catholic Church in *The Church and the Second Sex* (1968). Kate Millett argued that "sexual dominion obtains . . . as perhaps the most pervasive ideology of our culture and provides its most fundamental concept of power."[16] Phyllis Chesler, in her groundbreaking work on women in psychotherapy, put women's problems in a political perspective: "psychotherapy is a commodity purchasable by the rich and inflicted on the poor; . . . as an institution it socially controls the minds and bodies of middle-class women via the adjustment-to-marriage ideal and the minds and bodies of poor and single women via psychiatric incarceration; and . . . most clinicians, like most people in a patriarchal society, have deeply antifemale biases."[17] By these women and others, the lens was turned on the spiritual, social, economic, and psychological oppression of women in every layer of private and public life.

The point to emphasize is that this wave of the women's movement, from the beginning, was not unified: the agenda was various, the disagreements multiple, the discourse diverse—there was no golden age of harmony and unity of purpose. The radical edge was like a magnet, both drawing and repelling the moderate middle, fueling the energy for change. And the pressure exerted by women activists resulted in real change. Women chalked up an astonishing number of firsts during the early 1970s: the United Nations sponsored the first world conference on women; the First Women's Bank opened its doors in New York City; the U.S. Air Force Academy admitted its first women; the first women were ordained to the Episcopal priesthood; and Ellen Grasso became the first woman to be elected any state's governor on her own merits, not because she was taking the place of a spouse who had previously held the post and was now dead or incapacitated.

Academic institutions, already much shaken up by the war protests, also began to respond to the demands of women. The history of the Modern Language Association (MLA) at that time offers an exemplary tale. The foremost professional organization for professors of English and modern languages, the MLA had been founded in 1883, when "the original forty men gathered in Hamilton Hall at Columbia College," with the then-revolutionary aim of justifying and dignifying the study of modern languages and literatures in institutions of higher learning.[18] No woman presided over the association until the election of Louise Pound in 1955; and a woman would not serve again until Columbia's Marjorie Hope Nicolson held the presidency in 1963. The MLA's membership had expanded from about one thousand in 1911 to eleven thousand in 1960, and exploded to twenty-two thousand in 1965.[19] At that point, the association was primarily identified as serving the needs of a body of scholars (who also happened to be teachers); it produced, among an array of other supports for scholarly endeavors, an annual bibliography, academically dependable editions of texts, and the widely respected journal, *Publications of the Modern Language Association*

(*PMLA*); acceptance of a paper to be read at the MLA's annual convention was an honor accorded to relatively few.[20]

But what Paul Lauter called "the intellectual consensus,"[21] the foundation that held all this together, was already beginning to break down and by 1968 had collapsed, battered by the pressures for liberation and change. The disruptions at the MLA meeting in New York City that year reverberated throughout the profession, "resulting in massive correspondence with the Executive Council and Secretariat, meetings about MLA and the problems of the profession on dozens of campuses, and a spate of articles in the journals and the public press."[22] This profound disaffection eventually led to structural changes in the governance of the MLA and closer scrutiny of its policies and practice. The formation of the Delegate Assembly, the establishment of special-interest divisions, the increased numbers of committees, the appointment of the Commission on the Status of Women in the Profession and the constitution of a Committee on Minority Education helped make the MLA more responsive to the diverse needs of its burgeoning membership. Indeed, Germaine Brée would say in her presidential address of 1975, after the ground had shifted and settled, "I do not know of any association of higher learning that has proved more open to the expressed wishes of its membership, however unorthodox, if reasonably presented."[23]

The MLA survived the quakes of 1968 by developing a structure of governance that would enable the expression of oppositional views within the organization. The task of the association's officers and staff was (and still is) to try to contain the struggles, to hold things together, to find a way to accommodate the radical members without risking the loyalty of more traditional ones; the presidents, elected members of the professoriate, assisted, by expressing in their ceremonial speeches, a concern for "solidarity," "outreach," "professionalism," "historical examples," and the abiding value of the profession's work.[24]

In many ways, the MLA's present headquarters provides a fitting emblem for the association's operations over the past three decades. Located in a building on Astor Place in the heart of New York's Greenwich Village, the offices have an air of imaginative improvisation. Winding corridors run adjacent to asymmetrical offices, some spacious, some windowed, some barely enclosed by half-hearted partitions. Doors are almost always left open. There seem to be endless possibilities for adaptation. Searching for an office or an archive can be like following the mystery posed by research into a particularly recalcitrant problem or by the plot of a gothic novel: one never knows quite what will turn up around a corner. Everywhere, there is a sense of vigor and inventiveness: if a new function needs to be performed, a space will be created. The structure retains its outward shape, but its parts can be reconstituted, reformed, realigned.

Policies and practices could be reformed, but it was not clear if radical transformation were possible. When Louis Kampf took office in 1971, a radical was not merely haranguing the establishment from the (left) wings but had ascended to the president's podium. In his presidential address, Kampf made it clear that he despised the MLA's accommodations: "The monster has been shaken. But its response to every challenge is to create machinery that will absorb the shock." Kampf described himself as coming to the academy "with the hope of doing work which would not be alienating" but found that "control of our work has been wrested from our hands by industrial capitalism." Kampf's metaphors of machines and monsters have not worn well; but his wish to heal division and recover "wholeness" would resonate. His goal was the utter transformation of society, for only a new society could produce the academy he wanted; in this, he spoke of the "lessons to be learned from . . . the women's movement," for whom "changing consciousness is seen as part of the struggle to transform male-dominated institutions, and to humanize relationships between the sexes."[25]

Offering none of the mediations and conciliations of previous addresses, Kampf, to a degree, had an effect. The leadership of the MLA had been opened to other voices, and the subsequent advancement of Florence Howe to the presidency in 1973 represented a change even more startling than the election of Kampf. Howe, the first feminist to hold that office, had already distinguished herself as a founder of the Feminist Press and as the first chair (1969–71) of the MLA's Commission on the Status of Women in the Profession. By 1971, the commission had already surveyed the enrollments and graduation of women in doctoral programs, departmental hiring and retention practices, the kinds of positions held by women faculty, and comparative information on salaries and rank for men and women. The conclusions were predictable, but, for the first time, had been based on stark, statistical data: "Women in our profession find themselves, for the most part, in less prestigious, less privileged institutions, teaching mainly freshmen and sophomores, and earning less money than their male counterparts."[26] The solutions subsequently proposed by the commission included recommendations to impose affirmative action guidelines for hiring, abolish antinepotism rules prohibiting the employment of spouses, transform the curriculum, establish university-run day care centers, create parental leave policies, and develop more flexible patterns of employment for those juggling families and careers.[27]

By the time Howe became president in 1973, the Commission on the Status of Women in the Profession had already published its crucial agenda for change and, most importantly, had published that agenda under the auspices of the MLA and in the pages of its official journal, *PMLA*. Howe's presidential speech, addressed to teachers both within and beyond the MLA, focused on the connections between "the teacher of literacy and the professor of literature" and the ways such links can be fostered (particularly) in the women's studies classroom by evolving a curriculum that speaks to the lives of students. Howe spoke of the "extraordinary series of historical coincidences" that brought her, "a teacher rather than a scholar," to the head of the MLA; she might have added that such circumstances also propelled a feminist to that position. Certainly, as she points out in a dedicatory footnote, a talk framed to illuminate the relationship between women's lives and the texts they were required to read in institutions of learning "could not have been written without the women's movement."[28]

The Modern Language Association did seem hospitable to women's concerns and women's voices, especially at the annual conventions, which made room for more panels devoted to scholarship on women. Perhaps it went as far as a professional organization could go at that time. But the hierarchies still held; *PMLA,* for example, was slow to open its arms to women. As late as 1974, the editorial board and the advisory committee boasted only one token woman each and the journal printed few essays written from a feminist perspective. Indeed, it is arguable that the first overtly feminist essay to be published there (so identified by both title and abstract), Sandra M. Gilbert's 1978 essay, entitled "Patriarchal Poetry and Women Readers: Reflections on Milton's Bogey," was quickly neutralized in the editorial column, where William Schaeffer hastened to point out its parallels with another essay in the same issue also dealing with Milton's influence—not on women this time, but on Keats.[29]

Feminists recognized that professional organizations felt obliged to represent the interests of the whole membership and would only accept change to a certain extent. If *PMLA* and professional journals in other fields did not welcome feminist perspectives, then feminists would have to create their own structures and establish their own journals. In 1972, *Women's Studies* and *Feminist Studies* were founded. The editorship of *Signs: Journal of Women in Culture and Society* was offered to Carolyn Heilbrun, and she had to make an important decision about the direction of her career; ultimately, she decided against administration, and *Signs* produced its first issue in 1975 under the skillful editorship of Catharine Stimpson. Meanwhile, the Feminist Press, founded in 1970, had begun its campaign to recover and discover lost, forgotten, or marginal women's texts. Inside the classroom, feminists claimed curricular space; after Sheila Tobias organized a women's conference at Cornell in 1969, women's studies courses began to be offered in colleges and universities across the country.

The women's movement was gathering momentum, growing in power, and drawing the attention of the popular media. In the early 1970s, Kate Millett made the cover of *Time,* the first issue of *Ms.* magazine appeared, Helen Reddy won a Grammy Award for "I Am Woman," and the press flocked to watch the antics of Germaine Greer, Norman Mailer, Diana Trilling, and others at New York City's Town Hall, where "A Dialogue on Women's Liberation" was staged.

On the Columbia campus, the spirited association of women faculty, staff, and students known as Columbia Women's Liberation was actively lobbying to raise the collective consciousness. In 1969, this group prepared a report on discrimination against women faculty and, in 1970, a statement documenting the neglect of women in the curriculum.[30] In due course, after subcommittee reports and senate hearings, the University Senate Executive Committee formed the Columbia University Commission on the Status of Women (February 1972). It might have seemed as if Columbia were responding to internal and external pressures to address the legitimate concerns of women on campus, but in fact the spur was primarily economic. In November 1971, the Office of Civil Rights of the U.S. Department of Health, Education, and Welfare (HEW) ruled that Columbia University would be prohibited from receiving any federal grants or contracts; Columbia's Commission on the Status of Women was apparently formed in response to this crisis.

HEW had targeted Columbia because it (unlike other prestigious institutions, such as Chicago and Harvard) had ignored, for thirty months,
the department's requests for personnel data. According to the report
issued by the Commission on the Status of Women, "From the stand-
point of the Office of Civil Rights, the choice of Columbia University
could not have been better. To prohibit Columbia from holding federal
contracts would automatically spotlight the issue of sex discrimination
and affirmative action in the press" and "sensitize campuses across the
nation to their responsibility to correct the effects of past sex discrimination and to ensure future equal employment opportunity." In order to
stave off what was perceived as "economic chaos," the university developed a plan for affirmative action that was accepted by HEW.[31]

The atmosphere at Columbia was predictably tense: many women
wanted their long-held grievances about inequities in admissions, distribution of fellowships, hiring, salaries, promotion, and tenure redressed;
others warned against the encroachment of government bureaucracies
on the autonomy of an academic institution and feared the mass hiring
of unqualified faculty if affirmative action principles were followed.[32] In
this context, Lionel Trilling delivered on 22 April 1972 the first Jefferson
Lecture, under the auspices of the National Endowment for the Humanities, "Mind in the Modern World," protesting that the university had
accepted the imposition of affirmative action regulations without debate. In the 27 April *New York Times,* Nan Robertson reported that
Lionel Trilling "depicted . . . a crisis of confidence in the American academic community about its goals, its standards and its historic belief in
rational thought."[33] Trilling marked an important historical moment as
he set the terms of the opposition to affirmative action, invoking the
language of crisis, community, standards, and irrationality. Shortly after,
Trilling presented the same lecture to a Columbia audience; according
to the memory of Robert Hanning, still a member of Columbia's English
and Comparative Literature Department, the occasion was celebratory,
and Trilling spoke to a packed audience in the rotunda of Low Library.[34]
Some were delighted to hear him speak their mind; others left angry and
disappointed that he had not championed their rights. As we shall see,
Carolyn Heilbrun would present a public response to this lecture in
1986.

Heilbrun had not joined Columbia Women's Liberation in the
1970s, and she was far from advocating the solutions proposed by the

radical feminists. Still, with colleague Joan Ferrante, she initiated a meeting of Columbia's tenured women in December 1971,[35] acted as consultant to the original Commission on the Status of Women, and, in the later 1970s, served a term as member of the Commission. Unquestionably, she welcomed the women's movement, and much of her work of the late 1950s and 1960s clearly awaited that context in order to be fully recognized; but, at the beginning, she was understandably cautious. She was much closer to the aims of the more middle-class, reformist NOW than to those of the Redstockings. Her solution to the woman problem would be androgyny, a middle way that was designed to bring both men and women together; but, for the moment, she had turned her attention elsewhere.

In her role as scholar, Carolyn Heilbrun started the decade with a monograph on Christopher Isherwood for the series *Columbia Essays on Modern Writers,* edited by William York Tindall, Columbia's modernist expert, under whose supervision Heilbrun had written her master's essay on Isherwood. In *Christopher Isherwood,* Heilbrun continues to pay attention to the treatment of women characters,[36] but her remarks are tempered and, not surprisingly, she seems to be more fascinated by Isherwood's double persona, developing a lengthy analysis of his use of the mask "Isherwood" in such books as *The Last of Mr. Norris, Sally Bowles,* and *Goodbye to Berlin.* Noting that this literary device enabled Isherwood to achieve appropriate ironic distance and to write effective political novels, Heilbrun cautions that the persona, "Isherwood," is not to be confused with the author.[37] We might reasonably suppose that there is more at stake here for the inventor of Amanda Cross than the precepts of New Criticism that sever the connection between author and text. She, too, had invented another self, whose freedom to play could be more successfully maintained if the persona were seen as solely invention and not a reflection of the author who created the mask.

The year that Heilbrun published *Christopher Isherwood,* 1970, also saw the publication of Kate Millett's trail-blazing *Sexual Politics.* Heilbrun was paying attention and, in 1971, published her review, "Millett's *Sexual Politics:* A Year Later." Although Heilbrun was one of the first fully to appreciate the extent of Millett's achievement ("For the first time we have been asked to look at literature as women"), deploring the attacks on Millett by Irving Howe and Midge Decter, there is also some careful distancing ("Some in the Women's Liberation movement have been described to me as extreme in their anti-man attitudes") and a defense of Norman Mailer's view of male and female sexuality that will perhaps parry any charges of man-hating against herself.[38]

Similar caution is revealed in "Women on Women" (1972), the transcript of a discussion among a number of distinguished women invited by the editor of the *American Scholar*, Hiram Haydn, to ponder "the condition of American women today," and, in particular, the question, "If [women] win, what will [they] lose?"[39] Haydn assembled such luminaries as Renata Adler, Ann Birstein, Lillian Hellman, Elizabeth Janeway, Norma Rosen, Nancy Wilson Ross, Alice Walker—and the somewhat obscure English professor Carolyn Heilbrun.

The discussion form was politically appropriate, but, nevertheless, eight persons discussing complex issues from eight points of view created structural difficulties. The women tossed the question back and forth, digressing, diverting, and ultimately evading. Missing from the discussion was the clarity and passion of Gloria Steinem's article in *Time* magazine of 31 August 1970. Taking the same topic but not focusing on what women had to lose, Steinem set forth in "What It Would Be Like if Women Win" a vision of a world transformed to feminist ends. Such a vision eluded the eight women assembled by the *American Scholar*. Patricia McLaughlin, who assisted in the recording, put it well in her summary remarks: "The discussion I had come to listen to surprised me. It seemed curiously dispassionate and diffuse. A sense of all the incisive minds casting about for the point of it, spinning like tires in snow, failing to engage anything real or important."[40] Yet surely these women, highly placed in their various fields, knew all too well what, as professionals, they must lose, not even by winning, but merely by fighting on behalf of women: respect and reputation. It is one thing to fight conventional society from the outside; it is quite another to repudiate that society, having taken such pains to be accepted by it. Carolyn Heilbrun herself put the case succinctly with respect to tenured women at Columbia: "They've learned the gestures of survival in the male world, and if you take those gestures away, what are they going to do?"[41] A decade later she would take up in *Death in a Tenured Position* the very question of the reluctance of professional women "to appear unwomanly, to open themselves up to this pain" and would show the tragic consequences of the double bind professional women find themselves trapped in: to give up the gestures of assimilation is to risk ridicule and charges of triviality; to retain them is to deny one's womanhood.[42] Such an issue went straight to the heart of Heilbrun's personal dilemma at this time: Was her feminism compatible with her professional aspirations and the established image of a literary critic? Were her professional goals compatible with her feminism?

In *The Theban Mysteries* (1971), written very shortly after *Poetic Justice*, Kate Fansler, alumna of the exclusive Theban School for Girls, has been invited back to give a seminar on Sophocles' *Antigone*. As she has done in her previous books with exemplary literary texts or literary-cultural figures, Cross uses this play as a context against which to explore such contemporary resistance against the status quo as the antiwar movement and the women's movement. At this point Cross is still drawing upon the works of male writers, but in *Antigone* she has nevertheless selected a work with a dazzling female protagonist, one who stands alone (without even the support of her sister) against the laws of her society, against the fathers. Antigone's isolation may remind us that, even in as late a book as *Poetic Justice*, Cross allows a sympathetic character like Emilia Airhart to refer disdainfully to the collective women's movement: "There is now even an organization for liberating women—utter nonsense. Women are liberated the moment they stop caring what other women think of them."[43] In this book, too, Cross emphasizes the individual woman's quest for a destiny rather than collective action and expression.

The Theban Mysteries depicts a contemporary family drama that echoes the ancient Greek one in several ways. A patriarchal grandfather, Mr. Jablon, presides over an extended family of daughter-in-law and two grandchildren. He has lost his son to the war in Korea, but he is nevertheless committed to the war in Vietnam and expects his grandson to serve. The grandson has other ideas and hides out at the Theban School, protected by his sister Anjelica, the modern-day Antigone. The family conflicts have their source in generational as well as political differences just as in the Antigone prototype, but Cross does add one crucial ingredient: a middle-aged woman who is the children's mother and Jablon's daughter-in-law—the missing Jocasta. This woman plays a key role in Heilbrun's drama.

It is worth noting that the death in *The Theban Mysteries* is accidental and has nothing to do with individual acts. Crimes are instead committed by the government for prosecuting a war in Southeast Asia, and the arguments in favor of that war are put on trial. Interestingly enough, however, Mr. Jablon, an advocate for that war, is treated with considerable understanding by Cross. Like Heilbrun's own father, he is an immigrant who has worked hard to earn a place in American society, and she respects him even as she condemns his views. On the other hand, his daughter-in-law, an angry, "hysterical," unproductive woman, a demanding and devouring mother to her two children, is offered as the villain (together with Richard Nixon) of the piece. Anticipating the themes of Heilbrun's *Toward a Recognition of Androgyny,* Cross's *The Theban Mysteries* seems to say that, with such fathers and mothers, it is no wonder the world is in chaos. That this mother must die is no psychological accident. A parasite who does not contribute to society but feeds on the lives of her children, she is as dreadful a mother as Cross can imagine—and reminiscent of the middle-aged woman in *The James Joyce Murder* who preys on a young man to the degree that, within the terms of that novel, she invites her own death. It is not clear to what degree Heilbrun as Cross was conscious of "murdering" mothers in these two early books, but in an illuminating passage in Heilbrun's later book, *Reinventing Womanhood,* she would speak of the death of Clytemnestra in the following terms:

> May we not regard the overthrow of Clytemnestra by Orestes and Electra, and its defense by Athene and Apollo, as the symbolic moment when the institution of motherhood is overthrown? Motherhood is that institution in which woman has long been enslaved, which has doomed her children of both sexes to endless fears and fancies. Clytemnestra, a strong and wilful woman, like many women, has turned and twisted within the role of wife and mother, but found that individual selfhood is not attainable there. . . .
>
> Feminists will object that for a woman to suggest the "murder" of a mother, however symbolic, is to join with the worst male forces, including those who destroyed Clytemnestra and established male rule thereafter. But it is not a woman who is being symbolically murdered: it is the principle of motherhood. That principle, not its action in loving parenthood, but its establishment as an institution, must be demythologized and ritually destroyed. Orestes's and Electra's fear of mother-engulfment, which prevented their achievement of selfhood and individuality, is today still a real fear for both sexes,

but especially for women who have been institutionalized into a role where rebirth, initiation, and selfhood are impossible.[44]

Feminists have indeed objected to this killing of the mother. In "Feminist Murder: Amanda Cross Reinvents Womanhood," Jeanne Addison Roberts takes note of Heilbrun's reading of the death of Clytemnestra and the death of the mothers in *The James Joyce Murder* and *The Theban Mysteries*, arguing that "in theory the eradication of negative prototypes of femininity may be valid, but when one is dealing with fictional embodiments—even the most one-dimensional types—it causes real problems." Killing off women, even those who represent "antiquated modes of female behavior," leaves Heilbrun-Cross open to the charge of "anti-feminine rage . . . directed specifically and unforgivingly at the failures of the older generation of women."[45] The fact that the mother in *The Theban Mysteries* dies as an indirect result of her daughter's rage underscores Roberts's point.

In Heilbrun's assault on the institution of motherhood, she was in good feminist company. Adrienne Rich also took aim at the institution of motherhood in *Of Woman Born*, published three years before *Reinventing Womanhood*, though she would argue for the crucial distinction between actual mothers and the institution that bound them.[46] But despite Heilbrun's protests to the contrary, Clytemnestra the mother, as Roberts insists, is herself being murdered along with whatever she may represent. In that regard, the term Heilbrun uses to describe her effect is instructive: "mother-engulfment." She constructs this mother figure as powerful, consuming; as one who, having no autonomous self of her own, overruns her boundaries to swallow the selves of her children. In *The Unspeakable Mother*, Deborah Kloepfer offers this important insight into the psyches of women writers: "For the daughter's gift to be released, . . . for her to create not children but words, the mother must be slain."[47] Adrienne Rich, thinking along similar lines, suggests that fear of the mother is also fear of the mother within: "Matrophobia can be seen as a womanly splitting of the self, in the desire to become purged once and for all of our mothers' bondage, to become individuated and free. The mother stands for the victim in ourselves, the unfree woman, the martyr. Our personalities seem dangerously to blur and overlap with our mothers'; and in a desperate attempt to know where mother ends and daughter begins, we perform radical surgery."[48] Matrophobia thus leads to matricide. Killing the mother, the angry unfulfilled mother, may be, in Rich's terms, a means of avoiding the complexity of contradictions within—assuming anger is resolved or nonexistent because it has been conveniently projected onto another (a mother) figure.

Cross's use of the Antigone character is, of course, assurance of anger against the fathers as well. In that context, let us return for a moment to *Poetic Justice* to pick up one of the central themes of that tale. Inextricable from Fansler's exploration of her private and public forms of institutional loyalty is her relationship with Clemance, a beloved former teacher and present colleague who is aligned with the forces attacking University College. Fansler's interactions with this character, a thinly disguised Lionel Trilling, offer Heilbrun (through Cross) the opportunity to dramatize and explore her own complex attitudes toward Trilling. In making a stand for the importance of University College, Fansler must oppose her revered and wise teacher, her cultured and sensitive colleague. As Reed puts it, "Growing up consists in fighting our former heroes." That Clemance is presented as such a complicated figure, so prejudiced and yet so "large of soul,"[49] is a tribute to Trilling— and to Heilbrun—and yet Heilbrun does allow herself some sweet revenge on the man with whom she could have a conversation of the kind she wanted only by creating one between two fictional characters within the covers of a mystery novel. The conversation is initiated seemingly because Clemance thinks one of Kate's privileged background will appreciate his position on excellence and standards. This implicit indictment of Clemance, and thus, perhaps, of Trilling, on the grounds of snobbery, however, cannot fail to implicate Heilbrun, too, since she has created in Kate exactly the sort of character that Clemance would naturally seek out.

The boldest (some might even call it scandalous) stroke is to make the Clemance-Trilling character the murderer. He is not, one must hasten to add, an intentional murderer; he merely wishes to put temporarily out of action an overzealous disciple who goes mad in his feverish attempts to destroy University College. In light of Trilling's yet-undelivered Jefferson Lecture (it would not be heard until 1972), ironies abound: the failures of community, standards, and rationality, which he deplored as the consequences of not confronting the imposition of affirmative action guidelines on the university, are all provoked by those who oppose the existence of University College. Clemance's punishment is not delivered in a courtroom, since he is shielded from disclosure by Kate and Reed. Presumably, neither Heilbrun-Cross nor Fansler could face bringing him to trial. Instead, he must bear responsibility for the fanatical behavior of his disciple as well as for the accidental act of killing him, a fitting punishment for a Trilling character, perhaps. The man who taught generations of students to appreciate the moral force of literature must himself be forever morally compromised. Like the revolutionary students from whom he is alienated, he falls into the trap of justifying dubious means for the sake of the ends they will supposedly bring about.

Poetic Justice gave Heilbrun (as Cross) the opportunity to defend the School of General Studies, the "women's school," and to blame Trilling, not only for his own views but for the influence he wielded. That the standard-bearers of the men's college took extreme and even irrational measures to secure their goals is patently clear, but so is the fact that they were all originally Clemance's creatures. In this story, Cross has Clemance (poetic justice) repent.[50] What would the real Trilling do when publicly charged with exerting undue and pernicious influence, not by Amanda Cross but by Carolyn Heilbrun?

Heilbrun's criticism to this point has been marked by restraint and judiciousness. Certainly, nothing she has yet written in her role as scholar prepares us for Carolyn Heilbrun the woman, angrier than she has yet been, unleashing in the *Saturday Review* a scathing essay entitled "The Masculine Wilderness of the American Novel" (1972), nominally a review of James Dickey's *Deliverance*. At last, Heilbrun, who in that same year would become a full professor at Columbia ("belatedly by any standards") and would also be unmasked as Cross, gives full vent to the anger that has hitherto been disguised and deflected.[51] Deploring the ways in which American novelists and critics deny full humanity to women, Heilbrun launches a direct attack on Lionel Trilling. She quotes at length from Trilling's 1957 essay, "Emma and the Legend of Jane Austen," in which he declares "Women in fiction only rarely have the peculiar reality of the moral life that self-love bestows. Most commonly they exist in a moon-like way, shining by the reflected moral life of men. . . . Nor can we say that novels are deficient in realism when they present women as they do: it is the presumption of our society that women's moral life is not as men's. No change in the modern theory of the sexes, no advance in status that women have made, has yet contradicted this."[52] Heilbrun charges that by excluding women from the realm of moral action, Trilling (and other writers and critics) "lock us still more firmly not only into our prisons of gender, but also into a world that is now fatally dominated by the male-fantasy ideal," an ideal that leads to aggression and violence.[53]

Heilbrun also takes up in this article Trilling's theory about the young man from the provinces, the theory that had earlier made a dramatic appearance in *In The Last Analysis*. Now it becomes clear why this theory, which Trilling had developed in his essay on Henry James's *The Princess Casamassima* (1948), was so important to Heilbrun, why she had a special affinity for the young man from the provinces, described by Trilling as follows: "He need not come from the provinces in literal fact, his social class may constitute his province. But a provincial birth and rearing suggest the simplicity and the high hopes he begins with—he starts with a great demand upon life and a great wonder about its complexity and promise."[54] Yet the exclusive terms of Trilling's formulation can only disappoint: "Sadly," she says, "Trilling never considers that one of the provinces of which he speaks is womanhood."[55]

Let us register the full force of Heilbrun's public attack on Trilling in "The Masculine Wilderness of the American Novel," an attack presumably more than a decade in the making, since Trilling's article was first published in 1957. In 1972, Trilling was sixty-seven (he died only three years later) and, arguably, the most influential figure in American criticism, let alone at Columbia. By that time, Heilbrun had only published two scholarly books (discounting the detective fiction) and commanded nothing like the standing of Lionel Trilling. Heilbrun must have anticipated the explosion this article would cause in Columbia's world and especially in her department, where Trilling disciples were thickly planted. Her decision to take on Trilling in a public arena took enormous courage and must have seemed like nothing less than an attack on the institution of which Trilling, to Heilbrun's mind, was the most illustrious representative.

Why did she write the piece? Undoubtedly, she was impelled intellectually to resist ideas that were destructive to women, especially when propounded by one of Lionel Trilling's power and influence; to have confronted Trilling in the corridors of Columbia's Philosophy Hall would hardly have been a sufficient response. It is likely, too, that she acted from a personal need to assert herself to a department faculty that had, with very few exceptions, ignored her throughout her Columbia career.

Yet I would contend that Heilbrun had another important reason for writing this article: it marked a decisive step forward, the intimation of a larger ambition, first glimpsed in the 1962 essay on "Educating Female People." The publication of "The Masculine Wilderness of the American Novel" in the *Saturday Review* made the piece more accessible to a general audience than if it had been buried in the pages of a scholarly journal. Heilbrun was taking a public stand, and she was announcing it in a public way. Moreover, she was challenging the culture in a manner she never had before. What better way to proclaim her move into the role of public intellectual than to attack one of the most distinguished cultural figures of the day?

When I asked Carolyn Heilbrun about the angry assault on Lionel Trilling in 1972, she quickly replied that the piece was a review of Dickey's *Deliverance* and "not about Trilling." I reminded her that Trilling had figured prominently in that review and suggested to her that she must have been "enraged" in order to write it. Her response, not a denial but a query, "I was?" is telling. Later, she conceded, "You may be right," though she brushed off the notion that publishing such an article had required courage. No one at Columbia ever mentioned this essay to her: if people gathered in knots to mutter, she did not know about it; if individuals voiced resentment, she did not hear about that, either. Tom Driver, who describes himself as well aware of the "academic style" on Columbia's Morningside Heights, remarked that the silence of the Columbia faculty was not surprising and "doesn't mean that they didn't care. It means that they didn't care to go at it directly." Speaking two full decades after the event, he said, "It is maybe one of the things Carolyn's paying for now." If her Columbia department had calculated its response, it presumably could not have been more effective. She was negligible, unworthy of a reaction. Having written about the "masculine wilderness" of the American novel, she found herself exiled to the feminine wilderness.

Her remarks in "The Masculine Wilderness" on the polarization of the sexes and the exclusion of women from the moral sphere announced her forthcoming book on androgyny. Biographical notices accompanying her essays in the late 1960s and early 1970s indicated that she was working on a "book about the Edwardians." Presumably, that would have been another conventional line to add to her academic résumé. But that book has never, in fact, come to be. Instead, she decided to write a book about androgyny, a book with complex intellectual and personal sources, a book that would set forth intellectual principles to guide her for the rest of her life, and yet a book that would also threaten to marginalize her, both with respect to the mainstream and to the women's movement. Since the book represented an act of great courage on her part, the reactions to it were unexpected and disappointing.

The tone Heilbrun adopts in *Toward a Recognition of Androgyny* is extremely careful. The watchwords are "reconciliation" and "balance," the synthesis, perhaps, of the dispassionate scholar and the angry woman. In androgyny, she finds the means to heal the divisions in the self and the divisions between men and women. Heilbrun wants to embrace a larger critical and fictional territory, to keep an open mind, to acknowledge the justice in opposing claims, to retain what is best of the past, to look forward to a more enlightened future, and, finally, to offer a compelling, opposing argument to Trilling's view of women in such a way as to persuade all reasonable people to see the justice of her position. More theoretical, more speculative, more questing than her previous full-length critical works, the book celebrates the twin classical ideals of harmony and balance: "Androgyny suggests a spirit of reconciliation between the sexes; it suggests, further, a full range of experience open to individuals who may, as women, be aggressive, as men, tender; it suggests a spectrum upon which human beings choose their places without regard to propriety or custom." We should eschew received ideas about sex roles and sexual categories, and each of us, man or woman, should develop an individual self as fully as possible. In particular, "vital women" need to find appropriate public channels for their energy.[56] Heilbrun traces the idea of androgyny through myth and literature, examines its appearance in the novel, and hails its embodiment in the Bloomsbury Group. In *Toward a Recognition of Androgyny* she deals with social as well as literary life and moves further than she has before beyond the strictly defined limits of academic criticism.

The first and most important source for this book is Virginia Woolf's *A Room of One's Own*. The final movement of that extended essay moves toward a meditation on androgyny, the possibility that there are "two sexes in the mind corresponding to the two sexes in the body" that "require to be united in order to get complete satisfaction and happiness." Woolf's notion that "it is fatal to be a man or woman pure and simple; one must be woman-manly or man-womanly" is the starting point for Heilbrun's own exploration of the concept.[57] Not surprisingly, Lionel Trilling is also an important source for this book. Although the work contains only three or four references to Trilling, none of which expresses the level of anger in the *Saturday Review* article, it is nevertheless clear that in large part this book is, though unacknowledged as such, an elaborate argument against Trilling's view of women. In his preface to *The Opposing Self,* Trilling offers a memorable insight into the self in relation to culture. Speaking of the "frequency with which the image of the prison appears in the imaginative works of the nineteenth century," he elucidates the nature of that prison: "As soon as the Bastille had fallen . . . men began to recognize the existence of prisons that were not built of stone. . . . They learned to see that they might be immured not only by the overt force of society but by a coercion in some ways more frightful because it involved their own acquiescence."[58] Heilbrun takes up the prison image in *Toward a Recognition of Androgyny* (she does not refer to Trilling's use of it), but for her that prison is, as she has already indicated in "The Masculine Wilderness of the American Novel," "the prison of gender"; she asserts that "our future salvation lies in a movement away from sexual polarization and the prison of gender toward a world in which individual roles and the modes of personal behavior can be freely chosen."[59] In essays in *The Liberal Imagination* and *The Opposing Self,* Trilling had spelled out his notion of a self in resistance to culture. That self was essentially masculine, and Trilling locates it in "the free-ranging boys of Wordsworth's poems," in Whitman, and in Yeats, whose "long quarrel with the culture . . . made his passion and his selfhood."[60] Heilbrun's project is to revise Trilling's masculinist self (one might say feminize it, make it more androgynous), but even more to portray women as moral agents, as capable of significant action and destiny.

Heilbrun's intended audience is a relatively conservative one, and her goal is "recognition, not revolution."[61] She is confident that once she has named the problem, all reasonable persons will "recognize" it and agree with her solution. She still does not actively espouse feminism in this book; indeed, she carefully distances herself from it, perhaps seeing feminist ideology as one of those oppositional polarities she wishes to avoid, or viewing feminism as a more primitive stage than androgyny in the course of human development.[62] Heilbrun deliberately separates herself from the more radical positions taken by Firestone, Millett, and

Morgan; rather, she seems to build on the witty and subtle work of Mary Ellmann, which constitutes a third important source for this book. In 1968, Heilbrun enthusiastically reviewed Mary Ellmann's *Thinking about Women,* making two observations that are pertinent to our understanding of *Toward a Recognition of Androgyny* and of Heilbrun in general. The first is her disappointment that, in Ellmann's analysis of "male/female polarization," Ellmann provides "no conclusion," although she does "leave us . . . with an understanding that where polarization has been established, it is only the country in between which remains both fertile and uninhabited." The second is embedded in Heilbrun's witty statement that "Today's youth seem finally to have understood that only by freeing woman from her exclusively sexual role can man free himself from his ordained role in the rat-race: that of rat."[63] *Toward a Recognition of Androgyny* provides Ellmann's missing conclusion. Heilbrun's territory is indeed "the country in between," and her mission is to enlighten women, and men especially, as to the rewards of emigration.[64] Before leaving the matter of Heilbrun's sources, let us not forget that she was also drawing on her personal experience of mothering boy-and-girl twins; as often with Heilbrun, the writing project grows from an intersection of literature and history with the contingencies of her own experience, an intersection that marks a perceived injustice: on what basis could opposite-sex twins be denied access to identical destinies?

In Heilbrun's pioneering notion that gender could bend to the force of the imagination, she makes one of the first serious attempts to deconstruct "the prison of gender," anticipating a topic that would attract serious theoretical speculation in the 1980s and 1990s. But she presents her news in moderate terms. Her stance (well learned from Trilling) is liberal, reasonable, humane; her voice cool and dispassionate. This book, growing out of her personal experience, the influence of a growing women's movement, and her rebellion against her beloved teacher, Lionel Trilling, is Heilbrun's careful construction of a bridge between classical humanism and liberal feminism. But steering a middle course in the name of reconciliation proves perilous, and she propitiates neither conservative academics nor radical feminists.

More than two decades later, it may be difficult to gauge the full impact of Heilbrun's book on our intellectual life and on women's studies in particular. In the mainstream press, Joyce Carol Oates praised Heilbrun's "interesting, lively, and valuable general introduction to a new way of perceiving our Western cultural tradition," though she was not persuaded of the need for a term like "androgyny."[65] Feminists within the academy clearly regarded the topic as an important one. There were workshops and a forum at the MLA convention that year, and a full issue of *Women's Studies* was devoted to a discussion of androgyny. In that issue, the case for androgyny was supported by Nancy Topping Bazin (whose *Virginia Woolf and the Androgynous Vision* also appeared in 1973) and Alma Freeman,[66] but, for the most part, Heilbrun was attacked by feminists for producing (or reproducing) an idea that, historically, had served men more than women: men, it was argued, could now appropriate "feminine" values and modes, but women were still prohibited from seeking masculine ones.[67] Cynthia Secor, in a cogently argued essay, charged that androgyny proposes the image of "a man and woman, perfectly balanced, but devoid of context"; Secor refused "a static image of perfection in eternity, an image which cannot take into account the rough going of historical process." Androgyny is reactionary rather than revolutionary, claimed Secor, because it maintains the "old dualities" of sexual identity: it assumes a heterosexual model for human action and behavior; and it presents an abstract ideal or "goal without any road map for getting there."[68] Later in the decade, the moderate feminist critic Elaine Showalter, in her influential *A Literature of Their Own*, would dismiss androgyny as an ideal for Virginia Woolf, arguing that "androgyny was the myth that helped her evade confrontation with her own painful femaleness and enabled her to choke and repress her anger and ambition."[69] Showalter herself was attacked for her assault on Woolf, but the real casualty turned out to be the notion of androgyny. According to its critics, then, androgyny is an idea historically burdened with too much patriarchal baggage, an idea having little relation to social realities such as race and class and offering few possibilities for social change.[70] Elsa Greene, who reviewed Heilbrun's book for *Women's Studies,* credited Heilbrun with offering a "hopeful alternative" for those "who feel locked in a frustrating stand-off with the monolithic patriarchal establishment," and Sandra Bem, looking at androgyny in psychological terms, argued that "for full effective and healthy human functioning, masculinity and femininity . . .

must be integrated into a more balanced, a more fully human, a truly androgynous personality," but few then and since have paid tribute to Heilbrun for the ways in which she opened a new debate.[71]

In retrospect, that debate proved crucial; it was a debate about who would speak for feminism, a battle for the discourse between those who wished to emphasize the differences of men and women and those who wished to eradicate those differences. Heilbrun's ideas were born of the utopian imagination; the self she imagined for men and women was liberating, infinitely capacious, but not tied to the particularity of social and political circumstances. Moreover, though her rhetorical moderation might have been welcome in the 1990s, Heilbrun's nuanced and modulated tones of 1973 worked against her. Feminists wanted, needed, a more daring rhetoric, a more confrontational style. Ultimately, the androgyny model was declared an intellectual and political dead end; feminist critic Susan Stanford Friedman, working with Nancy Topping Bazin on two collections of essays on androgyny at this time, shelved both projects. Friedman recalls that advocacy of androgyny had become even more controversial by decade's end, by which time support for androgyny was perceived as an attack on lesbian separatism.[72] Thus Heilbrun, having entered the debate about the nature of women's roles as mediator, became a marginal figure in 1973, regarded as too radical by the academic mainstream, especially her Columbia community, yet sidelined by more radical feminists.

Toward a Recognition of Androgyny was written for an audience of educated, reasonable men and women; but those who debated its issues were primarily women. Heilbrun was being perceived as a feminist critic in spite of herself. If her next step was to define her own particular brand of feminist criticism, perhaps the key to the Heilbrun of this time may be located in a short essay (originally delivered as a speech) that she composed in concert with Catharine Stimpson. Entitled "Theories of Feminist Criticism: A Dialogue," the essay presents two feminist critics, X and Y, who "intend . . . to represent the sort of dialogue going on not only *among* feminists but within the individual feminist critic herself." The critics are not named within the text, presumably to underline their representative status, but it is nevertheless possible to identify Heilbrun's views as primarily those of X. Whereas Y commits herself to describing and changing the social situation, X wants to look beyond present social facts and transform imaginative consciousness—less pragmatic and immediate, perhaps, though no less fundamental. As in *Toward a Recognition of Androgyny* and, perhaps, like Kate Fansler, Carolyn Heilbrun demonstrates her allegiance to the world of ideas and perceptions rather than to the concreteness of political action, evincing an impatience to leap across present political inequities into an abstract future and an unwillingness to exclude from her calculations the potential role of men in changing the world ("Let us say that you, with your advocacy, will teach women the joys of action and I, with my disinterestedness, will teach men the joys of awareness," states X).[73] Although X and Y are probably farther apart in their political ideology and in the function they see literature performing than they acknowledge, much is accomplished politically by the form of their essay, a dialogue (in the interrogative mode Heilbrun loves) between two women communicating with each other and acknowledging mutual debts as well as mutual differences. This piece does not have the sharp-edged anger of "The Masculine Wilderness of the American Novel," but Carolyn Heilbrun, though still equivocal, has now identified herself with feminist criticism, albeit using the transparent alias, X.

In 1976, Cross, now fully revealed as Heilbrun,[74] published *The Question of Max,* the first of her novels to deal with female biography, and the first to draw inspiration from literary women rather than literary men. Heilbrun seems to be moving to a new stage of her feminism. *The Question of Max* weaves two plots: the story of an academic who will stop at nothing to write the biography of a woman writer, and the story of a high school senior who cheats on the college boards in order to gain admission to Harvard. Both plots, reflecting the so-called Watergate morality, link to expose those who will practice any means to achieve a desired end and who consider themselves beyond the reach of ordinary laws and rules. Illuminating one of Heilbrun's major arguments in *Toward a Recognition of Androgyny, The Question of Max* explores the arrogance of men bred to the "manly" virtues of domination and control. Yet here, as elsewhere, Heilbrun shows herself to be on the side of reform not revolution: society should not be completely overturned, and those codes that ensure decency and honesty must be preserved if civilization is to survive.

The word *civilization* is an important one for Heilbrun, whose most overused word is probably *elegant.* In Kate, Heilbrun presents us with a character who is irresistibly drawn to elegance and civilized sophistication, to a mannered world where (to give some trivial yet telling examples) people on short acquaintance do not presume to use first names and men of culture make fine grammatical distinctions (Kate notes an example of the latter even as she is being threatened with death). Furthermore, anglophiliac Kate is "besotted" by Oxford (which has no place for women), yearns for an invitation to eat at the high table of a men's college, and, in the United States, visiting a library that restricts women's access, remarks that it is "good for the soul" to revisit a "statelier era."[75] Clearly, Kate herself must do some soul-searching and question the price women have had to pay for the privilege of elegance and refinement. That question is central to *The Question of Max.*

It should be noted that convincing debates in this book do not occur between characters. Aside from Kate, characters are rather simply delineated, and most of those we can approve of talk exactly like Kate with similar wit and cadence.[76] At one point, Kate's nephew Leo remarks that Reed is beginning to speak as Kate does; later, two unrelated characters make comparisons between the enclosure of deer at Magdalen College, Oxford, and the place of women in that society, as if both thoughts had issued from the same mind.[77] Moreover, it seems clear that these same characters agree that there is only one way to think about Watergate, the Vietnam war, and women's rights. The interrogation of ideas reflected in the novel's title occurs not among or between characters but rather within Kate herself.

Kate's central conflict in this tale concerns her ambivalent attitude toward Max and the urbane cultivation he represents. In *Reinventing Womanhood,* published three years later, we find this: "[Christopher] Lasch does not . . . seem to recognize that the old, good life which he, Yeats, Trilling, and all today's new conservatives feel such nostalgia for, rested on the willingness of women to remain exactly where today's women, in fiction at least, will not remain: at home." This description certainly reminds us of Max, who claims he "was born a hundred years too late, in time to see all I might have treasured destroyed."[78] Kate is attracted to Max as the epitome of WASP elegance; he even has a royal English pedigree, his father being the younger son of an English Duke. But his polished manners and his old-world courtesy mask a violence that extends to the world of scholarship, whose direction he wants to manipulate; he will stop at nothing to write the biography of a woman

writer and thus control the story of her life. In particular, Heilbrun focuses on the conflict between fine manners and feminism. Kate goes to
Oxford to visit an American friend and to research the work of the
woman writer whose biography is in question. Once there, she is forced
to counter her infatuation with the city of dreaming spires with her realization of the Oxford establishment's treatment of women, especially
those women who have no academic connection with the university.

To what degree Kate's struggle with opposing tendencies mirrors
Heilbrun's own we can only guess, but there seems little authorial distance. Kate's complex relationship with Max may well reflect Heilbrun's
ambivalence toward another illustrious member of Columbia's world of
letters, Jacques Barzun, a man of French origins and impeccable style.
In 1953, Heilbrun had taken one of the famous Barzun-Trilling seminars, after which she and Barzun became friends—until they were separated by political differences, as Barzun became, like Trilling, more
conservative and Heilbrun became increasingly radical. Heilbrun admired Barzun in many ways, and some who know them both suspect
that Max is a portrait of Barzun. Clearly, Barzun would not have re-
sorted to Max's tactics, yet, through the figure of Max, Heilbrun seemingly finds a way to write out some of her conflicts with the temptations
that Barzun represented to her at that time. The fictional Max respects
Kate and seeks her out, albeit for nefarious purposes. Kate is flattered
by his attention, awed by his brilliance, and impressed by his superior
cultivation and taste. As Kate, during the course of the novel, learns his
true nature and the full extent of his disdain for women, however, she
is able (with Reed's help) to outwit him and to overcome her attraction
to him.

Heilbrun is not only battling her feelings about Barzun but also
challenging the very form she has been striving for in her fiction: the
detective novel of manners. A 1990 preface to "The Detective Story of
Manners," written in 1987 and included in *Hamlet's Mother and Other
Women,* casts light on Heilbrun's attitudes and on the themes of *The
Question of Max:* "[This essay] represents an important, earlier moment
for me when I finally faced the full implications of the English class
system and English imperialism in the novels I had long been teaching,
as well as in detective fiction. Lest I appear unforgivably naive in saying
this, let me mention that these themes are relatively new to literary stud-

ies. In my case, the anglophilia which had been a central part of my life from my earliest reading days loosened its hold on me."[79] Indeed, it does seem odd that Heilbrun has avoided noticing the "full implications of the English class system." Plenty of critics and observers have pointed them out; certainly, it would have been difficult for an academic to survive the 1960s without being aware, to some degree, of Marxist interpretations of the novel. Since anglophilia is a fairly common habit of mind in academia, particularly in English departments, one might imagine that someone like Heilbrun, an outsider both as American and Jew, might simply not see the negative aspects of a privileged class that seemed to embody the manners and traditions of a rich culture. Yet, even as Heilbrun admits her blindness to class with characteristic honesty, she is not doing herself justice. Just as we have seen that her struggles with her Jewish identity seem to have been carefully repressed, so were her battles with class. For *The Question of Max* makes it clear that Heilbrun was struggling with her ambivalence about class privilege and elegant manners a good ten years earlier. Indeed, that novel marks an important moment in Heilbrun's intellectual development. In *Sisters in Crime,* Maureen T. Reddy contends that "with *The Question of Max* (1976), Cross begins to ask what effects male-dominated society has on women" and proposes, in her analysis of *Death in a Tenured Position,* that the detective-story convention of "the restoration of order is a false ideal, as the order to which Harvard would like to return is built upon the systematic exclusion of women."[80] Heilbrun as Cross had questioned this order in *The Theban Mysteries,* but the real struggle occurs in *The Question of Max,* as Kate battles against the seductions of Max, and, in effect, against the soothing certainties of an elegant old world.

Before leaving *The Question of Max,* we must note that Jacques Barzun is not the only real figure to hover in the background of this tale. In depicting the lives of the women who were writers and friends during the first part of the century, Heilbrun draws inspiration from the childhood of Rose Macauley, the friendship of Vera Brittain and Winifred Holtby, the solitary life of May Sarton, the story of Dorothy Sayers's illegitimate son, and the lives of Brittain, Holtby, and Sayers at Oxford.[81] But of all these, the life of Sayers is predominant. This novel focuses, in large part, on whether the biography of a woman should be written by a man who is completely out of sympathy with feminist theory. In the 1970s, Heilbrun, who had become very interested in the life of Dorothy

Sayers, hoped to write her biography, but Sayers's executors chose a man instead; Heilbrun's criticism of James Brabazon's work centered on his inability to see Sayers outside the traditional script for women. In *The Question of Max,* Heilbrun sets forth a new script, focusing on accomplishment rather than on romance and marriage, as she recaptures the lives of dead women writers. Indeed, she initiates a practice she repeats in subsequent novels: recreating the life story of an absent or dead woman, offering new criteria by which to judge success.

Poetic Justice, The Theban Mysteries, and *The Question of Max* all examine the relationship of character to the changes of history. In fact, one could argue that, in *Poetic Justice* and *The Question of Max,* as well as in *Death in a Tenured Position,* the villains are precisely those who, in one way or another, refuse to adjust to the breakdown of old forms and the attempt to create more egalitarian structures. Neither Heilbrun, nor Fansler for that matter, is cavalier in regard to form. "I did not underestimate the price of what I sought to overturn," says Heilbrun in *Reinventing Womanhood.*[82] On many levels, Fansler, too, demonstrates her allegiance to structure and order: she deplores the extreme tactics of some college revolutionaries, not to mention their slipshod syntax; she is nostalgic for rose petals in finger bowls and the associated civilities of her privileged youth, and regrets the passing of order and proportion; she points out to her students in *The Theban Mysteries* that "It is dangerous to assume that the conventions of society are, despite our sneering use of the word 'conventional,' necessarily wrong. Without some conventions, each day would be a new battle back at the beginning of time."[83] Moreover, *Poetic Justice* reveals her own ambivalence toward radical change. But what lends Fansler's scrutiny of these matters such poignancy is the fact that, while appreciating the value of form and convention, she also knows that embedded in the received ideas and the old standards is much that needs to be changed: that in an ideal of educational excellence may be hidden the evils of prejudice, snobbery, and elitism (*Poetic Justice*); that patriotism may camouflage brutality (*The Theban Mysteries*); that civilized manners and a courtly demeanor may mask the ruthlessness ready to break any law to preserve the privileges of a fading way of life (*The Question of Max*);[84] and that traditional role differentiations for men and women, which maintain separate value systems in domestic and public life, may cause devastation at every level.

The Carolyn Heilbrun of this decade has become increasingly engaged with feminist issues in both her criticism and her fiction. Her novels of this time examine broader social concerns and show a marked leap forward in artistic control and complexity; but they are especially interesting for the ways in which Cross-Heilbrun explores Kate Fansler's gathering anxieties about many of the challenges thrown down by radical feminists with respect to marriage, class, and institutional loyalty. And although Heilbrun herself has a much more troubled and complicated relation to the institution since her stand on the steps of Low Library, her work demonstrates that she still wants to assimilate, still wants to succeed in the conventional academic way, and she is proving her ability to establish a professional reputation. But the locus of assimilation, the institution of Columbia, is proving ever more inhospitable, incapable of accommodating women. Reports Nancy K. Miller of her experience as a graduate student in French at Columbia, "despite pockets of local activity—the annual Barnard 'Scholar and Feminist' conference, the occasional undergraduate offering—the academic institution was impervious to the dramatic changes occurring in social relations wrought by 1968 and by feminism."[85] Yet not all members of the institution were impervious. During the 1970s, George Stade, another member of Columbia's English and Comparative Literature Department, was working on his novel, *Confessions of a Lady-Killer,* published in 1979. The protagonist-narrator announces at the beginning, "I am the hero or villain of the narrative to follow, depending on whether you are a feminist or a human being." The definition of "human being" is worth pondering as our protagonist embarks on a murderous rampage of revenge against feminists who have seduced his wife away from him. It is entirely possible to claim that, in this scathingly satiric book, the protagonist deserves as much censure as his victims; moreover, Stade was sufficiently open to Kate Millett's ideas to serve as advisor for the dissertation that became *Sexual Politics.* Still, he gleefully commits to print vicious caricatures of feminists. And perhaps the swipes at androgyny and androgynes are no accident—nor the fact that the most villainous feminist is a "science-fiction writer disguised as an anthropologist," who says of her son's education, "I shall see to it that the feminine side of his nature is properly nourished, that he grows up to be a complete human being, rather than just a man."[86] This could well have been one response to Heilbrun's feminism and her 1972 attack on Trilling.

This decade also sees the beginning of Carolyn Heilbrun's long connection with the Modern Language Association, an institution that would prove much more congenial to her than Columbia. In 1976, she was elected for a four-year term to the executive council, the main governing body of the MLA. In 1968, one woman, Liselotte Dieckmann, served on the council; by 1976, when Heilbrun was elected, six of the twelve at-large members were women. Among the matters considered by the council and the delegate assembly during Heilbrun's tenure were the desirability of implementing a policy of anonymous submissions to *PMLA* (eventually adopted); a review of the criteria for choosing members of the *PMLA*'s advisory committee and advisory board; a recommendation to develop guidelines for nonsexist language in MLA's official documents and publications; a resolution to reaffirm the importance of affirmative action; and a resolution to prevent holding the annual conventions in states that had not ratified the ERA.[87] Heilbrun is moving out of her study and becoming more actively engaged in the profession.

All around her, women are becoming increasingly insistent on their rights, and while Heilbrun's voice is generally more moderate and restrained, she is open to their demands and participates in some of them. Her review of Kate Millett's *Sexual Politics* was published not in a mainstream journal but in *Aphra,* and she contributed reviews to *Ms.* magazine as well. In 1971, she founded the *Virginia Woolf Newsletter;* that, in addition to her work on Bloomsbury, helped foster a new critical appreciation of Woolf at a time when members of the Bloomsbury Group were not highly regarded.[88] At this time, Heilbrun's anger against the mothers and the fathers is also beginning to show. These battles seem to be conducted first in the pages of the fiction and only then appear in the criticism. The ambivalence about Trilling emerges first in *Poetic Justice* and then in "The Masculine Wilderness of the American Novel"; the conflicts about motherhood appear first in *The James Joyce Murder* and *The Theban Mysteries* and then in *Reinventing Womanhood.* It is as if only the masked Heilbrun, Amanda Cross, can raise such powerful and painful conflicts. But then Cross, having opened the way to expression and exploration, can teach Heilbrun how to publish her anger.[89]

It is significant, too, that Heilbrun publicly revealed herself as Amanda Cross after *Poetic Justice* was published. The early 1970s was a time for women to shed disguises, and Heilbrun's act finds echoes in the 1972 publication of a book with the telling title *No More Masks! An Anthology of Poems by Women,* edited by Florence Howe and Ellen Bass, and in Adrienne Rich's intense self-exploration in *Diving into the Wreck* (1973). Presumably the Amanda Cross who wrote *Poetic Justice* about an institution so readily identified as Columbia wanted to throw off her protective covering, and the Carolyn Heilbrun who now had tenure was not so reluctant to disclose her true identity. Indeed, we shall see whether the unmasking of Cross will curb or fire Heilbrun's ability to speak out.

Yet, to be unmasked was also to deal in a public way with her complex attitudes towards Lionel Trilling and all that he represented as assimilated Jew, civilized humanist, liberal thinker, and defender of the autonomous self.[90] Heilbrun has begun to challenge his ideas directly, and, in the process, she is perceptibly transforming herself into a public critic of the culture. The writing self of "The Masculine Wilderness of the American Novel" can now brave combat and confrontation.

What compels about Heilbrun's story is that, while some other feminists of the time seem (at least, according to their written testimonies) to have experienced swift, radical transformations, Heilbrun's was a gradual evolution. This becomes especially clear in this phase of her life as she struggles with motherhood, patriarchy, class, profession, and academic institutions; as she tests her anger; and as she turns her lens (in *The Question of Max*) on women writers and the structure of women's lives, the project that was defining the second stage of this latest women's movement.

The ideal that Heilbrun-Cross seeks is balance, an infinitely expanding self that can accommodate multiple roles, multiple oppositions. This juncture of Heilbrun's development is graphically rendered by the cover illustration of the paperback version of *Toward A Recognition of Androgyny,* published by Harper Colophon Books. Above the title, framed by an enclosing (unifying?) arch is the depiction of a Janus-like head with three layered female profiles looking to the viewer's right and three male profiles looking to the left. No seam divides the sexes and there is little differentiation in the features of the profiles. The whole is pictured in shades of white, gray, and black, except for the (combined) male-female symbol placed midway between the profiles, which is red. The total effect is of balance, symmetry, synthesis, reconciliation, yet within this seeming wholeness we can see multiplicity, splits, selves pointing in opposite directions. It remains for the Carolyn Heilbrun of the following decade to practice selective exorcism and attempt to reinvent what she would call a whole self, a feminist writer and scholar. Later still, she would allow for a more complex play of selves.

5

Feminism in a Tenured Position

It is immediately plain that if there is no difference between men who earn their livings in the professions
and women who earn their livings, then this letter can
end.

— VIRGINIA WOOLF, *Three Guineas*

Women are human beings first, with minor differences
from men that apply largely to the act of reproduction.

— GLORIA STEINEM, "Sisterhood"

We, as a class, are tired of . . . protection . . . which
leaves us everything to do, to dare, and to suffer, and
strips us of all means for its accomplishment. . . . Undo
what man did for us in the dark ages, and strike out all
special legislation for us; strike the words "white male"
from all your constitutions, and then, with fair sailing,
let us sink or swim, live or die, survive or perish together.

— ELIZABETH CADY STANTON, "An Address to
the New York State Legislature"

At the cusp of the 1980s, the borders of feminism's terrain were
staked out by two works: Betty Friedan's *The Second Stage* and
Adrienne Rich's "Compulsory Heterosexuality and Lesbian Existence."
While Friedan argues that feminists have gone too far in alienating
mainstream women and thus, in effect, joins the forces of backlash she
purports to fend off,[1] Rich contends that feminists have not gone far
enough and, in particular, have neglected or denied the claims of lesbians. Obviously, other works of importance were produced at this time,
but, for the study of Heilbrun's development, I want to focus once again

on these two preeminent feminists of her generation: Betty Friedan and Adrienne Rich.

In 1981, the title and argument of Friedan's *The Second Stage* made a dramatic announcement: the first stage of the women's movement had come to an end. During the 1970s, Friedan had lost the center stage of the women's movement to more radical feminists; this book was an attempt to bring her moderate politics back into general focus and redirect the women's movement by naming what she saw as the crucial issues of the second stage just as she had named, for middle-class women, those of the first. In *The Second Stage,* Friedan made it clear that women had not yet achieved all their goals of equality and freedom, but that younger women, in particular, were identifying new problems.

Yet this book lacked the angry passion and conviction of *The Feminine Mystique.* Friedan argued that feminists, in extreme reaction to their years of entrapment in the roles of wife and mother, failed to acknowledge that women needed not only professional but also family lives. In Friedan's words, the feminine mystique was giving way to the equally rigid and unsatisfactory "feminist mystique." She attacked both "radical lesbian 'separatists'" and the "extremist supporters" of Phyllis Schlafly, contending that the women's movement had allowed itself to become side-tracked by sexual politics. She even went so far as to say that "men may be at the cutting edge of the second stage." Wanting to avoid what she called single-issue politics such as pornography, she emphasized the large themes (such as reproductive freedom and economic inequities) that would unite the majority of women. Anticipating a theme of election politics in the 1990s, she advocated a reclamation of what has become known as "family values" from the Moral Majority (though she made it clear that her vision of family was not necessarily the traditional one) and a commitment to transform (not merely invade) institutions in accordance with women's needs for family and profession. She saw her project as one of "human wholeness" for women who would transcend the "half-lives" of prefeminism and the overreactive first stage of feminism.[2]

If Friedan had once again put her finger on the pulse of middle America, her book met with derision from committed feminists who were astonished to be informed that the first stage was over and who found Friedan's solution to be reactionary. Simone de Beauvoir responded with a gesture that captured the sentiments of many feminists at the time: she flung Friedan's book across the room, declaring that she "rejected everything about it."[3]

A year before Friedan's book appeared, Adrienne Rich published "Compulsory Heterosexuality and Lesbian Existence," an essay issuing from a political position so entirely opposed to that of Friedan that it is still difficult to regard the two as part of the same movement. Friedan, seeing the issue of lesbianism as divisive and irrelevant to the concerns of most middle-class women ("not politics," "just sex"), wanted it excised from women's agenda. Rich, deploring the ways in which lesbian existence had been ignored, marginalized, or denigrated—even by feminist scholars—saw women's commitment to each other as central to that agenda. Rich exploded the ideological bomb that heterosexuality, contrary to widespread assumption, is not necessarily a freely chosen "preference," but "something that has had to be imposed, managed, organized, propagandized, and maintained by force." The notion that women are "innately heterosexual," according to Rich, must be questioned. Moreover, she argued, lesbian identity should not be narrowly defined according to sexual activity (it was not "just sex," as Friedan would have it), but along what she called a "lesbian continuum," a broader term that would "embrace many more forms of primary intensity between and among women, including the sharing of a rich inner life, the bonding against male tyranny, the giving and receiving of practical and political support."[4]

Friedan's book was addressed to a general, middle-class audience, to the housewife in Peoria she once was, and particularly to younger women, frustrated by the rhetoric of the women's movement. Rich's essay, widely discussed after its publication in *Signs*, was directed at a feminist scholarly community that Rich believed was continuing to neglect lesbianism, though her concerns certainly went beyond the academic.[5] Friedan wanted to find a broad base of agreement among men and women, a consensus that would allow small, incremental moves toward reform. Rich wanted to overturn comfortable assumptions about "normality" and free choice and unleash the power of women to resist constraints. Though both denied sentimental tendencies, Friedan romanticized her new concept of family and Rich romanticized lesbian solidarity. If Friedan alienated feminists who thought she had sold out to the patriarchy, Rich alienated feminists who embraced other forms of resistance and who refused the notion that they had been coerced into heterosexual unions.[6]

The arguments presented by Friedan and Rich in these curiously symmetrical texts had been developing within the women's movement throughout the 1970s. As the Reagans won the White House in 1980, proclaiming a return to their version of family values and intending to curtail women's reproductive rights and the advances made in civil rights and affirmative action legislation, and as the Equal Rights Amendment was defeated, at stake was nothing less than how women would live their lives—with what allegiances and with what personal, professional, and political power.

What I have construed as the debate between Friedan and Rich crystallized the significant feminist issues of the time. Should women focus on their connections to or their differences from men; on the transformation of male professions and institutions or on separation from those institutions; on female relations, traditions, and culture or on modifying relations with men, with male traditions and culture? And finally, should women attend to the differences among women (such as those constituted by race, class, and sexual preference) or to their common problems, needs, and values? Against this ideological landscape the drama of Heilbrun's own development is played out. I am not suggesting that these two works of Friedan and Rich directly influenced Heilbrun, but the tensions, issues, and anxieties at the turn of the decade as embodied in the works of Friedan and Rich were certainly both masked and expressed in Heilbrun's own work of this period. In some ways moving closer to Rich (she would deftly repudiate *The Second Stage*[7] and was rapidly becoming more radical as Friedan became less so), she was nevertheless still wary of the challenges Rich posed. Heilbrun's anxieties about what Friedan called the "whole self," about the tensions between men and women and women and women, would reverberate throughout her work of this period and particularly, as we shall see, in the pivotal works *Reinventing Womanhood* and *Death in a Tenured Position*.

Heilbrun's struggles of the time are captured in two pieces she published in 1981: "Virginia Woolf in Her Fifties" (portions of which were revised and included in a chapter of *Writing a Woman's Life*) and an essay for the "Hers" column of the *New York Times*. If the Woolf article presents us with a woman of increasing self-confidence and composure, the "Hers" column reveals the darker edges that may be the consequence of that public poise.

Of Woolf, Heilbrun concludes that "in Woolf's fifties, with great work behind her, she would no longer fear either the expression of her anger or its effects on the men who overheard her." *Signs*'s contributor Lynda Koolish, who reviewed the essay collection *Virginia Woolf: A Feminist Slant* (1983) in which this essay was reprinted, remarks that "Woolf's anger was undisguised long before her fifties . . . and that furthermore, Woolf . . . continued to be apprehensive about male opinion in her fifties." Whether Koolish is correct about Woolf is less important than the fact that Heilbrun is writing in this essay not only about Woolf but about herself, pointedly remarking that she will draw on her "own experience of being in one's fifties" in order to explain Woolf's. In noting her late-won appreciation of the angry *Three Guineas*, Heilbrun uncovers her own earlier fear of anger: "Woolf, like all women, had to fight a deep fear of anger in herself. For many years I was made uncomfortable by *Three Guineas*, preferring the 'nicer' *Room*, where Woolf never presses against the bounds of proper female behavior—where, it could seem, her art prevailed. I say this to my shame. What prevailed was not her art alone but her fear (and mine) of arousing the patriarchy to disgust, of acting wholly apart from the 'script' assigned to women." At last, Carolyn Heilbrun, who turned fifty in 1976 and was by then well established as both critic and detective-story novelist, felt free to engage her own anger, an anger that we have seen her express only fleetingly in the past. For Heilbrun, and perhaps for other women, contrary to conventional expectation, fifty was a "flowering."[8] Middle-aged women, according to Heilbrun, no longer regarded as suitable protagonists in the romance plot, could write other scripts, invent other possibilities. In part, Heilbrun's increasing radicalism is due to this middle-aged confidence. But it is also due to the context in which, in the late 1970s and early 1980s, she found herself.

The intellectual climate had changed. When Betty Friedan announced the so-called second stage, she could survey significant transformations not only in the social world but also, if she wished, in the academic one. Research on women had become increasingly sophisticated and influential, penetrating virtually every discipline from anthropology, history, psychology, and sociology to literature, philosophy, and religion. The works of such women as Adrienne Rich, Susan Brownmiller, Nancy Chodorow, Dorothy Dinnerstein, and Carol Gilligan crossed disciplines and made their way out of the academy and on to living-room bookshelves. Within the academy, journals such as *Signs: Journal of Women in Culture and Society, Feminist Studies,* and *Frontiers* provided forums for research on women, and contributions by feminists were increasingly finding expression in mainstream journals. Indeed, Jane Gallop was able to write in *Around 1981* of the "institutionalization of feminist criticism."[9]

Yet, if the inner and outer conditions were more conducive to the expression of Heilbrun's anger, we still must not underestimate its costs. For if she has been a representative feminist critic in her struggle to reconcile the demands of politics and profession, reflecting the tensions experienced by many women in the academy during these years, she has certainly not been representative of accomplished women of her own generation. One of the most poignant statements in "Virginia Woolf in Her Fifties" sounds a theme of isolation that, although mitigated by the presence of a strong women's movement, is nevertheless deeply felt. The "country in between" still has very few inhabitants: "There is a no-woman's land discovered by those who expound their feminism late in life. Occupied neither by the friends of their youth, who disdained the fight, nor by the youth of the day, who have not yet taken it up, this land is a lonely place."[10]

This darker note is sounded also in the "Hers" column mentioned earlier. Surveying her professional and personal accomplishments—the evidence, surely, the reader might think, of the "wholeness" she and Friedan have craved—Heilbrun finds not satisfaction but a central "lack." This "lack" is defined for her by John Updike who, in a discussion of Colette, praises Colette's "central firmness and clarity of vantage." According to Heilbrun, she (and other women) lack these qualities. As we listen to her strong, clear voice, she certainly seems to have battled her way to autonomy and "central firmness." About the nature of her pain, "a female pain, an angst indigenous to the sex," she is not absolutely clear except to attribute it both to those who suffer dependency and especially to those who have moved into lives of their own.[11] I return later to the nature of this pain, but for now, I simply want to recognize the complexity of Heilbrun's responses at this time: optimism and excitement edged in by pain and isolation.

Listen again to the rising spirits of one in her prime: "We recognize how extraordinary it is, in one's fifties, to search out a new creative vein, to allow one's anger to drive one to the discovery of new forms."[12] This is precisely what she does in *Reinventing Womanhood* and *Death in a Tenured Position*. I want to consider these two works at some length because, crucial in Heilbrun's own intellectual evolution, they illuminate matters of disguise (particularly women's disguise), displacement, isolation, and the need for community. If the critical *Reinventing Womanhood* points boldly in the direction Heilbrun wants women to take, the fictional *Death in a Tenured Position* dramatizes the underlying conflicts and anxieties. Both books reveal the ways in which Heilbrun's increasing commitment to feminism has altered the forms of both her criticism and her fiction.

Reinventing Womanhood (1979), a freer, more flexible criticism than Heilbrun has attempted before, takes up the theme first sounded in *Toward a Recognition of Androgyny*—the full development and expression of the self—except that she does now declare an unequivocally feminist stand, take account of the criticisms leveled at the *Androgyny* book, and insist that the self is female. Unlike *Toward a Recognition of Androgyny*, *Reinventing Womanhood* is addressed to women. In this book, Heilbrun sets out "to name . . . those strictures not wholly societal or cultural that inhibit women from the full formation of a self." It is important to note here that, for Heilbrun, the formation of a "whole" self is inextricably linked with the opportunity and capacity for accomplishment. The full self, the fulfilled self, is an ambitious, achieving self. Since the paths to achievement have been laid by men, and since Heilbrun believes one must take full advantage of the paths already tracked, she wants "to tell women that the male role model for autonomy and achievement is, indeed, the one they still must follow." But women must not become "honorary men"; they need "both to claim the male model and to deny its maleness" so that women can pursue professional and public work, too.[13] Once again, Heilbrun is arguing that men and women are more like than unlike one another and that to dwell on difference is to separate women from power.

The wholeness Carolyn Heilbrun aspires to is reflected in the unconventional form of *Reinventing Womanhood*. A blend of the personal and the critical, of autobiography and biography, *Reinventing Woman-*

hood ranges in disciplines though the fields of literature, religion, myth, history, theater, politics, business, psychoanalysis, and sociology, and in manner from condemnation through explication and inquiry to exhortation. Heilbrun seems to suggest that women's lives must be approached and discussed through precisely this kind of comprehensive method, a method that Heilbrun has doubtless learned from the interdisciplinary approach of women's studies as well as from other feminist writers. She is ready to abandon the once-comforting New Criticism that "demanded separation between the personality and the intellect." [14] By sharing her experience of being Jewish and female, Heilbrun seeks to open the professional to the personal, the scholar to the woman, and establish her critical self, not by masking aspects of her identity, but by stripping away many of the denials and disguises of the past. In this book, she has the courage to close many of the gaps between personal and professional and tells her own story in an attempt to explain the course of her own life and accomplishments to other women.

To the extent that Heilbrun introduces the personal, crosses disciplines, and exhorts women both to fulfill their potential and to encourage other women to do the same, she is attuned to the chorus of contemporary feminist voices. But, in more fundamental ways, her views are a counterpoint to that chorus. She is undoubtedly more radical than she has yet been, but, once again, Carolyn Heilbrun is writing against the grain of feminist scholarship of the period. As noted in the discussion of *Toward a Recognition of Androgyny*, the battle for the discourse had been won by the "difference" feminists, but Heilbrun was not yet prepared to give up her ground.

In order to understand what is at stake in Heilbrun's proposals for a reinvented womanhood, let us return for a moment to the differences between Rich and Friedan and, indeed, to the question of "difference" itself as that was being explored and debated in the feminist scholarship of the time. The early phase of feminist theory protested against the divisions of work and spheres for men and women and investigated the sources of these separations and exclusions. The pressure to open institutions and professions to qualified women was supported by a body of work attacking the images of women presented in serious and popular culture that suggested women were biologically and culturally unsuited to the work traditionally performed by men. The emphases, then, were

From the 1947 *Legenda.* Courtesy
Wellesley College Archives

In the early 1960s. Courtesy of
Margaret Heilbrun

New York City, December 1995. Courtesy of the photographer, Cathleen Rountree

on the capacity of women to do so-called men's work and the injustice of their exclusion; or, if women were employed alongside men, their lower pay and certainly less-frequent chances for promotion.

Protests of this kind are, of course, not new. From the English Mary Wollstonecraft to the American Charlotte Perkins Gilman, women had, from time to time, sometimes individually and, in the nineteenth century, as part of a movement, insisted on their ability to work side by side with men. What, asked the feminists of the 1970s, would make their protest different this time? What would make it stick?

Heilbrun, among others, had pointed out that earlier struggles for women's liberation had failed because they were unsupported by a body of theory.[15] The growing number of feminists in the academy ensured that theory would be supplied, and the development of that theory served to legitimate both feminism and the place of feminists in the academy. But the question is why feminist theory chose in the late 1970s and early 1980s to emphasize difference rather than similarity between the sexes. The simple answer is, of course, that the analysis of oppression was more or less at a dead end: the villains were marked and the systems exposed. Moreover, this analysis also focused on men as the primary agents of control and on male theoretical principles. In "Feminist Criticism in the Wilderness," Elaine Showalter made the case for moving to a new stage: "The feminist obsession with correcting, modifying, supplementing, revising, humanizing, or even attacking male critical theory keeps us dependent upon it and retards our progress in solving our own theoretical problems. What I mean here by 'male critical theory' is a concept of creativity, literary history, or literary interpretation based entirely on male experience and put forward as universal. So long as we look to androcentric models for our most basic principles—even if we revise them by adding the feminist frame of reference—we are learning nothing new."[16]

It was imperative to respond to attacks claiming that feminism had no comprehensive theory of its own, no thinkers like Marx or Freud, and that it fed, instead, on systems and theories created by men. To quote Showalter again on the subject of literary criticism: "I do not think that feminist criticism can find a usable past in the androcentric critical tradition. It has more to learn from women's studies than from English studies, more to learn from international feminist theory than from another seminar on the masters. It must find its own subject, its own system, its own theory, and its own voice." Coining the term *gyno-critics,* Showalter argues for a focus on women rather than men as subjects. Her subject is women writers: "To see women's writing as our primary subject forces us to make the leap to a new conceptual vantage point and to redefine the nature of the theoretical problem before us," a problem which is "the essential question of difference." Asks Showalter, "How can we constitute women as a distinct literary group? What is *the difference* of women's writing?"[17] The argument for "difference" produces theories based on women as subjects and asserts the intrinsic value of women's activities and expression. The emphasis falls on women's affinities with each other (as mothers and daughters, as friends and lovers, as participants in women's traditions) and on their difference from men.

Showalter had already followed her own dictum by producing *A Literature of Their Own* (1977). Patricia Meyer Spacks's earlier *The Female Imagination* (1975), Ellen Moers's *Literary Women* (1976), and Showalter's 1977 book proposed the existence of female traditions in literature whose characteristics Showalter, Spacks, Moers, and then Sandra M. Gilbert and Susan Gubar, in *The Madwoman in the Attic* (1979), would codify. Scholars in other disciplines were also pursuing the study of women's difference from men. Carol Gilligan's *In a Different Voice* (1982) held up for scrutiny the standards by which moral development was measured. Gilligan discovered that, in the model designed by her Harvard professor Lawrence Kohlberg, women were usually found wanting. Arguing that women based moral decisions on their experience of relationships with people, their sense of need and obligation, whereas men decided moral questions according to abstract principles of justice, she concluded that women's values were different from, not inferior to, men's. In fact, Gilligan pointed out that the "different voice I describe is characterized not by gender but theme. Its association with women is an empirical observation, and it is primarily through women's voices that I trace its development." But in spite of her wish not to offer a "generalization about either sex," her work has been used to underscore gender differences.[18] Similarly, Jean Baker Miller in *The New Psychology of Women* (1976) noted that conventional theories of psychological development valued the autonomous self (male) and denigrated the relating self (female). Miller formulated a "new psychology" that would honor the modes and expressions of female behavior. Another influential proponent of difference was Susan Brownmiller who, in *Against Our Will* (1975), explored the distinctions between male and female physical power and aggression. Finally, Mary Daly, in her passionate *Gyn/Ecology* (1978), resisted all things patriarchal and insisted on the intrinsic and extrinsic differences of women: "Radical feminism is not reconciliation with the father. Rather it is affirming our original birth, our original source, movement, surge of living. This finding of our original integrity is re-membering our Selves. Athena remembers her mother and consequently re-members her Self. Radical feminism releases the inherent dynamic in the mother-daughter relationship toward friendship, which is strangled in the male-mastered system." [19]

It is against this feminist course, charted by moderates such as Showalter and radicals such as Daly, that Heilbrun writes *Reinventing Womanhood*. Not interested so much in celebrating what women are as selves, what they have learned from each other, how they relate to each other—or even what some of them have already achieved, she is concerned with the need to change, to reimagine. Unlike Showalter, who is stimulated by the "many theoretical opportunities" afforded by the term *gynocritics,* [20] Heilbrun is absorbed not by theory but by the practical consequences for women's work in the world. When Elizabeth Abel edited a collection of essays from *Critical Inquiry* that she entitled *Writing and Sexual Difference,* Carolyn Heilbrun was one of two critics (Jane Gallop was the other) invited to publish a response to the essays in the volume. She is characteristically generous to the essay writers in the book but nevertheless deeply concerned about the emphasis on difference: "Men, taking unto themselves all adventure, leaving women each other, the children, and the laundry, will further enslave women if women identify all adventure as 'male' and not for them. Women must discover their difference and their own culture. No doubt that, as Showalter knows, is the next important phase for feminist criticism. But if women forfeit the culture men have dubbed 'male' when it is, in fact, human, they will have deprived themselves of too much." Further, Heilbrun objects to the emphasis on differences among women: "I fear lesbians who insist upon what separates them from other feminists, even from more conciliatory lesbians." [21] About other separations—those of class and race, Heilbrun has little to say either in this response or in other essays of this time.

Now, of course, in a very particular sense, Heilbrun is interested in difference: not in the differences between men and women or the differences among women but in a different female self—a self different from the conventional female self and similar to the conventional male self. Her project is nothing less than the reinvention of the self—her own and that of women in general. But does such a utopian enterprise inevitably entail new fictions of the self? In what sense is it possible to reinvent the self? What is changed, what stays the same, what is suppressed, what invented? Indeed, is the quest for "wholeness" and the reinvention of the self a contradiction in terms? To some of these questions I return presently.

Given Heilbrun's identification with the male world of adventure, it is not surprising that her first and primary example of a reinvented self is her father. She tells of his emigration from Russia, his self-education, his break from family and Jewish roots, his making and losing and making fortunes. It is an immigrant's success story, from Russia to riches, though with an important difference: it involved the complete suppression of the old self and the creating of a new by sheer will and imagination. Says Heilbrun, "Like Gatsby, my father had been his own creation."[22] But Gatsby is haunted by the past, as is Heilbrun's father. He suffers a nervous breakdown, and though Heilbrun declares he is healed through analysis, the collapse reminds the reader that the past clings more closely than we consciously know, that new selves are won at a price, that severed roots may produce the "lack" Heilbrun laments in the "Hers" column.

That these new selves are, to some degree, fictions, is precisely Heilbrun's point. In *Reinventing Womanhood* (she would develop this point further in *Writing a Woman's Life*), Heilbrun expresses the belief that, in order to become characters and to act in the world, we need scripts. Literature ought to help us find them. However, in a chapter entitled "The Failure of Imagination," Heilbrun holds to account writers such as Willa Cather, Edith Wharton, and George Eliot, who led unconventional lives of independence themselves but who were not able to imagine female protagonists with the same powers. In another chapter, "Search for a Model: Female Childhood," Heilbrun presents capsule biographies of famous women, among them Helene Deutsch, Golda Meir, Phyllis Schlafly, and Frances Perkins. All led exceptional lives but, in their public utterances, failed to see their choices as open to other women. But if public narratives of female achievement are misleading, if private narratives are unavailable, and if fictional narratives are often conventional, where are women to find scripts? If they are to follow male scripts, how should those scripts be adapted? Indeed, can women follow male scripts without changing the very structure of society so as to make such actions possible?

Given this problem and this context, Nancy Chodorow clearly emerges as one of the heroes of Heilbrun's narrative of reinvention.[23] She is able to show how changes in child-rearing practices can lead to changes in development of the male and female self. Not rejecting but revising Freud, Chodorow sets herself the task, in *The Reproduction of Mothering* (1978), of examining the bases of the current arrangements that produce "daughters with mothering capacities and the desire to mother" and "sons whose nurturant capacities and needs have been systematically curtailed and repressed." Chodorow suggests that, if both fathers and mothers rear children, the cycle of reproducing social arrangements that inhibit the development of both men and women will end: "My expectation is that equal parenting would leave people of both genders with the positive capacities each has, but without the destructive extremes these currently tend toward. Anyone who has good primary relationships has the foundation for nurturance and love, and women would retain these even as men would gain them. Men would be able to retain the autonomy which comes from differentiation without that differentiation being rigid and reactive, and women would have more opportunity to gain it."[24] This sounds much like the kind of program Heilbrun was urging in *Toward a Recognition of Androgyny,* though Chodorow does not speak about general principles of androgyny, providing instead a theoretical basis in psychology and sociology for her ideas. And Heilbrun celebrates Chodorow precisely because she is able to show that Freud's drama of the developing female and male selves is not only psychologically but also culturally determined; that, indeed, the female self is as capable as the male self.

In addition to her father, there is another important man in Heilbrun's intellectual world, one who also insists with Freud on the essential differences between men and women, one whose life's work was also devoted to the drama of the self in culture, one to whom Heilbrun owes a huge intellectual debt, and one with whom in *Reinventing Womanhood* she resumes her long, defiant quarrel.[25] That man is, of course, Lionel Trilling. In *Reinventing Womanhood,* Heilbrun opens two areas of personal vulnerability: her rejection of her Jewish identity and Lionel Trilling's rejection of her. I have dealt with both experiences in previous chapters; of the two, the latter seems to have been more painful. But in *Reinventing Womanhood,* Heilbrun makes the effort to turn both negative experiences into positive ones, to show how both contributed to the evolution of her feminism.

Trilling's death in 1975 "released" Heilbrun, she declares, "to frank disagreement with his disciples, [her] colleagues," and to the "dialogue" that "did not require his presence." In *Reinventing Womanhood,* she produces, for the first time, an extended discussion of, response to, and denunciation of Lionel Trilling. True, she had called him to account in her *Saturday Review* piece and she had implicitly challenged him in *Toward a Recognition of Androgyny,* but this book provides the occasion for a fuller, and much more eloquent, commentary. Most striking is the personal tone she takes and the personal revelations she is willing to make. I have indicated in earlier chapters some of the details of these disclosures—her sense of exclusion and utter invisibility. With *Reinventing Womanhood,* it was time for Heilbrun to unmask the pain and the anger ("I can still feel . . . the desire I then felt . . . to let him know that the anger of women, wholly displaced from power, was also a cultural fact"[26]), time for the invisible woman to become visible. It was one thing for Lionel Trilling in the 1950s to ignore a graduate student; but quite another for Trilling in the late 1960s and 1970s to ignore a colleague. In that regard, it is instructive to note that, in *The Beginning of the Journey,* Diana Trilling seizes the occasion to rap the knuckles of several young males who had criticized Lionel Trilling—but she never mentions Heilbrun's criticisms of him. No matter that Heilbrun's actions took considerable courage; no matter that she was, to my knowledge, the first woman to challenge Trilling in this way; it is as if, once again, she did not exist.[27]

Heilbrun does not, however, simply wish to record a personal experience; her goals are more complicated. She wants to acknowledge Trilling's "greatness as a teacher and critic" and yet oppose the ideas he taught; she wants to spell out his concepts of the self in relation to society, and then use them against him. To teach other women how to apply Trilling's ideas in the formation of their own strong selves would be to exact a delicious revenge: "The woman who goes to [Trilling], as intelligent readers do, for insights into life and culture must avoid any specific comments of his on women as women, and listen to the advice he gives, or records others as giving, to 'young men.' She must look especially to his descriptions of the quests and dreams and desires of young men in search of a self. It is in these accounts that a woman will learn most of what she needs to know about the search for sincerity. Its history is her history, though Trilling never considered the matter in that light." In short, Heilbrun wanted to reinvent Trilling, to put him to the service of women, he who "never took the opportunity to comment on . . . the feminine revolution without disparaging it, seeing in it profound dangers to the proud, masculine life." But the task of feminizing Lionel Trilling was not easy. She knew that Trilling, especially in *Sincerity and Authenticity,* had begun "to shift his sympathies away from the self and toward the culture"; that "when Trilling sets the community against the self, and backs the former, he is backing the male world of power that women ought to understand and accept as adversary."[28] She requires demanding intellectual acrobatics from her women readers: that women learn from the Trillingesque self when that is appropriate and, even when he transfers his approval to the culture and away from the self, to stick with the self and resist the culture. Heilbrun is not unaware of the dangers of recommending male patterns of action to women, and she seems to be alert to the fact that some will claim that what she has achieved is merely "translation" rather than significant "transformation"; but the Heilbrun of 1979 can see no other way forward for women. Whether or not her advice will work for other women, it is nonetheless the case that working through her own relationship with Lionel Trilling contributed to the making of her feminism. If Adrienne Rich was radicalized by motherhood, Carolyn Heilbrun was radicalized by her experience at Columbia. She learned to resist with greater daring, to renounce assimilation, to claim a public voice with fuller range, with anger in its repertoire. She learned to take her place in the public debate.

Explicit as a unifying theme throughout *Reinventing Womanhood,* then, is the record of a woman's education. Out of the materials of her life—her experience of displacement, of being an outsider as woman and Jew, her education at Wellesley and Columbia, her professional commitment—Heilbrun accounts for "the formation of this kind of feminist,"[29] and in so doing shares the process with other women. Responding to the criticism of *Toward a Recognition of Androgyny* that she had proposed a self that had its life primarily in the mind and in imaginative literature, she wanted to delineate a self embedded in the particularities of a personal and social context. To those who argued that the androgynous ideal could not work for women in practice, she tried to show how it could be applied. She *is* the protagonist of her own story,[30] and her success is presented in such a way as to demystify the image of the lone woman whose accomplishments are mysterious as they are strange. In the preface, Heilbrun deplores, as she will do in *Death in a Tenured Position*, tokenism and the failure of sisterhood, claiming that "the failure of woman's movements, past and present, to retain the momentum of the years of highest accomplishment can be attributed to three causes: the failure of women to bond; the failure of women to imagine women as autonomous; and the failure of even achieving women to resist, sooner or later, the protection to be obtained by entering the male mainstream."[31] The body of Heilbrun's work, especially that produced after 1976 (her fiftieth-birthday year), represents her own battle against these odds.

What, finally, is *Reinventing Womanhood*'s contribution to the feminist debate? Clearly, Heilbrun intends not so much to advance theoretical speculation as to break free of disciplinary bounds in order to reach a much wider audience of women. Her approach is positive; she will not be content merely to record victimization and assign responsibility, but will set herself to construct new ways of seeing and doing. In effect, the book is a critique of the way things have been and still are in many aspects of women's lives: of women writers who have not been able to imagine female protagonists with the same powers they themselves have exhibited; of marriages based on romantic love that lock women into subordinate roles; and of the professional world that excludes women from full participation. But interwoven in that very critique is a plan for the way things might be. Heilbrun has built on the work of other feminists such as Nancy Chodorow and Dorothy Dinnerstein and contributes to the belief that child-rearing must be shared both to allow women to work side by side with men and to allow daughters to develop strong identities. She does not advocate that women should live separately from men, believing that a separate culture means powerless women, and she presses for reform rather than abolition of marriage. While she argues that women must revise the counsels of cultural figures such as Freud and Trilling and must claim the culture and achievement of the fathers rather than the mothers, she has learned from the woman-identified women to celebrate sisterhood as an essential component of her feminism.

Reviews of *Reinventing Womanhood* were mixed, with many academic feminists objecting that Heilbrun's plan for women to adopt or adapt male patterns of achievement would leave the present structures of our society, as well as present routes to, and definitions of, success fundamentally intact.[32] But her emphasis is not so much on the ways society can be changed as on the transformation of the self; she is, after all, the daughter of a self-made man. But she expects that self not to merge its colors, chameleon-like, with those of the dominant culture. This quest for the whole self is seductive indeed, especially for women who have felt constrained, limited, and cut off from their full powers of expression and possibility. Yet Toril Moi, in examining the work of Gilbert and Gubar (I do not want here to engage the justice of that assessment), offers a provocative critique of "wholeness":

> [According to Gilbert and Gubar], women's writing can only come into existence as a structured and objectified whole. Parallel to the wholeness of the text is the wholeness of the woman's self; the integrated humanist individual is the essence of all creativity. A fragmented conception of self or consciousness would seem . . . the same as a sick or dis-eased self. . . .
>
> But this emphasis on integrity and totality as an ideal for women's writing can be criticized precisely as a patriarchal—or more accurately—a phallic construct. . . . The Phallus is often conceived of as a whole, unitary and simple form, as opposed to the terrifying chaos of the female genitals. Now it can be argued that Gilbert and Gubar's belief in unitary wholes plays directly into the hands of such phallic aesthetic criteria.[33]

Heilbrun clearly subscribes to Moi's more dynamic conception of self, for the self she presents in *Reinventing Womanhood* is hardly "whole." This self is a yearning self, struggling toward feminist positions, a working self, aspiring to "the greatest accomplishment of which [she] was capable."[34] Little is said of domestic life and less of domestic satisfactions. Pain and lack characterize this self as much as optimism and self-confidence. Damaged, this self is forged in opposition to neglect and disregard. Heilbrun revisits the matter of her Jewish identity, reflecting or anticipating the moves of other secular Jewish feminists, but, unlike, say, Rich, in "Split at the Root," she would not seek to incorporate, however uneasily, that aspect of identity into her self; instead, she cast off her Judaism all the more forcefully.[35] One might say that what Carolyn Heilbrun offers in *Reinventing Womanhood* is a deconstructed self; that, in spite of her stated ideals, she critiques the wholeness she seems to desire. Certainly, in *Death in a Tenured Position,* the fictional counterpart to *Reinventing Womanhood,* she works out feminist issues, especially those she finds disruptive, through the mode of split and double selves and self-interrogation.

Death in a Tenured Position is a novel rooted in the sexual politics of the late 1970s, the ideological landscape described at the beginning of this chapter. Kate Fansler's increasing radicalism results in deepening anxiety as she attempts to negotiate between a powerful male-dominated academic institution and the challenges posed to that institution (and others) by a relatively powerless all-women's commune. Indeed, I would contend that the main character in this book is the academy.[36] *Death in a Tenured Position* is Heilbrun's most compelling fiction since *Poetic Justice;* both deal primarily and explicitly with Kate Fansler's relation to the academy in general and to an academic institution in particular. Clearly, this was a theme that fully engaged Carolyn Heilbrun, and it does not require much of a leap to suggest that she wanted to work out her own highly complex attitudes.

The novel opens with a familiar situation. A large, prestigious university, which in this case is named—Harvard—suffers from the usual dire (if desired) lack of women at the upper levels. An anonymous donor (this more fanciful, though, apparently, it has happened) offers to endow a chair in the English Department, provided the professorship is held by a woman. Shock waves reverberate through the predominantly male department and occasion the following language in a letter from a Harvard professor to a colleague at Columbia: "The dame we seek ought to be well established and, if possible, not given to hysterical scenes. We are firmly told that stalling will not be allowed, but in exchange for an agreed-upon deadline, I am allowed to have no women on the search committee. Howls will go up from the Radcliffe quarter—they have, of course, been promised a say in *everything* to do with women (if only women had stayed happily confined within those female ranks)—but I hold firm. This department *will* make one final all-male decision."[37] Harvard chooses what it takes to be a "safe" woman, Janet Mandelbaum, a scholar with a national reputation, who has no affinities at all with feminist scholarship. To her, matters of gender are irrelevant, and, conveniently, she has had a hysterectomy in her youth, presumably making her less prone to "hysterical scenes," not to mention happy confinements.

But, some time after her arrival at Harvard, Janet Mandelbaum is found drunk in a women's room, attended by a member of a local women's commune. Rumors of Janet Mandelbaum's disgrace circulate and eventually reach Kate Fansler, who agrees to come to Harvard to help in response to appeals by her friend Sylvia Farnum (a powerful member of the Washington bureaucracy, presently advisor to the Harvard Government Department), by Joan Theresa (a member of the women's collective), as well as indirectly by Janet Mandelbaum herself. She does try to make contact with Janet Mandelbaum, but the attempts fail, and the next we hear, Janet Mandelbaum is found dead, this time in the men's room, poisoned by cyanide, and Kate Fansler has a murder to solve. We might expect this novel, then, to turn into a conventional whodunit, albeit with female main characters, but, as Kate Fansler plucks out the heart of this mystery—and it is worth pointing out that she operates for the first time without any assistance from Reed—she also manages to anatomize sexism at Harvard, and, by extension, in the academy at large. "Beginning for the first time in a life devoted to language and ideas, to question the efficacy of both" (6), Kate Fansler moves out of the world of ideas and into the world of social action.

Indeed, to a large extent, the novel explores what it means for a woman to be placed—or rather displaced—in this alienating world of the academy. Kate Fansler tries out, as it were, a number of different environments and reports on her findings. At the beginning of the novel, we find Kate at a meeting of a "prestigious" (4) committee at her own university in New York City, a supposedly much more progressive institution than Harvard. Yet she is the only woman present among a large group of men. The situation for women and minorities is summed up in a bleak, witty aside: "The other woman member of the committee was black, female, and absent today. She had so many demands on her time and attention that occasionally her committee assignments overlapped" (4). Kate imagines her own "tombstone with 'The Token Woman' engraved in the marble" (4).

When Kate goes to Harvard, she notes that Warren House, home

of Harvard's English Department and locale of Mandelbaum's first disgrace and subsequent demise, "spoke loudly of long-held power and
patriarchal attitudes" (28–29). Fansler's office at the institute for female
scholars, where she has wangled an unpaid fellowship through the
string-pulling of her friend Sylvia, is pleasant and comfortable. Her
room at the Faculty Club is definitely inhospitable: "no room could be
that uncomfortable and inconvenient by accident. The degree of casual
malevolence pointed to a sinister mind at work. Kate was . . . prepared
to suppose that Harvard's general attitudes toward women were not
badly represented by this room" (27). She is relaxed with Moon, an ex-
lover (and, coincidentally, Mandelbaum's ex-husband), who is himself
made extremely uncomfortable by Harvard, and she is also at ease at a
small dinner party where the ratio of men to women is one to three—
and the only man, Andy Sladovski, seems unconscious of the fact that
he is outnumbered. On the other hand, Fansler feels out of place at the
all-women's coffee house called, tellingly enough, Maybe Next Time:

> Kate sipped her coffee and tried to decide why she did not feel com-
> fortable. Nothing could have been more reassuring than this humble
> restaurant, with the cooks in the back and notices all over the
> wall—rock concerts, discussion groups, apartments needed. No,
> the problem wasn't entering an unknown world, it was that, being
> here, one defined oneself too sharply: either one was an observer from
> the outside, automatically "other," or else one qualified to be a mem-
> ber of the club, which limited one in a different way. Was this how
> a Leftist felt in England in the thirties, attending the first Socialist
> meeting? Hard to stay away, impossible to join? (63–64)

This is a crucial passage, demonstrating that Kate is by no means ready
to identify herself fully with women. Note how she feels like an outsider
in a women's place; note that to be a member would limit her, though
she does not precisely say how; note the anxiety about self-definition;
and note the retreat to a reference to the 1930s—and another country—
to avoid confronting her unease.[38] Thus Kate Fansler gauges a range of
social situations and political atmospheres, expressing her discomfort
with both the all-male and the all-female settings. In this polarized landscape, Kate's anxiety about where she belongs and if she belongs is palpable. "I absolutely refuse to consider myself either" (25), says Kate
in a discussion with Sylvia about male- and female-identified women.

Apparently, she wants to distance herself from Janet Mandelbaum, who sees herself as an honorary male, and from Joan Theresa, who has, in defiance of the patriarchy, taken her mother's name and named her dog Jocasta, presumably in celebration of all silenced mothers. But Sylvia reminds her that she cannot slide away from her label: "You live with a man, you work with men, you support the patriarchal institutions" (25).

Janet Mandelbaum is, of course, unambiguously male-identified, and defends her position with all the old clichés: "I honestly do think that if women have the ability and are willing to pay the price they can make it. I did. You did" (37). But to win, in the terms of this world, is finally to lose (to return to the discussion from "Women on Women") and, under the tired rhetoric, Kate Fansler senses a very lonely and defeated woman, a woman profoundly out of place and out of her time. Indeed, after Mandelbaum's death, Fansler inspects her home and office and recognizes that Mandelbaum could not have felt at home in her apartment and only somewhat more so in her Harvard office. This recognition of what it means to be an outsider (Heilbrun is simultaneously working out this notion in *Reinventing Womanhood*), this woman's understanding of displacement, rather than any linear logic, propels Kate Fansler to the solution of Mandelbaum's death.

If "proper place" is significant, then to one like Janet Mandelbaum, the horror of being discovered dead drunk in a women's room with Luellen May, a woman from the commune, by her side could not be measured. Here she was—and the symbolism is crude—relegated to the bathroom, the clarity of her mind, that most precious possession, and the nature of her sexual preferences, both called into question. When Mandelbaum weeps out her disgust at being perceived a "dyke," Kate responds grimly,

> "Janet, is that bothering you still? You've been a professor for years, maybe not at Harvard, but in a university. What did you think men said about women like us, particularly unmarried women? When we were graduate students we had balls, and now we're lesbians. You can't still be bothered about that."
>
> "I am bothered. I can't even bring myself to say the words you say." (40)

While Kate Fansler is able to name names and face facts for Janet Mandelbaum, she is nowhere near as comfortable, as her response to the coffee house shows, in dealing with her own fears of being identified as a lesbian. Heilbrun defuses the anxiety with a witty episode: Kate, meeting Joan Theresa by chance in a Cambridge street, takes a "large bite" of the apple Joan Theresa offers her (48); but Kate cannot be tempted away from her institutional connections, her individuality, and her heterosexuality.

If Kate Fansler shows an increasing level of anger in this book, she is still hardly a radical. She is, in a term she appropriates from sociology, an "interstitial person" (69), a woman in the patriarchy but not of it, a feminist opposed to the system but not out of it—and some might say she takes the best of both worlds, wanting the rewards of the patriarchal system but not wanting to ally herself with its values. She is married, and in this way her heterosexuality is comfortably assured, but her husband is conveniently absent throughout the book; since he is touring Africa, he could hardly be much farther away. In fact, Fansler renews her friendship with Moon Mandelbaum, a man she knew from graduate school days, who subsequently married Janet Mandelbaum. This relationship raises questions. It is, after all, difficult to imagine Kate Fansler, who refuses to use the first names of mere acquaintances, who loves elegance and witty conversation, having a sexual relationship with Moon, a guitar-toting man in his fifties (he fought in World War II) who offers her the following, apparently irresistible invitation: "'All I have,' he said, 'is a lousy room almost at Central Square. Also a kitchen and bath. I've got a mattress on the floor, my guitar, a bottle of Tequila from a student who graduated last semester, male, he may learn to write, and a lemon. You busy?'" (45) Moreover, having "give[n] way" (45), as she obliquely puts it, Kate seems to suffer her only discernible monogamous guilt in an ambiguous parenthetical aside "(Kate groaned to herself)" (88). Since her marriage to Reed, this is the first time (in print) that she has been seduced. Yet, surprisingly, the affair seems to be preceded by, or to result in, little reflection, even though it is an important act, an important choice.

Why then is it in the book? Presumably, Kate's independence and freedom must be affirmed; she is married, but not possessed, and this remarkably enlightened marriage can accommodate unconventional behavior. As Heilbrun has pointed out in her articles on marriage written about this time, marriage should not be based on lust or romance or sexual attraction, but on friendship.[39] And she makes a point of stating that explicitly about Fansler's marriage at the beginning of the novel: "she had married a man who offered companionship rather than dizzy rapture; they had neither of them chosen to view marriage as an unending alternation between lust and dinner in the best restaurants" (5). But more important, in this climate of male- and female-identified women, Kate's heterosexuality must be made absolutely clear. Nonetheless, her choice of Moon is significant. He is not a manly man, a male-identified man. He does not want power or worldly success. He is happy to live and work far away from the bastions of academic prestige and influence. And his name is Moon—or, rather, he has become Moon (since his given name was, tellingly, Milton)—and Moon is a name that foregrounds the feminine aspects of his presumably androgynous personality. Finally, unlike Reed, unlike Kate, he is Jewish. In *Reinventing Womanhood* (1979), Heilbrun finally reclaims (if only to deny again) her Jewish self. In *Death in a Tenured Position* (1981), Kate, too, embraces a Jew, Moon, her opposing self, but leaves him in the morning.

Kate's friend, Sylvia, also insists on her heterosexuality. She, too, is married, but again on her own terms; her husband drops in for occasional conjugal visits, fleeing at dawn. Nevertheless, in spite of their attachment to men in marriage, both Kate and Sylvia acknowledge that, in these times and in these places, their primary support must be given to and sought from women. Yet both also feel cut off from community; indeed, some of the most striking imagery in the book reveals Kate in rooms of one sort or another, looking out through glass, cut off from the world beyond. To Sylvia, she confides, "The fact is . . . women, at least around here, live in a never-never land, not certain where they belong, where their allegiances lie, not even what their hopes are" (61). Thus again, this time through Kate Fansler, Heilbrun expresses her sense of the profound isolation of that "country in between."

Kate is isolated in part precisely because she is an "interstitial" woman: she resists alliances and bravely insists on articulating her differences from any extreme political position. To Joan Theresa, she says, "You've just finished telling me, and you told me even more clearly in New York, that you'll use men and women who work with men any way you can to get what you want. Why should I let you use me?" (70). To Janet Mandelbaum, she mingles support and insult, "I am now here. Sylvia is now here. We will try to comfort you, we can be consulted, we promise not to argue feminism, if you'll at least try not to sound like

Phyllis Schlafly on one of her more histrionic days" (41). And to Clarkville, member of the Harvard English Department, who expresses his relief that Janet Mandelbaum was not a "real feminist, always being offended if one held the door for her," Kate responds, "I don't think any woman feels offended at that. . . . It's always the stupidest men, quite frankly, who make jokes about that, hold the door for you and then say coyly that they hope they're not being male chauvinist pigs in doing it. Such a bore. Do you find me particularly difficult to talk to? If you do, say so, and I'll spare you my theories" (128–29). In her deliberate opposition to extreme positions, Kate tries once more to mediate. Paradoxically, the effect is not of safe, inoffensive negotiation of conflict, but of profound loneliness, a feeling of being on the edge because she is allied only with her own principles and not with any group. If she is loathe to abandon power and privilege, they bring her scant comfort.

Kate Fansler's vantage point serves her well in solving the mystery of Janet Mandelbaum's death.[40] Some of the evidence is literary. Kate discovers from books found in her apartment and her office that Janet Mandelbaum was reading George Herbert, in particular the poems "Love" and "Hope," and a biography of Eleanor Marx. Kate also remembers that a student told her that he had consulted Mandelbaum about the connection between Herbert and Simone Weil, who had a mystical experience in connection with the poem "Love." And Kate rereads a biography of Marx and recalls that Marx had translated *Madame Bovary*. From this complex interlayering of texts and writers, Kate reconstructs the long story of "despair" that led to Mandelbaum's death. She concludes that Herbert's "Love" can be read as an "invitation to death" (145), and we might add that the poem, depicting Love offering welcome to the reluctant sinner, shows Mandelbaum's yearning to find a place where she can be fully accepted, finally at peace. Regrettably, that apparent acceptance comes not in this world, and certainly not at Harvard. Brooding on the suicides of Eleanor Marx and Madame Bovary, Kate notes that the latter suffered "despair at having no place to live her life, and no life to live" (146); similarly, Simone Weil "died in part from not having a proper place in which to suffer" (145). But further, Weil, as Kate points out, while identifying with a whole range of human deprivation, refuses to identify with "the only kinds of suffering she had experienced personally: as a woman and as a Jew" (145). What Kate does not say is that Weil actively renounced her Judaism, that while she was resistant in some ways (even wanting to be a resistance fighter in World War II), she was anxious to assimilate in others.[41] As Heilbrun here touches on these figures who provide the key to Mandelbaum's death, we may assume that these monitory figures have their place in Heilbrun's development, too: that salvation cannot come from male poets, however seductive; that being the daughter (Eleanor Marx) of an achieving father does not necessarily show one how to live; that women cannot live by and through the old rites of romance (*Madame Bovary*); and that although assimilation can be a tool for survival, it must be resisted ultimately.[42]

Interpretation of all the available evidence of text and place leads Kate to realize how Mandelbaum has died. Yes, the male establishment has killed her, but Mandelbaum must also take her share of the responsibility.[43] And here we see the extent to which Heilbrun has taken liberties with the formal conventions; for, in most detective stories, when we discover the murderer, we breathe a sigh of relief and close the book with a sense of completion. Not here. Kate and Sylvia ponder their own complicity in the crime, agreeing that they have failed Janet Mandelbaum by not providing her with support. It has been a failure of sisterhood.[44] And the feminists on campus have been as dangerous to Mandelbaum as her hostile male colleagues. After Mandelbaum's death, Kate and Sylvia have one of the most important exchanges in the book: "'Kate, my dear,' Sylvia said, with less than her usual flippancy, 'if you want to know, friendship or the lack of it is going to be what it will all turn on in the end. Whether or not women change their lot will depend on their future friendships'" (102–3). The fact is, however, that, in spite of good intentions, Kate and Sylvia are unable to befriend Mandelbaum, and one of the strengths of the book is that it never underestimates the difficulties of friendship, particularly with one like Janet Mandelbaum, who retreats from intimacy and who cannot share Kate's values.

Themes of friendship and community shape the book, which depicts many women of different ages and varying political views. These characters are not caricatured, even though some are scarcely developed, and the novel as a whole presents a kind of full-scale debate about women's roles engaged in by these women—and by some men, too. What Heilbrun and her distinguished colleagues could not manage in reality in "Women on Women," Heilbrun replays and achieves with her fictional characters here. And it is a genuine debate, a form (characteristic for Heilbrun) of women, selves, talking with one another, and all the women (if not all the men) are granted the seriousness of their positions. Certainly, the woman-identified women from the commune are not dismissed but are appreciated as women whose views are justified by public and private histories; their devotion to one another is cause for celebration, and Kate by no means comes off best in their exchanges. Even Janet Mandelbaum, who has wrongheadedly tried to deny her womanhood, is seen, finally, in her self-hatred and despair, as an object of pathos rather than condemnation, a woman who grew up in a different world with different rules and who has been unable to adjust. Moreover, the point is repeatedly made that, even if politics is a game of large power blocs, particular women and what they do matter. Women can talk across their ideological barriers; indeed, Kate can help Luellen May in her custody suit and be a friend to the radical Joan Theresa; and Sylvia and Kate can come to the aid of Janet. If some object that the notion of friendship and community explored here smacks too much of an E. M. Forster's liberalism, with expressions of "goodwill, goodwill, and more goodwill" that are unlikely to lead to political change, we should remember that Heilbrun has always regarded individual change and individual action as the more significant.

After all, Kate herself has demonstrated significant change. She, too, was bound by the same rules that formed Janet Mandelbaum; indeed, there are many close ties of identification between them. Both are professionals, both are beautiful and successful by established standards, both were (and Kate still is) involved with Moon Mandelbaum, both have unsympathetic brothers and no (biological) sisters. Kate is like Janet, too, in the degree to which, like a true academic, she often seeks to judge, dispose, categorize, declare. I underline this identification between Janet Mandelbaum and Kate Fansler because the death of Janet Mandelbaum can be seen as the exorcism of the kind of scholar that Kate Fansler's (and perhaps Carolyn Heilbrun's) training prepared her to become. That self, like Carthage, had to be destroyed. It is not clear, however, that Kate realizes the degree to which she and Janet are similar or that she recognizes that this identification assists her in solving the mystery of Janet's death.

Yet Kate Fansler is also unlike Janet Mandelbaum; she is more sensitive to the moral pressures of change, and she has earned a new perspective. Torn between the claims of radicals and liberals, between academic judgment and human compassion, between homosexuality and heterosexuality, attracted by structure and convention but welcoming revolution, Kate tries to be a kind of go-between, understanding those identifying with the system, those within it who work against it, and those outside it. In a sense, she aspires to the same equipoise she sought in *Poetic Justice,* where she anatomized the self in relation to the academic institution. But the world of *Death in a Tenured Position* is far different and is one where the luxury of reconciling polarities and mediating between oppositions is near impossible. If the institution in *Poetic Justice* was able, finally, to admit University College, it is still not ready to commit the revolutionary act of fully including women. Kate's dogged faith in institutions has been shaken, though it is worth noting that she has to leave her own beloved New York institution in order for that to happen. But there is no hint that Kate will abandon the academy and continue the fight from outside; she prefers to be an outsider on the inside. Perhaps then, Kate Fansler still has no place by the end of this novel, but, as the form of the novel demonstrates, she has the beginnings of a community, of a dynamic debate among women, and she has testified to the ability to change of one who was like Janet Mandelbaum.

This is, then, a novel about sexism, male sexism on the part of men, male sexism on the part of women in the person of Janet Mandelbaum, and female sexism on the part of those feminists who wanted Janet to be one of them; and it is a novel about the ways in which sexism kills. Heilbrun paints a scathing portrait of Harvard, an institution that should assume moral leadership in our society but instead lags far behind in an altogether unpromising field. Headnotes to some of the chapters, extracts from a report on the status of women in the university, underscore the dismal reality that in many ways women's lot has not changed very much from the days of Woolf's *A Room of One's Own.* *Death in a Tenured Position* is a bleak book about death, despair, and deracination. Janet and Kate are both successful women, members of the privileged classes and well established in their professions. Yet they are outsiders, unable to belong. For them, there is no such thing as a tenured position, and at the end Kate is still a token woman, going to yet another committee meeting.

Ultimately, the novel seeks a proper mode for women's actions and expression. As part of her obligations to the institute, Kate Fansler must give a lecture, and she chooses as her topic, one that she dedicates to

Janet Mandelbaum, "the new forms possible to women in making fictions of female destiny" (148), an indication that Heilbrun had already begun working on the book that would become *Writing a Woman's Life*. We are not privileged to hear that talk, but Heilbrun's own novel is testimony to the way even such a fixed form as the detective novel can be changed.[45] Indeed, in the friction between old forms and new revisions, we discover that the old forms are just that, forms, which we have ourselves made.

In her work of this time, then, Heilbrun reveals herself to be, quite explicitly, a feminist. *Reinventing Womanhood* unfolds the process of her own evolution, her directions for the evolution of other feminists, and *Death in a Tenured Position* lambastes an academy whose members disparage women. Like Kate Fansler, however, Carolyn Heilbrun cannot be described as a radical. She writes against the grain of the most influential feminists of this period. Indeed, Heilbrun's work does not often appear in the selected bibliographies of "key" works in feminist criticism and theory. Her goals in *Reinventing Womanhood* are the transformation of marriage, motherhood, and the professions, and she is thus still staunchly loyal to those middle-class ideals. While distancing herself from the ideals of Betty Friedan as set forth in *The Second Stage* and moving closer to the position of Adrienne Rich, she still resides mainly in the isolated middle ground. As for differences among women, she is more responsive to the claims of lesbians but shows relatively little awareness of distinctions in class and race. The absence of the black woman in the first chapter of *Death in a Tenured Position* proves prophetic. Heilbrun was clearly paying little attention to the work of black feminists and scholars. Nonetheless, while individual achievement is still important to her, Heilbrun has moved toward an ideal of sisterhood, though this vague and perhaps even sentimental notion is exposed as fraught with tension and anxiety in *Death in a Tenured Position*. If Heilbrun's anger at the recalcitrance of systems and institutions is sharper and clearer at this stage, leaping out to castigate the women of Wellesley for valuing only the conventional housewife and the men of Columbia for valuing only the achievements of men, she also has the courage to explore her self-doubt and pain. As she describes it in the "Hers" column of the *New York Times* in February 1981, she has achieved both professional and domestic satisfactions, but they are, somehow, not enough. There is a gap, a lack: "My lack is rather of something central, interfused, vital, something I feel is not there, has never been there." Heilbrun describes the pain even successful women suffer for claiming a life and work of their own: "The reward for remaining conventionally womanly is to be allowed to avoid pain; the price is to avoid life." [46] The confidence of *Reinventing Womanhood,* with its opening salvo of exhilaration ("Fifty is a flowering"), is belied by the raw pain bared in this article, the sense of hollowness at the center.

Heilbrun marks this "lack of central firmness and clarity of vantage" as general to women who move out into the world. This seems accurate enough. But, as we read the personal history set forth in the opening chapters of *Reinventing Womanhood,* and as we think about Heilbrun's career, we might conclude that Heilbrun's pain comes, in part, from a more personal source. She was, as we know, deracinated, cut off from her own history. Her father and mother wished to reinvent themselves and so did she. Indeed, as I have suggested, she tried on several identities, made reinvention a theme of her life and work. As the only daughter of immigrants (her father was first-, her mother second-generation American), she was disposed to succeed; and she wanted success to take the form of professional achievement. As one whose identity was deliberately emptied, she might well seek to identify herself with an institution that would encourage and value the achievements she set such store by. But what if that did not happen? What if the hard-won achievements were scarcely noticed? What if the achiever were all but invisible?

When Carolyn Heilbrun announced her resignation from Columbia University in June 1992, she gave the reasons for her decision: the department failed to award tenure to a woman in Heilbrun's field whom Heilbrun had supported and it failed to admit several of Heilbrun's graduate students to the doctoral program. But more than this, Heilbrun charged that her colleagues ignored her, failed to acknowledge her. She was an invisible woman suffering a kind of death in a tenured position. In light of our later understanding of Heilbrun's experiences at Columbia, it is not surprising that two of her most absorbing novels, *Poetic Justice* and *Death in a Tenured Position,* cast the institution as a central character and develop Kate Fansler's struggles with the institution as a central theme. To be sure, the institution has proved a mighty opponent. Moreover, the theme of *Death in a Tenured Position* may be perceived as even more poignant in retrospect. In the novel, Kate draws a distinction between her New York institution and Harvard in the former's favor: Heilbrun also implies that while self-destruction may be the consequence of the antifeminist position taken by Janet Mandelbaum, hope is possible for women like Kate Fansler and Sylvia Farnum (who have changed themselves) to make gradual changes in the institution. Given subsequent events, Heilbrun might well have been writing obliquely of Columbia while directly condemning Harvard. And did she believe then that the treatment meted out to a Janet Mandelbaum might easily be dealt to a Kate Fansler (and thus to a Carolyn Heilbrun) as well?

Nevertheless, in 1981, while discouraged, Heilbrun was still trying to stay in the fight: "As Updike wrote, 'It's not easy to be another Colette.' There are times when I find it hard even to be myself, with my accomplishments in place like so many service stripes, and the chance now, in late middle age, to let loose my strength. Rather there is the temptation to feel strength an illusion, to retire from the field and nurse one's wounds. But Colette, with her clarity of vantage, tells us a different story; she assures that, if it is not easy to be another Colette, it is at least not impossible."[47]

6

Stepping Out of the Circle

Winifred Ashby disappeared and hasn't been heard of
since. By anyone.

— CAROLYN HEILBRUN, *No Word from Winifred*

One day it seems we really have transformed "our" institutions; the next day it's quite clear that we've been
had, swallowed whole.

— GAIL B. GRIFFIN, *Calling: Essays on Teaching
in the Mother Tongue*

It would just be so interesting for all those white folks
who are giving blacks their take on blackness to let
them know what's going on with whiteness.

— BELL HOOKS, *Yearning: Race, Gender,
and Cultural Politics*

In the dead of night, three women vanished without a
trace from a neat suburban home. . . . Two years later,
they're still missing.

— ALBANY TIMES UNION, 20 November 1994

We expected this second wave of feminism to be a wave that would
carry us forward on a grand voyage of discovery and progress,
not a wave that inevitably receded, pulling back, pulling us back with
the tide. This, in spite of the lessons of history that show support for
women's rights ebbing and flowing, and in spite of postmodern theories
that teach us to distrust grand narratives. This time we could not fail,
we told ourselves. Our analysis was persuasive, our cause just, our energy boundless.

What did it mean, then, to come upon a cover story in the influential

New York Times Magazine for 1982 entitled, "Voices from the Post-Feminist Generation"? Postfeminist? Had the age of feminism come and gone? Had the goals been achieved? Susan Bolotin, the thirty-something author of the article, had interviewed a number of women between the ages of eighteen and twenty-five from her Pennsylvania hometown and from her own university, Cornell, and discovered that most of them kept their distance from feminism and certainly did not want to be known as feminists. While some supported the ERA and all were in favor of equal pay, many of these women were, according to Bolotin, "unwilling to act, to speak up, to fight against the inequalities that affect not only them but the rest of the world's women."[1] A number of articles appearing in the mainstream press during the 1980s followed the same pattern, and, of course, this was the situation Betty Friedan had taken note of in *The Second Stage,* when she had recommended that women return to "family values" in order to attract the young women who felt so alienated from feminists of an earlier generation.

Four years later, in another *New York Times Magazine* cover story, this one entitled "The American Wife," Anne Taylor Fleming, also in her thirties, conducted an informal study of American wives. "How quickly," she notes, "it all seems to have changed . . . or changed back. Big weddings are back; Rambo and his like are the male cultural icons while the tenderized men of the 70's are now scorned as wimps." Fleming acknowledges that some marriage patterns have been influenced by the feminist movement toward a more equitable partnership but, she concludes that "Right now . . . there is no discernible women's movement left" and that women themselves seem uncertain whether they want to aim for the old or the new model of marriage.[2]

What had happened to the feminist movement in the 1980s? Were these writers picking up a real current of the times, or were they just cashing in on what they thought were trendy topics? Which was more newsworthy: the changes that had taken place or the institutions and attitudes that had failed to change? In fact, the decade could boast an impressive number of victories: in 1981, Sandra Day O'Connor became the first woman appointed to the Supreme Court; in 1983, Sally Ride became the first American woman in space, aboard the shuttle *Challenger;* in 1984, Geraldine Ferraro was chosen by Walter Mondale as his vice-presidential running mate—the first woman to be so named; in 1985, Amy Eilberg became Conservative Judaism's first woman rabbi, and Reverend Maria-Alma Copeland was ordained as the first female African-American pastor of the American Lutheran Church; also in 1985, Wilma Mankiller became Chief of the Cherokee Nation of Oklahoma, the first woman to preside over a major Native American tribe; and in 1987, Barbara Mikulski of Maryland became the first woman Democrat elected to a Senate seat that was not previously held by a spouse. This was not simply a case of exemplary women rising to positions of leadership in a man's world. Women were also making inroads into many blue- and white-collar jobs traditionally held by men; women were now police officers, firefighters, and construction workers—as well as surgeons, architects, and engineers. Women had also become much more actively involved in politics; and while the number of women in the House and Senate remained small (24 in 1983 as opposed to 11 in 1971), the number of female legislators at the state level nearly trebled, rising from 362 in 1971 to 992 in 1983.[3]

At the end of the decade, Vivian Gornick wrote an article, demanding "Who Says We Haven't Made a Revolution?" Reminiscing on the exhilaration of being a feminist in the 1970's, Gornick recalls thinking that "any minute now the whole country would be converted to the rightness of our cause." But "the 70's passed into the 80's and the revolution began to seem a bit farther off than I'd imagined. . . . I began to see it was going to take longer than any of us had expected. Much longer." Nevertheless, Gornick contends, "Contemporary feminism is a piece of consciousness that can't be gone back on."[4] She points out that the success of the women's movement can be measured by what now is taken for granted, and by what now can be said. Feminism, she argues, is part of the cultural scene; the analysis has made a difference in our ideas, our language, the ways we structure our relationships and our lives.

Yet Gornick is also right about the slow rate of change. Who would have believed, in the heady days of 1970, that, in 1982, the Equal Rights Amendment (ERA) would fail to be ratified? Who would have imagined that the U.S. Census Bureau would report that in 1984 the average woman still only earned 64% of the median male income? What had happened to the belief that women deserved equal pay, equal opportunities, equal rights?

The fact remained that while the women's movement had changed many lives, its progress was much more complicated than anyone had anticipated. The two most divisive issues of the decade for women were the ERA and the struggle for abortion rights. One full decade after the passage of *Roe* v. *Wade,* abortion rights were still squarely on the political agenda. In 1985 alone, no fewer than 224 assaults on women's clinics were reported, and in 1986, Randall Terry founded Operation Rescue, an organization committed to halting access to abortion.[5] In 1986 and 1989, tens of thousands of women converged on Washington D.C. to demonstrate in favor of abortion rights, and the issue loomed large in political battles throughout the decade, most notably in the defeat of Robert Bork's nomination to the Supreme Court and the election of Doug Wilder as the governor of Virginia. The Republicans controlled the Senate from 1980 to 1986, but that changed when ten Democrats, the majority of whom were pro-choice, were elected to the Senate for the first time in 1986.[6]

The battle mounted against the ERA was just as devastating. According to Susan Faludi, "the people who defeated the ERA were not ordinary women but a handful of very powerful men in three key state legislatures";[7] in *Where the Girls Are,* Susan Douglas also makes the point that the opponents of ERA were primarily men, but she argues that the media seized upon one highly visible woman, Phyllis Schlafly, whose "Stop ERA" campaign successfully capitalized on the fears of women worried about alimony payments and the possibility of being drafted into the military, even though these protections were not guaranteed without ERA. Douglas cleverly exposes the maneuvers of the media in casting the ERA struggle as a "cat fight," with Gloria Steinem challenging Phyllis Schlafly.[8]

The battle over ERA sharply dramatized the ways the issue of women's difference could be used to shape public policy. To defeat the ERA, Phyllis Schlafly had successfully taken advantage of what she defined as women's need for different (protective) treatment; indeed the debate about difference was continuing to polarize the feminist community, especially within the academy. When the Equal Employment Opportunity Commission brought a discrimination suit against Sears for failing to promote women to the better-paying sales positions, Sears countered that women generally preferred positions demanding less ambition and risk. But the significant aspect of this suit was that two feminist historians were brought in to offer expert testimony, with Rosalind Rosenberg testifying for Sears, and Alice Kessler-Harris testifying for the plaintiffs.[9] At stake here were whether women's natures and needs were essentially different and whether such differences justified different economic treatment.

In another corner of the academy, feminist lawyer Catherine Mac-Kinnon joined writer Andrea Dworkin in drawing up ordinances that would allow civil suits to be filed against purveyors of pornography. MacKinnon and Dworkin argued that pornography violated the civil rights of women; thus they advocated the kind of protective legislation championed by the opponents of the ERA. The efforts of MacKinnon and Dworkin found some support in the feminist community, most notably from Susan Brownmiller and Robin Morgan; but Betty Friedan, Adrienne Rich, and Kate Millett "opposed court-imposed limitations on free speech," fearing that any kind of censorship would work to the detriment of women.[10] Clearly, the media relished the "catfights" even more when the women involved were feminists; the 1980s provided plenty of examples of the genre.

The struggles among women, especially those within the feminist movement, suggested disarray. The movement needed focus and new supplies of energy for the long haul. But those who had started the fight could not rely on younger women to carry on because those women were declaring themselves alienated from what they imagined feminism's agenda to be; besides, as Carolyn Heilbrun herself had pointed out, women came to feminism later rather than sooner, usually after they had had some experience of life. The movement lacked the vision provided by strong leadership, but the idea that the feminist movement needed leaders, central figures to motivate and inspire, seemed a contradiction in terms, and indeed one could argue that the movement had "trashed" its leaders.[11] Yet, without leaders, the movement was apparently floundering.

What happened in the 1980s to those women whose books had revived the women's movement with such force and energy? What happened, for example, to Betty Friedan, Kate Millett, and Germaine Greer? All three had produced powerful critiques of culture and society; all three later wrote other books, but none of those works had the impact, the transformative power, of their first big books. Meanwhile, other once-prominent feminists such as Susan Brownmiller, Shulamith Firestone, and Ti-Grace Atkinson withdrew to the sidelines or dropped out of sight completely. Many women were, of course, working quietly on different fronts—setting up rape crisis centers and battered women's shelters, joining political campaigns, struggling to break through the glass ceiling—but the movement, as a political force, seemed to have lost its intensity. The media kept Gloria Steinem center-stage; she lectured, wrote, and organized, but she was unable to focus the movement in such a way as to mobilize and direct energy.

Nevertheless, feminism as an object of legitimate scholarly inquiry had lodged itself in the academy. A new generation entering the academy turned its attention to theoretical studies, and feminist scholarship recharged almost every field and discipline. The number of women's studies programs multiplied; more journals dealing specifically with women's issues were established; publishers, even the most prestigious ones, developed special series on women; more graduate students sought concentrations in women's studies or in feminist criticism; and untold numbers of articles and books on women and women's issues were published. But despite the increased presence of women and the growing influence of feminist scholarship, the academy was not as feminized as these data suggest.

Note, for example, that by 1986 at Harvard, only 54 (7%) of the 787 tenured faculty were women.[12] And in 1990, Derrick Bell of the Harvard Law School took a leave of absence until, as he said, Harvard tenured an African-American woman lawyer; two years later, he resigned, when the woman lawyer was still unhired and Harvard refused to extend his leave. Columbia itself, Heilbrun's institution, did not open its doors to women undergraduates until 1983—and it was the last of the Ivy League colleges to do so.[13] Beginning in 1982, Bernice Sandler and Roberta Hall wrote a series of now-famous articles on the campus as a "chilly climate" for women, drawing attention to the status of women in academic institutions, sexual harassment on campus, attitudes toward male and female students in the classroom, and the general inhospitality to the needs of women.[14] By the end of the decade, charges that academic feminists were members of the "thought police," coercing everyone to a "politically correct" line, would make the climate, in some cases, positively frigid.

Determined not to be intimidated, Carolyn Heilbrun forged another pattern from the one set by some of the feminist leaders already mentioned here. She did not begin her career with a strong, revolutionary book and then slowly become more moderate or allow herself to be diverted into other paths; instead, she became increasingly radical, especially in this decade, writing about the issues of the day in all the genres available to her: the critical book, the polished public speech, the stinging essay, the detective novel, and the short story.

It is fair to say that, at the beginning of the 1980s, Carolyn Heilbrun, though well known and highly regarded, was not yet a leading figure in academic feminism. By 1981, having published five works of criticism (including the edition of *Lady Ottoline's Album*), seven novels, and numerous essays and reviews, she was certainly an established figure in the field. But by the end of the 1980s, her status had been dramatically enhanced: in a great burst of activity, Heilbrun produced a spate of essays, three novels, and her pithy *Writing a Woman's Life*. Late in the decade, she achieved that rarest of distinctions for an academic when, in some parts of the country, both her critical book, *Writing a Woman's Life*, and her detective novel, *A Trap for Fools*, appeared on best-seller lists at the same time. By 1990, her critical reputation was sufficiently secure to merit publication of her selected essays as *Hamlet's Mother and Other Women*.

Three basic themes drove Heilbrun's work in this decade. Her long interest in women's lives and choices now focused on the constructions of those lives found in biography. In the 1980s, Heilbrun wrote numerous reviews of biographies and autobiographies and articles about the challenges of writing lives of women, these efforts culminating in the enormously successful and influential book *Writing a Woman's Life*. The second theme grew out of Heilbrun's fascination with the stages of women's lives. In 1986, Heilbrun turned sixty, for many women the age of dread. Typically enough, Heilbrun preferred to see aging from another perspective, one that would enable women rather than suggest that their productive lives were effectively over. Indeed, her ideas about aging would prove among her most influential. Finally, Heilbrun's increasing prominence in the profession, her rise to various positions of power, provided opportunities to battle for the inclusion of feminists and feminist culture in the academy.

The Modern Language Association offered a stage for some of these professional and institutional battles. By the middle of the decade, Heilbrun's reputation was certainly secure. She had been named by Columbia to the Avalon Chair of the Humanities in 1986, received honorary degrees from the prestigious University of Pennsylvania, Bucknell, Rivier, and Russell Sage, and appeared as the keynote speaker at a host of conferences and seminars. At that point, Heilbrun would certainly have been seen by most members of the profession as an established figure, a figure of influence, an acknowledged insider. By the time Carolyn Heilbrun became the ninety-fourth president of the MLA in 1984, the immigrant's daughter, by any measure, had "made it" at last.

In the ten years since Florence Howe's presidency, five more women had served as presidents of the Modern Language Association: Germaine Brée, Edith Kern, Jean Perkins, Helen Vendler, and Mary Ann Caws. The climate had changed dramatically since the late 1960s. Heilbrun herself had served a term on the MLA's executive council from 1976 to 1979, and she was impressed by the MLA as an organization that was capable of evolution. When I asked her what had drawn her to run for the presidential election, she responded matter-of-factly: Joel Conarroe, then executive director, called to say that her name had been put forward by the nominating committee, and he asked her to run. "One does not," she said, "refuse." Clearly, the presidency of the MLA was (and is) still one of the highest honors the profession can confer. Catharine Stimpson, who took office in 1990, remembers being "thrilled to bits" to be elected president.[15]

By the time Heilbrun agreed to run in 1981, the forces that had propelled Florence Howe to the forefront some ten years before had lost some of their momentum; in an article published for the centennial issue of *PMLA* in 1984, Paul Lauter laments that, even though more women attend and give papers at the annual conventions, this development does not mean "that women and minority professors are now, in significant numbers, at the top of the hierarchy, much less that the hierarchy has itself been altered. On the contrary, the profession remains as stratified as ever."[16] Running for the presidency thus offered an important challenge. Given the state of the profession of that time, Joel Conarroe does not find it surprising that Heilbrun agreed to run: "She is a professional, conscientious person who had served as a pioneer in many ways; I cannot pretend to read her mind (Carolyn is wonderfully inscrutable), but I suspect that being an out-feminist president probably appealed to her."[17] She had said, as part of her ballot statement, "Within the MLA, the young lack faith and the old fear change."[18] Presumably, what attracted her to this office was the honor of assuming the foremost position in the foremost professional organization in her field in the country, the opportunity for risk, for testing herself—and the chance to speak out publicly for change. In the fall of 1981, Heilbrun's name appeared on the ballot to elect the second vice-president. She ran against Gordon Ray, then president of the John Simon Guggenheim Foundation and former professor of English at New York University, and William Schaeffer, executive vice-chancellor of the University of California at Los Angeles and a former executive director of the MLA. Former executive directors were thought to have the edge in such elections, according to Joel Conarroe, but Heilbrun won and, in accordance with MLA procedures, became second vice-president in 1982, first vice-president in 1983, and president in 1984.

Still, the power of the president is carefully circumscribed. The president serves only a short term, and the office involves few official responsibilities beyond presiding over the meetings of the executive council, and, of course, delivering the presidential address. The opportunity for the president to shape an agenda is limited, and Heilbrun does not recall bringing specific items to the table. During her terms as second vice-president, first vice-president, and president, the executive council and delegate assembly considered many matters having to do with hiring procedures, recommended the continuation of the *PMLA*'s anonymous submissions policy, and endorsed a proposal from the Commission on the Status of Women in the Profession that the MLA create a minority clearinghouse to assist in minority recruitment and hiring.[19] Significantly, during the Reagan years, the MLA took an increasing role in national politics. In his executive director's report for the year of Heilbrun's presidency, English Showalter noted that, in 1984, the MLA had protested against censorship, had "authorized the preparation of an amicus curiae brief . . . in a case involving the Helms Statute, an Oklahoma law against homosexual teachers," and that the executive council had met with then director of the National Endowment for the Humanities, William Bennett, in order to voice concerns about the direction of national policy. That national policy, as English Showalter phrased it, was "a very clear, openly stated, hostile policy towards education": the Reagan administration wished to abolish the Department of Education and eliminate the National Endowment for the Humanities. These moves were defeated by a Democratic Congress, with ammunition supplied, in part, by the MLA. Showalter remembers Heilbrun as a strong and effective leader in that important campaign.[20]

Phyllis Franklin, now executive director of the MLA and, in 1984, director of English programs, admires Heilbrun's skill in running the council meetings. Both she and Joel Conarroe (who had resigned from his post as executive director in the year Heilbrun became president but who had previously worked with her on the council and in other committees) independently describe Heilbrun as warm, witty, fair, and forthright. "A good president," said Phyllis Franklin, "is rather like the conductor of an orchestra," and praised Heilbrun for working effectively with a wide range of people and moving the agenda along efficiently, while still making space for minority views. Both Franklin and Conarroe agree that Heilbrun has the first and most important qualification for an MLA president: a lively sense of humor.[21] Certainly, Heilbrun must have enjoyed the MLA joke she slipped into her 1986 novel, *No Word from Winifred*. Kate Fansler's sleuthing takes her to the MLA headquarters, where one of the staff members remarks to her, "You've been recommended several times to the executive council for positions on some commission or committee, but the impression seems to be that you would turn it down. In fact, I think you have."[22]

Heilbrun may not have remembered coming to the presidency with an agenda, but she knew she could have an impact with her presidential address, and she took full advantage of the occasion for public visibility. There were two decisive moments of the 1980s for Carolyn Heilbrun: in 1984, she delivered her address as the departing president of the Modern Language Association; and in 1986, she gave the University Lecture, a singular honor bestowed on one of its professors by Columbia University. These addresses, declared Heilbrun, "constitute, collectively and separately, the bravest acts of my professional life."[23]

Heilbrun seized the opportunity offered by the occasion of the presidential address to expose the politics of gender. Just at the moment in her life when she might have been coopted, content to bask in earned appreciation for her achievements, she determined that she would speak, "not just as the president of the MLA but as a woman president."[24] This is an act of aggression, the conjunction of the margin with the center.[25] Its potential for offense may be measured by the "noisy" exit from the hall of "one woman academic of some renown," and by the angry letter published in the *PMLA* "Forum," March 1986, a response summing up the import of Heilbrun's speech as a feminist "Final Solution."[26]

Addressing both women and men, Heilbrun interposes herself between feminists and "those prominent male critics who have ignored fifteen years of feminist criticism." Indeed, the burden of this talk is a double one: to challenge those who still think gender is "merely a property of linguistic discourse" and to celebrate the revolutionary work of feminism. Heilbrun speaks with many voices in this address, paying tribute by quoting nineteen women, including Sandra M. Gilbert and Susan Gubar, Adrienne Rich, Nancy K. Miller, Catharine Stimpson, Elaine Showalter, and Helen Vendler. Thus the very form of her address celebrates not the woman as "hero" but the chorus of voices that builds a movement: "For the very heart of feminism . . . has to do with solidarity and identification with other women."[27]

The emphasis on multiple voices, multiple selves brings us to a more complex theoretical notion underlying this speech. In *Reinventing Womanhood,* Carolyn Heilbrun had aspired to a transformed, whole self, a self in balance. Now, perhaps influenced by contemporary psychoanalytic and literary theory, she implies the more complex notion of selfhood dramatized in her fiction. Beginning her speech with an ironic dismissal of the unitary "one—that wonderfully neuter, transcendent, hegemonic one," she acknowledges that privileging "oneness" for women might lead to the same dead end. She then invokes Whitman's "I celebrate myself and sing myself / And what I assume, you shall assume" and Dickinson's ironic hymn to invisibility, "I'm nobody."[28] Implicitly, Heilbrun stakes out for women the territory between these opposed self-definitions, a space where a woman can be somebody or even somebodies, urging a more expansive concept of self for women, a play of selves who must take on a multiplicity of (sometimes) conflicting tasks and roles: president, mother, writer, teacher, scholar, sister, friend, and mentor.

The question of difference has also become more problematic. If, in the great debate about women's difference, Heilbrun has previously cautioned against too great an insistence on difference, knowing all too well that difference is the weapon that has been used against women in the past, her position here has modified.[29] She quotes Jonathan Culler who, in acknowledging for feminists the "urgent question" of whether to "minimize or to exalt sexual differentiation," advocates the "importance of working on two fronts at once." Heilbrun points out that for "earlier women presidents of the MLA . . . their professional personas required that they meld into a male 'whole' in which their womanhood would be unnoticed and inoffensive," but that now, using Myra Jehlen's words, "contradiction is the norm." [30] Note here the indictment of assimilation, the shift in Heilbrun's vocabulary; she implies that progress no longer depends on unity, synthesis, and balance, but on contradiction and deconstruction. The old humanist notion of the whole, autonomous self, which Heilbrun, too, had cherished, has fractured into postmodernist pieces.

In this speech, taking on the men and women of the profession who refuse to acknowledge the feminist "intrusion into the patriarchal world," Carolyn Heilbrun honors what has been accomplished and points to what remains to be achieved. Turning to the biblical text of Jacob's struggle with the angel, she transforms this story with male protagonists into a story for women, as she often did in *Reinventing Womanhood*. Woman's identity is always, for Heilbrun, what she, woman, makes it: protean, capable of adaptation and reinvention. So here, Heilbrun claims, "We women intrude on the narrative of male hegemony, as Jacob did, to be wounded and to demand a blessing." That the angel in question is also "the angel in the house" is implied in the seeking of recognition and "blessing" for feminist work from the profession as well as from "the female past . . . all female refusal to acknowledge the new state of women." [31]

Two years later, ready to deliver the University Lecture, Carolyn Heilbrun stood once again in a place rarely occupied by a woman. She has said of Lionel Trilling that his characteristic pronoun, "we," was intended only "to encompass the entire male intellectual community," excluding women.[32] Now, ironically, a woman takes his place, since she is the forty-third University Lecturer, as Trilling was the first. Nevertheless, she chooses not to continue his tradition but to challenge and expose its assumptions—and especially those about who should be included in the "intellectual community." Selection of those who would constitute the august intellectual community of the University Lecturers was made by the provost; to be chosen was a high honor. With the exception of the inaugural year (1971–72), in which Trilling was the only lecturer, three lecturers were appointed each year; in the fifteen years since Trilling's lecture, Heilbrun was only the third women to be so honored, following Diana Trilling in 1977–78 and Edith Porada in 1979–80.

Heilbrun's speech was, with one exception, more polemical, more daring, than the published version.[33] She marks her adversarial posture, what she calls "the effrontery of [her] presence" in the male sanctum of the academy by declaring "I am sharply aware, as I stand here, of the names above the entrance of Butler Library just opposite, and of the togaed figures behind and above me here, and I sense that they, together with the still vibrant and beloved memory of Trilling, gaze upon me now with horror, wonder, and amazement."[34] Three years later, Laura Hotchkiss Brown, a student from the School of General Studies, protesting the lack of a single female name among those inscribed in stone, would hang a white frieze, emblazoned with the names of women writers, from the high windows of Butler Library.[35]

I have already referred in chapter 4 to Trilling's University Lecture, the one previously given as the first Jefferson Lecture in the Humanities, and the one that caused such a stir in 1972. In that speech, entitled "Mind in the Modern World," Trilling contended that our "diminished confidence in mind" proceeds from a variety of causes: the "disaffection from history"; the devastations of 1968; the pronouncements of Louis Kampf who, as president of the Modern Language Association, could declare that "the teaching of literature . . . is now virtually at its end"; the attacks on authority, objectivity, and rationality; and, most particularly, the threats to "standards of excellence," posed by the intrusion of an affirmative action program into university affairs by the U.S. Department of Health, Education, and Welfare.[36] Heilbrun's reply, fourteen years later, was pointedly called "The Politics of Mind: Women, Tradition, and the University." Eleven years after Trilling's death, Heilbrun's anger has not abated. For her, at Columbia, his influence is still pervasive. Using against him his concept of "the opposing self," the self opposed against culture, and taking culture now to mean "the culture of the university," she opposes herself to all that he still represents in that culture.[37] Deconstructing a phrase often used by Trilling, "the life of the mind," Heilbrun argues that mind is not a transcendent category as he had implied, but is, instead, formed by gender, race, and culture. She explains, "The life of the mind is a synonym for what is referred to as the universal—treated, revered, accepted as though it had been engraved somewhere as eternal and unchanging truth. But we must ask, what is lost to this 'life of the mind,' to mind itself, to colleges and universities, to that proud contemplation of texts and culture to which Lionel Trilling devoted his life, when women are excluded from taking their full part."[38] Framing her remarks in the context of a response to the calls for a return to our "intellectual heritage" from William Bennett, then Secretary of Education, and A. Bartlett Giamatti, then President of Yale University, as well as in the context of the unwillingness to include even one text by a woman in Columbia's famous humanities course, Heilbrun sees her role once more as goad, urging that men not fear domination or usurpation by women and that women be welcomed to the university's life of the mind. Seeking dialogue, the play of selves once more, she declares, "Women do not ask for a new harmony with the major theme always in the soprano range, but for counterpoint." [39]

One sentence calls particular attention to itself: "Women within the university need not only to pass from the margin to the center of intellectual life, they need help from the University in confronting the problems of being female in our culture, and especially in the culture of the University at this time." That help will prepare them "to cope with the inevitable inequalities of work, marriage, child-rearing, and aging." [40] Echoing the spirit, if not the letter, of her early essay, "The Education of Female People" (1962), Heilbrun asks for nothing less than the transformation of the culture of the university to make it hospitable to the needs of women. It is not enough merely to include women in the university; the very structures must be changed.

To appreciate the defiance of Carolyn Heilbrun in these speeches, we should turn to her review essay, "Women's Biographies of Women," where she takes up Phyllis Rose's biography of Virginia Woolf: "Rose's biography is the first to see Woolf's sense of her own displacement as a woman from the center of established institutions as *essential to her achievement*" (emphasis added). [41] Does this mean that assimilated women cannot achieve? I suspect that the energy for these risky speeches came not only from Heilbrun's conviction that an insider, praised and prized by other insiders, could not effect changes in the university culture but also from a fear that cooptation would mean the end of significant achievement for her. Thus, in both these public speeches, Heilbrun uses the power of the center to turn the circle inside out. Both speeches speak of struggle: with the institution, with female critics, with male critics, with Trilling. Both are the speeches of an outsider, an opposing self—bold, confrontational, polemical. [42]

Viewed by anyone far outside the academic circle, of course, Carolyn Heilbrun appeared to have the position, the credentials, the power, and the reputation of a snug insider. Yet, just as surely, Heilbrun did not feel she belonged, even though she is not quite the outsider she felt her-self to be some forty years before at Wellesley College. In the University Lecture, she carefully deconstructs the exclusive "we" constructed by Lionel Trilling, a "we" in which there was no space for her; and in the presidential address, with her repeated use of the phrase "we women," she implicitly reconstructs a "we" of which she could be a part. The members of this group are inside the circle though not necessarily of it; they are academic feminists. For, as Heilbrun reminds us, the female "intrusion" in the academy has made a difference; after the long years of isolation in "the country in between," Heilbrun notes "We have today something like . . . a country. There are now enough of us to constitute a women's space into which one can cross."[43] Close readers will not miss the resonance for Heilbrun of that final verb.

If Heilbrun expresses some limited optimism here, the view of the academy expressed in two of her novels of this time is much bleaker. *Sweet Death, Kind Death* (1984) is set, in part, at Clare, a women's college, giving Heilbrun the opportunity to have Kate Fansler question the value of a women's college: "If women's colleges aren't concerned with women's advocacy, what are they doing, except protecting the male idea of womanhood?"[44] At the center of the novel is Patrice Umphelby, who challenges one of these orthodox ideas of womanhood until her mysterious death. Her research upsets the conventional notion that youth is generally the most intense and important period of one's life. Indeed, according to her, "Many women's lives particularly were lived by another pattern: beginning again just when it was all supposed to be over. A life wholly apart from youthful sexual attractions and domestic services."[45] *Sweet Death, Kind Death* offers Heilbrun's boldest and most elaborate account of her theory of aging: if one jettisons the romance plot that claims women's lives are over once physical attraction fades, and if one substitutes the accomplishment-quest plot, then aging can open up new possibilities for women. Patrice extols living in the present, not looking back to the past, and welcoming death even voluntarily, when productive and healthy life is no longer possible. Although she may seem to underestimate the pains of aging, her work is revolutionary enough within the context of this women's college to cost Patrice her life.

If Clare College offers dismal prospects for women, except for women scientists, the picture drawn of Kate Fansler's institution in *Trap For Fools* is bleaker still. *A Trap for Fools* continues the story begun in *Poetic Justice* of Kate Fansler's relationship with her own academic institution. The tone is dark, despondent; in this novel, everyone seems to be at odds—black and white in the United States and South Africa, Arabs and Israelis, men and women, middle and working class, with conflicts arising from race, religion, nationality, class, and gender. One character has an interest in the Crusades; another, an Irish security guard, cannot fail to call to mind the inveterate hostility between England and Ireland; and a British novelist discusses with Kate Fansler the fact that contemporary England is composed of two nations just as Disraeli's was. Since the novel's setting is Kate Fansler's university, we also learn about the discord among faculty, administration, and students. Even a good female friend, one whom Kate Fansler trusts absolutely, turns out to be an enemy. For the first time in nine novels, Kate Fansler's instincts about people prove wrong.

Within these fields of contention, Kate Fansler wages her own battles with race and class. In this novel, African Americans have more than a walk-on role; indeed, the news that an African-American colleague and a group of African-American activist students are the most likely suspects persuades Kate to investigate the murder of Canfield Adams, Professor of Islamic Studies. In this turn of plot, Heilbrun may well be responding to criticism that persons of color have been, to a large extent, left out of her criticism and fiction.[46] Nonetheless, Fansler's interactions seem forced; when it emerges that Fansler participated in civil rights marches in Mississippi during the mid-1960s—a fact that had not been revealed in previous books—one has the sense that Fansler's past has been reinvented to project a more radical temperament.[47] That radical past feels unearned, as does her grief for the death of Arabella, a black student activist whom she met only once. Yet a note of authenticity is struck when she claims, "black women . . . don't like me."[48]

If Kate Fansler is more enlightened with regard to race politics, she still has some distance to travel with regard to class politics. Careful to recognize that "nostalgia for old times and old values was little more than a yearning that poverty, despair, and desperation might keep themselves decently hidden from those lucky enough to have escaped them," Kate Fansler still does recall, with some pleasure and satisfaction, the hockey games in Central Park and the visits to friends at exclusive addresses.[49] She enjoys her elegant tea (complete with uniformed maid) at Mr. Witherspoon's. Able to strike up a relationship with the aristocratic

Mr. Witherspoon ("despite her often outspoken differences with the establishment, she was one of them by birth, and they sensed it"[50]), she also appreciates her conversations with the security guard, Mr. Butler, whose views differ from hers in every possible way. Kate Fansler has come a long way from the Kate of *In the Last Analysis,* in which she dismissed the police "who must all have staunch lower-middle-class backgrounds" and who therefore could not possibly understand her values and those of her friends.[51] Regarding Butler, she was "pleased, as academics often are, to have established a relation with a working man or woman." Nevertheless, Heilbrun adds a revealing sentence: "Kate didn't delude herself about the permanence of the relationship, or the depth, but she felt good, nonetheless, as when one is welcomed into their home by strangers in a foreign country."[52]

In investigating the murder, Kate Fansler remarks that professors of literature "deal in subtexts, in the hidden story," but what is the subtext of Heilbrun's mystery? I would suggest that this novel has to do not so much with the solution of a murder but, once again, with Kate Fansler's ongoing battles with the institution. Early in the novel, Kate Fansler reveals her feelings about the university: "Why should I help a university that I have been forced to honor less and less as the years go by? Not that that means I despise it. In the beginning I honored it this side idolatry." Throughout, we get a sense of Kate Fansler's growing exhaustion with "the long march through institutions," her confusion and despair that she no longer understands the institution ("I more and more have the sense of taking part in someone else's play," of being controlled like "puppets or marionettes"). As always, we hear of loneliness and marginalization. Kate Fansler is faced with a university divided by the hostilities of groups and individuals, a world given up to rancor and antagonism, all jagged edges and oppositions. The story that emerges from these pages suggests that the institution has changed little over time. Even brave women who can make a difference must still "play the game."[53] True, more women and African Americans have been hired, but the game is still what it was: the old structure self-perpetuates. Corruption seeps through the system, seducing with money and power even those who seem most immune, such as the female dean much liked and admired by Kate Fansler. Ultimately, even when the culprits are unmasked, the university administration does everything possible to avoid attracting negative publicity and offending donors. Punishment is light; one offender is even helped to another position. The wheels grind on.

Clearly, Kate Fansler's disillusion with the "long march through institutions" is echoed in Heilbrun's own speeches and essays of this time. But she has always focused not only on systems and institutions but also on individual selves, individual women. Fascinated by the patterns and shapes of women's lives, Heilbrun turned her attention more and more, in the 1980s, to biography, the literary construction of a life. For Heilbrun, this decade proved to be a rich period of reflection on biography through reviews, articles, and the process of working on *Writing a Woman's Life*. As earlier chapters have made apparent, Carolyn Heilbrun is not drawn to biographies of women who were interesting only for their *relation* to a person of influence or accomplishment; thus she did not focus on biographies of the wives, lovers, sisters, or daughters of famous men even when those biographies brought to the foreground the life of a woman hitherto unseen and unheard. Her interest is primarily in the lives of women of accomplishment, in how such women have managed their lives of accomplishment, and how the story might be told in such a way as to be exemplary. Like other pioneers in the field of biography, she knows that the story of a life is not simply the factual recounting of a chronology from birth to death but a "fictional" (her word) construction constrained by conscious and unconscious assumptions about the norms of a woman's life; that is to say, traditional biographies are (usually unwittingly) tied to traditional views of women's lives and women's roles. Heilbrun set out to offer a radically different construction of selected women's lives.

Writing a Woman's Life came about as a result of complex influences and motivations, and, though I do not want to oversimplify, I would propose that one influence was particularly powerful. In chapter 3, Heilbrun offers a remark that illuminates the genesis of this book. In the context of exploring the lives of several women poets of her own generation, she asserts that "when a woman sought a female model for self-realization and achievement, she had to find it in a woman who had died."[54] For Heilbrun herself, I would suggest that that woman was Dorothy Sayers. Heilbrun has been vitally affected by a number of women writers (both living and dead)—such as Virginia Woolf, who taught her about women's anger; May Sarton, who unfolded the possibilities of solitude; Vera Brittain and Winifred Holtby, who gave her a model for women's friendship—but none, I would contend, has touched her quite as profoundly as Dorothy L. Sayers.

Heilbrun's disappointment in not being chosen as Sayers's biographer by Anthony Fleming, Sayers's son, is recorded in a number of places, most recently in *Writing a Woman's Life.*[55] A biography of Sayers would have focused Heilbrun's abiding interest in the women of that period, in the first women to earn degrees at Oxford, and especially in a woman whose pattern of achievement she emulated. Prevented from writing this biography, she wrote and rewrote fragments of Sayers's life in *Sweet Death, Kind Death, The Question of Max, No Word from Winifred,* and in several critical pieces; and she obliquely wrote out her disappointment in *The Question of Max,* which, at one level, investigates the question of whether a man can write the biography of a woman.

Yet perhaps out of her disappointment, out of her attempts to conceptualize Sayers's unconventional life, and out of her response to the official biography of Sayers, written by James Brabazon, emerged Heilbrun's increasing absorption in the subject of biography in general and the challenges of reading and writing a woman's life in particular. In due course, she would take up the challenge of writing the life of Gloria Steinem, but, first, she would develop her theory. In *Writing a Woman's Life,* she would explore what happens when a critic with a feminist's conceptual tools defines the structuring story behind female biography: the problems facing a woman who chooses work as the central focus of her life; the stages of such a woman's development; the connection between her domestic and professional lives; the nature of her intimate relationships with both men and women; and the risks of choosing a very different life pattern from that followed by most women. In *Reinventing Womanhood,* Heilbrun suggested that women needed to expand their possibilities by claiming male patterns of action. Now, in *Writing a Woman's Life,* she argues not so much that women should have access to male plots but that women should (urgently) reread and rewrite the lives women have lived.

This shift of critical focus from male to female is a crucial one. In her own life, Carolyn Heilbrun had valued her successful father over her mother. Later, in her progress as a feminist, she replayed and revised the Oedipal plot. She was influenced first by her revered teacher Lionel

Trilling, against whom, as a woman, she had to struggle, reappropriating and revising his work for women's purposes in the course of inventing her own female voice; but she also embraced the example of Dorothy Sayers, who provoked an interest not only in the work (as Trilling had) but also in the life of the woman who had produced that work. The nature of that life, its splits and fragmentations, proved endlessly intriguing. For Sayers, in her secret personal life, produced a child out of wedlock, an act, argues Heilbrun, that freed her from convention and enabled her to embark on a life of accomplishment.[56] Sayers's life thus dramatized the positive consequences of a life lived against the grain, and Heilbrun's interest in that life, in such lives, produced *Writing a Woman's Life*.

In the book, Heilbrun recalls the autobiographies and biographies of famous women (such as George Sand, George Eliot, Willa Cather, Virginia Woolf, Adrienne Rich, and, of course, Dorothy Sayers), women whose lives have formerly been told only as accommodations to or deviations from the accepted female plot. She suggests, however, that these women's accomplishments did not compensate for their lack of sexual success or attractiveness, nor were thrust upon them as they passively lived conventional lives; instead, they were the result of powerful choices, whether or not the women consciously knew they were making those choices. Heilbrun coins the richly suggestive word "ambiguous" for women whose lives have marked another pattern, who "did not make a man the center of their lives."[57] Indeed, Carolyn Heilbrun's principal contribution to biographical theory is to see the unorthodox logic in lives that hitherto might have seemed incoherent and even dysfunctional, offering in the process exemplary texts for exemplary lives.

Since I have used the word *exemplary,* I need to ask, exemplary for whom? Who was the intended audience for this book? Heilbrun had always written in such a way as to cross disciplinary lines and to be accessible to a broad readership of women, but in this book, she must have succeeded beyond her hopes since it sold over 150,000 copies. If this is Heilbrun's most popular critical book, it is also her most theoretically sophisticated, although she always presents the theory in clear, accessible terms. She makes a conscious (and risky) decision not to use texts in her book but the lives of actual women; she tells the stories of lives but tells them in such a way that those lives are seen not as anomalous departures from accepted female destinies but as texts (or models) for other lives. She struggles, as she has throughout her life, to find the answer to constructing female selfhood, meditating on unitary and multiple identity, on capacity for achievement, on pushing the boundaries assigned by gender.

"Women come to writing, I believe, simultaneously with self-creation," declares Heilbrun. For Heilbrun, of course, the self should not simply happen; it must be created, imagined, improvised, reinvented. Moreover, she has come to the conclusion that "For women who wish to live a quest plot . . . some event must be invented to transform their lives, all unconsciously, apparently 'accidentally,' from a conventional to an eccentric story."[58] Thus George Sand took lovers and dressed as a man; George Eliot set up house with the married George Henry Lewes; Dorothy Sayers had a child outside of marriage; Vera Brittain married a man who took a position in the United States while she lived in London with Winifred Holtby; Adrienne Rich understood she was a lesbian. Even if they did enter conventional marriages, like Woolf and Sexton, these women did not behave like conventional wives. Probably because they crossed the line of convention, almost all these women are perceived to have androgynous qualities in their actions, dress, style, in the force of their work. Indeed, the work itself (as in the case of writers like Woolf and Rich) might be the means by which they defy convention. All these women allow themselves larger selves than convention dictates; what emerges strongly from the narratives Heilbrun presents is a story of multiple selves: think of George Sand, as mother, lover, cross-dresser, always leaving her lover's bed in time to put in her routine hours of work; think of Sayers with her hidden mother self; and think of all those women with secret selves that have other names: George Eliot, George Sand, Amanda Cross. Cynthia Ozick has spoken of the good citizen and the wild writer; her essays and her fiction, she says, come from two different selves who have "nothing to do with each other."[59] Finally, fifteen years later, in *Writing a Woman's Life,* Heilbrun has rewritten her androgyny book, but by keeping the word firmly out of sight and by focusing on the (re)writing of women's lives, she has succeeded in claiming the freedom for women's actions and development that she imagined in *Toward a Recognition of Androgyny.*

What must also be clear from this analysis is that the women whose lives Heilbrun has reconstructed are outsiders. But while Heilbrun was writing about women who had deliberately chosen to be outsiders so that they could lead lives devoted to work, she was also, in her fiction, choosing to write about quite another kind of outsider. Heilbrun's androgynous protagonist, Winifred Ashby, may well be her most unusual and most shocking character, and *No Word from Winifred*, taking place at the farthest remove from academic and literary life and providing no dead body at all, may well be the most unconventional of Heilbrun's detective novels thus far. *No Word from Winifred* gives us what is called a "new" story, a story of two contented women, Winifred and Biddy, who share a deep friendship with each other and who also share Martin, Biddy's husband (without his knowledge). Yet the novel has an apparently conventional ending: unable to bear what he sees as betrayal by the two important women in his life, and obsessed with Winifred to the point where he will kill either her or his wife, Martin banishes Winifred to India. She, in spite of her courage and independence, agrees to be silenced and sent to a place where independent women are scarcely welcomed.

Heilbrun's narrative may have been inspired by two similar triangular relationships: the fictive one in Alice Walker's *The Color Purple* and the real one among Vera Brittain, Vera Brittain's husband, and Winifred Holtby (whose name echoes Winifred Ashby's) recounted in Brittain's *Testament of Friendship*. The differences between Heilbrun's story and those mentioned here are instructive, however. Heilbrun has provided a model of female friendship with a man at its center, and when that man pulls away, the friendship is destroyed. But in both Walker's novel and Brittain's memoir, the women are the key figures in the triangle; in both, the women's friendship persists; and in Walker's book, the man's violence is tamed by the courage of the women.

Heilbrun's book thus poses serious questions for the feminist reader: Why does Heilbrun allow Winifred to remain a shadowy figure whose options are managed, finally, by a man? Does it not seem implausible that, in a book written in the mid-1980s, these two women would disappear out of one another's lives without a fight? Is Heilbrun reaffirming a heterosexual model that seems threatened by the friendship of these women?[60] Is this a "new" story or the old formula once again? Carolyn Heilbrun has told me that she includes *No Word From Winifred* among those novels she regards as her best; clearly, the book has a particular significance for her. Yet the novel seems to call into question some of the more dominant themes in Heilbrun's work.

For example, whereas Heilbrun has always extolled women of accomplishment, Winifred's goals seem much more modest. When we first hear of her, she has been hired by a dairy farmer and is working a few hours a day in return for a cabin, a small wage, and the opportunity to spend part of her time writing. She has retreated to the cabin because her lover has discovered her friendship with his wife. Her needs are few, and, like Thoreau, she is not interested in exceeding them. But what does she write? There are a few chapters of a journal, the signs of a woman setting down her life, but no evidence of anything else in progress. Winifred has "a gift for friendship and for solitude,"[61] we are told, but she gives up her relationship with Biddy, the most important friendship in the book, when it is threatened by the husband. The person who notes that Winifred is missing is not a friend but the biographer of Winifred's aunt, and as far as we know, no one except Biddy and Martin notice Winifred's retreat to the cabin. Her gift for solitude seems of greater consequence.

That Winifred's identity is mysterious is carefully established. She wanted to be a boy when young and, as an adult, wears pants and tailored shirts; and, of course, she takes a job as a "hired man." Indeed, one character is surprised that she is involved in a passionate heterosexual love affair—presumably, no one would have been surprised if she were a lesbian. This is, then, an androgynous woman whose identity is fluid, mysterious, and finally, contradictory. She cannot be pinned down.

What ultimately seems most interesting about Winifred is not who she is but the fact that she has disappeared. Unlike so many of Heilbrun's heroes, she is not achieving, aspiring, becoming; she is not forming a self, inventing a self. Instead, she is absent. There is no word from Winifred. She has slipped out of her familiar life into a new identity where no one knows her and where she can live a safe, solitary, routine existence, where she can work with animals and avoid the pressures and constraints of ordinary existence. The novel is not about female friendship but about disappearing out of a self.

Two short stories written during this period explore similar themes. In 1987, Carolyn Heilbrun wrote "Tania's No Where," which returns to the motif of the disappearing woman. At the age of sixty-two, Tania disappears from her ordinary life as a professor of Russian, a wife, and a mother of grown children. Called in by the head of Tania's department, Kate Fansler solves the mystery. Tania has stolen into the identity of a man who drives a horse-drawn carriage around Central Park. We note the similarities with Winifred Ashby's disappearance: Tania, too, decides to disappear without telling anyone; she, too, picks a not-particularly-demanding job with a set routine, dealing with animals not humans, and a job performed mostly by men. Indeed, in Tania's case, she decides to cross-dress for the part, donning the costume of an Edwardian cabbie.

Why do these women slip out of their lives without a word? Why does Kate's niece Leighton, the narrator of this story (who also, as it happens, has a larger-than-usual role to play in *No Word from Winifred*), say that "only Kate could have solved it"? Why does Kate say to Tania, after her true identity is revealed, "I understand more than you'll ever know about how you felt"?[62] Perhaps Kate, too, wants to escape her life without a word; and it is significant that Leighton is narrating this story, that Amanda Cross is silent, has, in effect, disappeared.

This story produces no murder, no violence, no foul play, no ill-gotten gains; a woman with a good job and congenial family life simply disappears without a word of explanation to family or friends. The motive given is that Tania seeks "adventure." Her husband has told Kate that they live a "regular" life: "every day was just like every other," varied only by the demands of Tania's teaching schedule. And so Tania plans her "escape" into a "dream," a move that Kate Fansler, to Tania's surprise, fully understands.[63] The routine of driving a Central Park carriage seems scarcely to provide adventure; surely there are more daring forms of rebellion. But Tania's choice enables her to stay in the same city, just a few blocks away from her former (and Heilbrun's present) home.

Perhaps this is simply a fantasy of escape from a mundane life, a move out of a public self with a network of relationships, a self whose outlines are predictable and safe, to a self that appears to be the opposite of the abandoned one. This self is private as opposed to public, solitary as opposed to socially and professionally connected; this self chooses work that exercises the body not the mind, work that is typically undertaken by men rather than women; this self has snipped itself out of the web of obligations and responsibilities and assumed a life without professional or personal pressures. It is perhaps the textual equivalent of that double-headed illustration on the paperback cover of *Toward a Recognition of Androgyny,* or the "psychic space" that Heilbrun found by inventing a secret pseudonym, Amanda Cross, who provided her with a whole new writing life. It is perhaps the equivalent of stepping out of the circle once one has reached its center.

When Tania returned and was welcomed back by colleagues and students, "she found out she was loved." The story's last sentence reads "Maybe that made her return more rewarding."[64] Would she not have left had she known she was loved and would therefore be missed? Perhaps leaving is the only way to know if one will be missed, if one will leave a space that others will notice. If one does not leave a space, then one can fill a space somewhere else, pouring identity in and out of selves as if it were a magic fluid.

Another short story of transposed identity is "Murder without a Text"(1991), in which a middle-aged professor, Beatrice, is accused of murdering one of her students.[65] She hated the student, and indeed, all the students in that particular women's studies class—who, in turn, hated her—but she has not committed the murder. In fact, we learn, the murder has been committed by a homeless woman. Her motive: anger against a student who wanted to invade her life and interview her for an academic project. Beatrice is mistaken by a young male student for the homeless woman and therefore implicated in the murder. Heilbrun has made the point before that middle-aged women are either invisible or indistinguishable from one another;[66] but the further implication in "Murder without a Text" is that the professor is also "homeless" and does not belong; she is without a place, "without a text." We are told that this professor suffered pain as an early feminist, and, unlike Tania Finship, she is not beloved, at least not by this particular group of students. She is, then, "homeless" despite her institutional affiliation.

Beatrice is thus related to Winifred, Tania, and the homeless woman, except that they have chosen to disappear and she is perceived as having already done so. Why do such women appear in Carolyn Heilbrun's writing at this point in her career? Is disappearance—the self as unmarked, insubstantial, evanescent—the logical next fantasy for a writer who has spoken so eloquently of not having a history, of always inventing and reinventing the self? Or is this the nightmare of the writer who has extolled the importance of autonomy and selfhood for women?

In tracing the curve of Carolyn Heilbrun's accomplishments in the 1980s, I confess to the same wish for a narrative of progress in this private story as I did in the more public narrative of the women's movement. But if the women's movement has shown disarray, a scattering of energies and impulses, Heilbrun's career produces a clearer line of development. She has become increasingly influential and increasingly radical. Heilbrun's story in the 1980s is, in short, a story of triumph, compelling in its outline though complex in its details.

Yet signs of another story, interwoven with this bold narrative of a feminist's evolution, also must be acknowledged. The résumé tells one story—that of the accumulation of achievements, a synthesis of themes—but reveals nothing of the disappointments, the failures, the fears. The conventional script declares that we become more moderate with age, more jealous of our reputations, less energetic about resisting injustice, less willing to take risks. Heilbrun concludes *Writing a Woman's Life* with a telling passage: "it occurs to me now that as we age many of us who are privileged—not only academics in tenured positions, of course, but more broadly those with some assured place and pattern in their lives, with some financial security—are in danger of choosing to stay right where we are, to undertake each day's routine, and to listen to our arteries hardening. I do not believe that death should be allowed to find us seated comfortably in our tenured positions."[67] With these words, Heilbrun deliberately writes herself into a place of risk, a place from which she is obliged to act.

She does not enumerate here the costs of the radical life, the endless battles to be fought, the energy required to keep resisting, the dearth of models for one who is, as Heilbrun often puts it, the oldest woman in the room. Some of these anxieties are reflected in the world conjured in the Kate Fansler mysteries: in that world, a feminist is murdered for her work, her revolutionary theories on aging; a powerful woman administrator is implicated in corruption; and a bold, independent woman is forced to give up her friendship with a woman and simply disappear. This world is hardly utopian, nor do the feminists always toe a feminist line. It is a world riven with discord and conflict, one in which hostility can take a deadly turn. But this fictional world sometimes reflects the real one with stunning force: was it only a bizarre fiction, or was it a terrifying fact when a young student at the University of Montreal Engineering School in 1989 walked into a class and shot fourteen women? His parting words: "You're women, you're going to be engineers. You're all a bunch of feminists. I hate feminists."[68]

"I hate feminists." That sentence resonated ominously in the 1980s as the backlash gathered force; yet in defiance of that backlash, Heilbrun stood her ground even as she became more powerful in the profession. Perhaps the notion of power provides a clue to Heilbrun's stance in her important public speeches and to her fascination in *Writing a Woman's Life* with outsiders. The outsider who has struggled to become an insider generally must toe the line and observe the rules in a way that born insiders do not need to do. And those not born insiders know full well what the rules are and exactly where the line to be toed is. But, although assimilation confers a certain kind of power, the assimilated one is, in fact, relatively powerless unless she becomes fully aligned with the agenda of the group. Perhaps only the outsider can have the kind of polemical edge that can lead to change.

Thus all the moves in this period of Heilbrun's work have been about stepping back, stepping outside, not belonging. Heilbrun has deliberately refused to become an insider in a group whose values she wants to transform. If the academic world had not changed to some degree, a woman such as she could not have become the president of the MLA, and she is no longer really an outsider with hungry eyes wide against the glass; moreover, she has constructed an oppositional "we," a group like Woolf's Society of Outsiders. Nevertheless, while she acknowledges it is hard, quoting E. M. Forster, "after accepting six cups of tea from your hostess, to throw the seventh in her face,"[69] she has determined not to sit at the table even though a place has now been laid for her.

The outsider's position provides not only political but what Heilbrun herself has called "psychic space." In *Writing a Woman's Life,* Heilbrun spoke of having little "space in a small city apartment"; presumably there was also little space in the expectations for a tenurable professor at Columbia. Thus she created Amanda Cross and Kate Fansler, identities that would give her "psychic space."[70] But once she was discovered to be Amanda Cross, that psychic space necessarily narrowed. Heilbrun stepped back from the circle because doing so preserved a larger space for action and expression.

In that context, it may not be surprising that the Heilbrun of this period keeps telling the story of the woman who disappears or fails to belong. Just when Heilbrun's own professional identity seems most publicly marked, just when she has created a writing self most willing "to take risks, to make noise, to be courageous,"[71] she imagines women who have the magic capacity to give up words, to disappear. Just when she is giving, as critic, her most successful account of womanhood, she describes, in her fiction, not exceptional women but women who have vanished into the clothes and lives of unexceptional men. In her professional life, Heilbrun has stepped back in order to resist, but, in fiction, she is drawn to the depiction of characters who step outside completely, characters who need not be public, who need not find the energy to resist, to refuse, or to oppose—but who are anonymous, invisible, silent.

In her review of *No Word from Winifred,* Susan L. Clark makes the perceptive point that, in the novel, "the covert story treats the difficulty of finding (missing) women in general, women who are left out of both the recorded history of literature and of the written history of 'doing.'" [72] To be sure, Heilbrun-Cross has written poignantly of the woman without a text. She knows the attractions of disappearing, but she has also written of its terrors: women killed, their revolutionary work lost but for Kate's detection. And while Heilbrun has celebrated the invisibility that aging brings to liberate women from their dependence on the romance plot, she has written of the pain of professional invisibility as well. As a metaphor for the contradictions of this stage of the women's movement, the disappearing woman surely has an eerie appropriateness. For example, when Marina Angel was casting about for a title for her 1988 article on the presence and absence of women in law schools, she picked "Women in Legal Education: What It's Like to Be Part of a Perpetual First Wave or the Case of the Disappearing Women." [73]

At about this time, too, mainstream feminism was fracturing under the assaults of those who questioned its universalist assumptions. In theoretical terms, the "subject" was disappearing. As Nancy K. Miller observes, feminists in the 1970s had "pose[d] a massive challenge to the regime of the universal [male] subject. . . . But the 1980s revealed that the universal female subject could be just as oppressive as her male counterpart and under accusations of first-world imperialism and essentialism her reign was quickly dismantled." [74] In other words, just as men had made women invisible, so mainstream feminists had failed to make visible the differences of class, sexual preference, race, and ethnicity among women. Above all, indeed, they had been blinded by a "vast encircling presumption of whiteness." [75] New and exciting work would come from this recognition of diversity, but also an edge of fear and loss, a sense that a tide might be turning that would engulf us all. In this moment, Heilbrun's quotation from Emily Dickinson in her MLA presidential address has added resonance: "I'm nobody."

In *Writing A Woman's Life,* Heilbrun declares that the invention of Kate Fansler permitted her "to write my own life on a level far below consciousness, making it possible for me to experience what I would not have had the courage to undertake in full awareness."[76] The quotation leads to a final question: Was Carolyn Heilbrun herself preparing to step out of her accustomed life? Was she planning, unconsciously or consciously, to leave Columbia University, where she had spent her working life since 1949?

7

A Rhetoric of Risk

I am sitting at a table in an empty room at the moment
between daylight and darkness, having come to the end
of the journey. I survey the books on my table, which
have become companions along the way, and I touch
the talismans there that have done the same.
  — LOUISE BERNIKOW, *Among Women*

When those who have power to name and to socially
construct reality choose not to see you or hear you . . .
there is a moment of psychic disequilibrium, as if you
looked into a mirror and saw nothing.
  — ADRIENNE RICH, "Invisibility in Academe"

I was looking forward, with never a glance behind
me. . . . Behind me a door had slammed shut. Doors
had been shutting behind me all my life.
  — DORIS LESSING, *Under My Skin*

What does it mean to a women to write? For the real
person Anais Nin and the fictional character Anna
Wulf, writing represented the only viable possibility
for freedom.
  — PATRICIA MEYER SPACKS,
  The Female Imagination

A Meeting

In chapter 1, I took us as far as the foyer of the Kenilworth, Carolyn
Heilbrun's New York City residence. When I wrote the first draft of
that chapter, I had not met her, though I had tried to arrange an inter-

view, and, at that point, I did not know if I ever would get any closer to her than the Kenilworth's imposing front entrance. But in January 1992, Carolyn Heilbrun agreed to meet me; indeed, our initial meeting lasted about three hours, and we had dinner together two days later. Subsequently, we have spoken frequently on the telephone and met from time to time both in New York City and in Troy, New York, where she had agreed to run a monthly class for Russell Sage College in spring 1994.

It is now possible to be taken up to the second floor of Heilbrun's New York City apartment building by an obliging doorman, to knock on the door, to be greeted by Heilbrun herself, and to step inside her apartment. Heilbrun is a little shorter than I have pictured her; she is wearing leggings, black ballet-style shoes with a strap across the instep, and a loose-fitting black tunic. Her crinkly hair, from which the color has faded to a brownish-gray, is pulled back into a serviceable bun. She wears lipstick but not much else in the way of makeup as far as I can tell—and she has a dazzling smile. Behind the spectacles, her eyes are bright, sharp, intelligent. The energy is palpable.

I am scarcely aware of the foyer of the apartment on this first occasion, but I register the low bookshelves on which a few porcelain objects are tastefully placed. By the door, a dark wooden table holds a small pile of letters to be posted. Order prevails, and Heilbrun tells me later that she hates disorder; everything must be tidy, in its place. I give Heilbrun a bottle of Beaune wine. I have thought long and hard about this gift. "Give her a bottle of wine," said Sandra Gilbert, who had come to talk at my college a few weeks earlier and to whom I had confided this upcoming meeting. "She loves white wine." In the end, I settle on the Beaune even though it is red, because that is what Kate Fansler demands of the publisher who takes her to an expensive lunch at the beginning of *The Players Come Again;* the publisher, Simon Pearlstine, wants something from Kate Fansler: he wants her to write a biography. I knew Heilbrun would recognize the joke behind my gesture.

We sit in the living room, a very large room extending from the foyer, with two big windows overlooking Central Park. I wish I knew the dimensions of the room—perhaps forty by twenty-five feet?—but I do not ask. The question seems, at the time and now, a tasteless one, yet it is relevant to her status as an academic woman with more material privilege than most and to our sense of her as a person who has spoken of needing "psychic space." You should, then, imagine her living room as a grand, luxurious space, a generous expanse of the parquet floor covered by an oriental rug. One wall is lined floor to ceiling with books. Velvet-upholstered furniture is comfortably disposed for conversation: a burgundy sofa and two dark blue armchairs. In the middle of the room, a bright peach chaise longue reposes. A coffee table is set in front of the sofa, bearing a small stack of porcelain coasters. There is no clutter, either of furniture or objects; no plants to water, no flowers; no hired decorator's flourishes. The focal points of the room are two original paintings, both self-portraits: the Vanessa Bell hangs over the fireplace; the Duncan Grant is situated above a grand piano. Heilbrun points out the distinctive ways the male and female artist present and reveal themselves, the male arrogant, looking down his nose, the female unassuming. I note the confidence with which she insists upon difference and watch for the other ways Heilbrun will reveal herself, shuffling a sheaf of questions in my hand and worrying about whether the tape recorder will actually work. Throughout our talk, the noise of an invisible clock intrudes, ticking away Heilbrun's precious time with a sound as loud and as inexorable as a metronome.

Memory

Some time later, I pay another visit and, seated in Heilbrun's living room, look around in surprise. The room is smaller, for one thing, the ceiling seems lower, and what I remembered as a chaise longue has shrunk to an ordinary armchair with a hassock. The colors are different, too; the carpet is bluer, and the once burgundy sofa has a lighter, rosier hue. More unexpected: a wall of cupboards and bookcases has sprung up, quite out of thin air, between the windows. "Was that there before?" I ask. "Oh yes," she says. "Nothing has changed, except we've now given away the piano, and brought the TV in," nodding toward a television just inside the archway leading to the foyer. "And I have acquired two small pieces of jade left to me by May Sarton." I examine the carved jade objects, try to fix them in thought: a pair of kittens, intertwined, and a solitary frog. These I won't forget, I say to myself, as I reflect on the deceptions of mind and memory.

A Rhetoric of Risk

Departure

On this second visit to Heilbrun's apartment, I pause in the foyer before a lithograph I had not noticed before. Had that, too, been there on my first visit? Heilbrun told me the work was entitled *Departure*. Did I only register it because of Heilbrun's 1992 resignation from Columbia, because of all the instances of disappearance and departure I had been finding in her later novels and short stories? The lithograph depicts three versions of a woman with a suitcase in the act of departing; all are walking away from the viewer; one of them, the middle one, has her face turning in profile. Are these three separate women? One woman split in three? One woman changing as she changes motion? Heilbrun says ("of course") they are the same person, a woman leaving her marriage; in any case, as I see it, the lithograph depicts three distinct figures, different selves—departing, turning back, moving on.

Looking Backward and Forward

Is Heilbrun a person who can leave things behind? In a variety of places, Heilbrun suggests that her attitude to the past is a simple one: she does not look back. *Reinventing Womanhood* recounts the fact that she did not dwell on her parents' past or on her own; they were self-made people who had snipped away their history, always forging ahead, eyes on the future not the past. To dwell in the past is to dwell in nostalgia and anxiety. "We do not reminisce," said Tom Driver of his conversations with Carolyn Heilbrun. Sympathetic characters in several of Heilbrun's novels voice similar sentiments: Kate in *Poetic Justice* and Patrice in *Sweet Death, Kind Death* disdain nostalgia; in *An Imperfect Spy*, Kate is reminded that "Some English writer had commented that nostalgia was a 'disabling pressure which signifies retreat' and Kate concurred with that wisdom."[1] Love of the past is associated with conservatism, with an attachment to things-as-they-are, with an unwillingness to change. The villains of Heilbrun's life and fiction are those who refuse the challenge to reconsider the assumptions of the past.

Heilbrun's attitude to the past is also reflected in the form and method of her writing. She does not "outline an entire mystery" before she begins writing; she simply sets to work.[2] Tom Driver remarked that once, in conversation, she had divided writers into clean-paper writers and dirty-paper writers. The dirty-paper writer writes slowly with lots of revisions and adjustments, always laboriously going back and back again over what has been written. Heilbrun is a clean-paper writer. She does revise, of course, but not excessively, and she writes each draft quickly. Even when she is writing, then, she prefers not to look back. In the Amanda Cross detective stories, Kate and Reed, of course, appear in all the novels; a few assorted family members reappear in some; but no other character from one novel reappears in another, even when Kate has formed a friendship. Although Kate herself develops and changes, it is as if each novel is a fresh start, a discrete slice of history. In an earlier chapter, I mentioned that Heilbrun was stunned when she learned that she had used an unflattering reference to a homosexual in *The James Joyce Murder.* The point is not only that Carolyn Heilbrun would never make such a reference now, and would not have done so in the recent past, but also that she does not remember the person who would. The portraits on her living-room wall measure the stages of a journey, too; the Heilbrun of today would presumably not have purchased the Duncan Grant; its presence is the reminder of an earlier self. At a public celebration marking her resignation from Columbia organized by Jane Marcus and Nancy K. Miller in October 1992, Heilbrun began her remarks with these memorable words: "Once a day, or a year, or an academic life is over, it's over—and the hell with it!"

Nevertheless, an attitude to the past cannot be quite so simple. In the final paragraphs of *The Players Come Again,* the character Nellie has this to say about the past: "the three of us didn't want to remember back to when we were children in order to understand our childhood. We want to think forward together; is there a word for the opposite of remembering?" The past is not explored for its own sake ("not to belabor the past," "to replay old injuries") but "reconsider[ed] for the future," as Kate Fansler remarks in the same novel.[3] In an essay on May Sarton's poetry, delivered at a conference in honor of Sarton in 1992 (Heilbrun also delivered an address), Sandra M. Gilbert spoke of the woman writer's relation to her literary past. In Sarton's poem "Letter from Chicago," she deals with the death of Virginia Woolf, with her complex relationship to Woolf, writing, "I send you love forward into the past." Gilbert points out that in the first volume of their three-volume *No Man's Land,* she and Susan Gubar had seized upon Sarton's phrase to "help explain what we called a 'female affiliation complex,'" the complicated relationship of the twentieth-century woman writer with her "female literary history" and her own "literary future."[4] Such a notion, according to Gilbert, explains the woman writer's conflicted relationship to a past in which she wants to find her roots so that she can assure her own literary future, but a past to which she does not wish to return.

In Heilbrun's case, one might say she returns to the past only in order to convert its use for the future. She does this both in terms of her personal past—as when she describes in *Reinventing Womanhood* the ways in which her Judaism contributed to the making of her feminism— and with respect to the cultural past. One could argue, for example, that her critical books constitute attempts to review, revise, and retell the past. Thus, in *Toward a Recognition of Androgyny,* she shows that androgyny has a long and deep history, a history that can now be revived for cultural purposes; in *Reinventing Womanhood,* she proposes that the past, in the form of myths, of Greek drama, of the writings of Lionel Trilling, must be revised so that it can be made usable for the future of women; and in *Writing a Woman's Life,* she resees and rewrites the scripts of women's lives in order to rescue them as exemplary patterns. There is a fundamental optimism in all this, a determination to put the best face on things, not to be limited or trapped by the past.

The Players Come Again, published in 1990, can be seen as just such an act of revisiting the past in order to move on into the future; but this time, Heilbrun is revisiting both the cultural past and her own writing past. This, Heilbrun's tenth mystery, marks in a dramatic and palpable way the degree to which Heilbrun has changed, departed from an earlier self. The very title, its words taken from Virginia Woolf's *The Waves,* gives a clue to the novel's project: the book revisits, revises, and reinvents material covered in Heilbrun's second mystery, *The James Joyce Murder,* published twenty years earlier; moreover, the explicit reference to Virginia Woolf suggests that Heilbrun wants to remind us that there were (at least) two great giants of modernism and that Joyce did not have the field to himself. Indeed, in the controversial "Virginia Woolf and James Joyce" written two years before and published for the first time in *Hamlet's Mother and Other Essays,* Heilbrun had argued that despite all its technical innovations, its "new and ultimate language," *Ulysses* "looks back to an old cosmology and an old faith," whereas

"Woolf's characters, on the contrary, are aware of all the texts that preceded them. . . . Aware of the entire western culture behind them . . . also aware that it is not for them."[5] Heilbrun does not deny that *Ulysses* is a "masterpiece, in some sense *the* masterpiece," and for that very reason fills women with "terror" because Joyce is incapable of hearing "the voice of a woman passionately intellectual"; the battle between Joyce and Woolf, as Heilbrun constructs it, is to decide "whether the destiny of women is to serve man as inspiration and comfort, or if it is to create themselves and new, joyful female lives."[6]

Joyce, like Milton, is the writer women must "write against";[7] but Heilbrun did not always "write against" James Joyce. *The James Joyce Murder,* built on the framework of Joyce's *Dubliners,* was an homage to James Joyce. The *Players Come Again* returns to the world of Joyce but with very different intentions. It is a going-back in order to go forward. In the writing of this book, Heilbrun has been influenced by Brenda Maddox's *Nora,* by the revisions of modernism performed by Gilbert and Gubar in the multivolume *No Man's Land,* by the discussions of archeological findings in Crete by Sylvia Horwitz in *The Find of a Lifetime* and by Sir Arthur Evans in *The Palace of Minos,* by Joseph Campbell's *The Masks of God,* by the novels of John Le Carré, by Ellen Glasgow's *Barren Ground,* and, of course, by Virginia Woolf's novels, especially *The Waves* and *Mrs. Dalloway.*[8]

The plot turns on the approach to Kate by a publisher who wants her to write the biography of a woman very like Nora Joyce, a woman who was married to Emmanuel Foxx, one of the central figures of high modernism. The woman, Gabrielle Foxx, was said to be the model for the character at the center of Foxx's major novel, *Ariadne.* As Nora did for Joyce, according to Brenda Maddox, Gabrielle supplied her husband with the language, experience, and actions on which he could base his female protagonist.[9] Maddox has Bennett Cerf recalling a memorable line of Nora's: "'Sometime *I'm* going to write a book . . . and I'm going to call it *My Twenty Years with a Genius—So-Called.*"[10] Heilbrun makes that book happen.

In Heilbrun's review of the Maddox book, she deplores Nora's fate in her own inimitable terms: "But to read of her life married to the biggest egoist, not to say shit, who ever put pen to paper . . . is to wish that feminism had reached Ireland sooner, if indeed it has reached it at all."[11] Moreover, we know that Heilbrun is not usually impressed by biographies of women important only for their relation to a genius and not for any notable accomplishment of their own. Thus it comes as no surprise that in Heilbrun's reworking of this material, when she has the opportunity to take things into her own hands, Gabrielle turns out to be a writer herself—with a manuscript of a novel that, when it is published, will offer the perspective of the real "Ariadne" and "counter" the male view presented by her husband, Emmanuel Foxx.[12]

The key to all this is the lost story of Ariadne. If Joyce had to tell the story of father and son, then Woolf had to write the script of mother and daughter—and Heilbrun argues that Ariadne is forgotten in the myth that Joyce constructs in *Ulysses*. "Woolf's task was to remember Ariadne." Heilbrun acknowledges that "Woolf did not ask the question [about Ariadne] either, not in so many words, perhaps not even consciously," but that is her legacy to later women writers, Heilbrun seems to imply, and that is the charge Heilbrun will take up in *The Players Come Again*.[13] In effect, Heilbrun will provide Nora with the work she might have written and will offer the story of Ariadne that Woolf only "unconsciously" sought.

With the sense of fun born of fictional power and possibility, Heilbrun rewrites the struggle for the culture, the struggle for modernism. This new document will "question the whole masculine bias of high modernism," "bring gender to the foreground of what had previously been a rather reactionary and male literary period," and thus provide the missing piece of the puzzle that will change the map of modernism.[14]

At one point in *The Players Come Again*, Kate Fansler declares that the English novel is "all about second chances,"[15] and this novel, too, makes much of second chances, as Heilbrun writes her "counter" novel to *The James Joyce Murder;* as she has Gabrielle, in effect, write the female *Ulysses;* and as Heilbrun herself retells the story of Ariadne, recapturing it as a story not of love and abandonment but of will and resistance. Indeed, Heilbrun even rewrites one of Woolf's characters from *Mrs. Dalloway;* Dorinda, Heilbrun's version of the Sally Seton character, sees the folly of her accommodations to a bourgeois conventionality and begins her life again, seizing a second chance.

Another "second chance" offered in *The Players Come Again* is the opportunity to resee the relationship of mothers and daughters. In Heilbrun's earlier work, she had argued that women were entitled to a life beyond the cradle and the sink, punishing those mothers whose energies were confined to the maternal. In the late 1980s and in the 1990s, Heilbrun returns to the idea of motherhood, but this time she revisits in order to focus on the relationship between mother and daughter. She sets the tone in a short essay she wrote in 1988, "*To the Lighthouse:* The New Story of Mother and Daughter," in which she argues that "Joyce seized on the father-son drama, allowing it to diminish other themes, particularly those concerning women. *To the Lighthouse . . .* can now marvelously be read as the untold struggle and love of mother and daughter, that other story of the family romance which did not interest Freud or Joyce, for which they had no room, for which women, before Woolf, had no language." Heilbrun now reads *To the Lighthouse* as the story of Lily Briscoe, the daughter, the artist, who must struggle through to her own identity and vision, taking what she needs from Mr. Ramsey and avoiding the "engulfment" of the mother. But she must choose "to quest without ceasing to love," learning "to reject that part of the mother which the patriarchy has claimed and to identify with . . . what reaches out to other women, supports them in their quests." Heilbrun also revisits the story of Electra and Clytemnestra. Heilbrun is now arguing that women can mend their relationships with mothers and has turned away from her earlier disturbing analysis of the murder of Clytemnestra which, for Heilbrun, represented the killing of the institution of motherhood. Now, writing her 1994 review of Strauss's *Elektra,* she seems to have forgotten that earlier reading. In this review, she sees Elektra becoming "willingly, eagerly . . . a tool of patriarchy." The story is no longer read as a triumphant destruction of the institutionalized maternal principle, but, as feminists have typically read it, as a triumph for patriarchal power. Elektra destroys not an institution but her mother, and is allied with her father and her brother. Her mental collapse, the focus of Heilbrun's essay, is seen as that of "the woman who thinks the male world will thank her for her compliance, and too late goes mad facing the truth."[16]

The Players Come Again tells the story of reconciliation between mothers and daughters, especially when those daughters have reached middle age. *An Imperfect Spy* tells a similar story of estrangement and reconciliation. In this novel, Heilbrun returns to mythology—this time the relationship between Demeter and Persephone. In *Reinventing Womanhood,* Heilbrun had argued that this myth was "not about 'motherhood' but about the sturdy loyalty and application of power that the older woman can use on behalf of a younger one."[17] It was, in other words, a story about mentorship, a public or professional bonding of women, not a private one. In *An Imperfect Spy*, the myth is revived, this time so that a mother can use power on behalf of a daughter. In this context of celebration of the bond between mother and daughter, it is worth noting that Heilbrun's dedication in her biography of Gloria Steinem is to her mother and to her new granddaughter.

A Mother

I ask Carolyn Heilbrun if she had felt "nurtured" by her mother; I know the question is banal but I ask it anyway, noting several occasions in *Reinventing Womanhood*, where she seems to speak of neglect. "Oh yes," she says quickly. "But she was not overprotective. And that is what allowed me to become what I am." She then tells me the story of taking her bicycle to a garage to have the wheels pumped up when she was twelve years old. Riding the bicycle, she accidentally fell into the car pit, and her mother leaped forward to the rescue. Heilbrun was unhurt.

We laugh together as we note that this odd and extreme example is the one Heilbrun chooses to let me know her mother cared.

The Present

A definite shift can be perceived in Heilbrun's work of this period. She is writing from the place of risk she had written herself into at the end of *Writing a Woman's Life;* she would "take risks," "make noise," "become unpopular."[18] Her focus now is directly on women, especially on women's traditions and relationships; that emphasis characterized *Writing a Woman's Life* as well, but the goal there was to show women ways of achieving, not to assert that women are essentially different from men. We detect a new kind of polarization in Heilbrun's work of the 1990s; she seems to have landed firmly on the side of the essentialism she resisted in *Reinventing Womanhood*. In her criticism, Joyce and Woolf are utterly opposed; a review of *Richard III* speaks of "raw masculine ambition and the suppression of feminine wisdom and gentleness";[19] in her fiction of this time, sons kill their fathers (*The Players*

Come Again) and men batter women (*An Imperfect Spy*); on her walls, the self-portraits of Bell and Grant prove the contrasts between male and female artists. Mothers and daughters, on the other hand, although certainly not perfect, are capable of renewal and reconciliation. It should not surprise us, perhaps, that Heilbrun's commitment to change has driven her in this direction, nor that her affirmation of difference comes at a time when some feminists are reconsidering essentialist positions, finding their way back to a middle ground.[20]

In another ironic conjunction of timings, Heilbrun is ready to celebrate the mothers as mothers just as the "real-life" daughters, in their own plot, are staging a rebellion. Some of the daughters, such as Katie Roiphe in *The Morning After: Sex, Fear, and Feminism on Campus,* are charging that women of her famous mother's (Anne Roiphe's) generation have wrongheadedly emphasized speech codes, sexual harassment, and victimization—in short, that they have taken the fun out of being a sexual woman. Her peer, Naomi Wolf, in *Fire with Fire: The New Female Power and How It Will Change the Twenty-First Century,* sounding a little at times like the early Heilbrun, urges that women aspire to the wholeness of their natures and claim their power. She, too, calls to a stern accounting the academic feminists who have dwelled on oppression and who are targets for cultural critic Camille Paglia with her menacing flamboyance and her undiluted scorn for feminists of the academic variety.

But it is not only the disaffected daughters and the occasional way-out slasher who are acting up in the 1990s. In 1993, Karen Lehrman exposed what she saw as the sloppy thinking in women's studies programs in an article in *Mother Jones;* her conclusions seem tenuous because she had surveyed only four colleges, but Elizabeth Fox Genovese, a well-respected scholar, has also been reporting her disaffection from women's studies programs.[21] Daphne Patai and Noretta Koertge have weighed in with their *Professing Feminism* (1994), telling horror stories of the politicization of women's studies programs; as professors teaching in women's studies programs themselves, their criticisms carry more weight than Lehrman's but, again, the generalizations from their research depend on interviews with only thirty women out of the hundreds who teach in women's studies programs—and none of those interviewed agreed to be named.[22]

In 1994, Christina Hoff Sommers published her attack on what she called "gender feminists," and her book, sensationally entitled *Who Stole Feminism?*, was joyfully seized by the media. Sommers's point is that life is now much better for women but that gender feminists are determined to believe they are constantly "under siege" and will do whatever is necessary to spread this propaganda.[23] Sommers opened her book with a vignette of Heilbrun's retirement-from-Columbia celebration-conference, scoffing at what she perceived as the prevailing talk of anger and oppression from so privileged a group. Earlier in the decade, Heilbrun had a more serious adversary in the eminent critic, Helen Vendler, who in 1990, reviewed eight works of literary criticism in the mainstream *New York Review of Books*. With the essays in *Hamlet's Mother* she is not impressed, accusing Heilbrun of teaching not literature but "moral propaganda"; for Vendler, Heilbrun's conclusions in the essay on Woolf and Joyce are, quite simply, "lamentable."[24] Ironically, the Heilbrun who wrote *Toward a Recognition of Androgyny* was attacked in the 1970s by feminists as not being radical enough; in the 1990s she is attacked for being too much of a feminist. The Heilbrun who had railed against victimhood in *Reinventing Womanhood* is in 1994 accused by Sommers of wallowing in victimization.

What is most striking in the writings of these critics is the rancorous, even contemptuous, tone. It is reasonable to expect that, at this stage of feminism's history, there will be honorable and legitimate disagreements, that there will be excesses and abuses. But these critics suggest that feminism, especially as it is practiced on college campuses, has something rotten at its core: self-indulgence, narcissism, puritanism, authoritarianism, and dogmatism. If this is the counter-plot from sophisticated women who might conceivably be sympathetic to the goals of feminism, what then from those who are absolutely antipathetic? Try a vicious caricature of Catharine Stimpson as pinup in the April 1993 pages of *Heterodoxy*, a magazine committed to the opposition of "political correctness," and a new sobriquet for feminists coined by Rush Limbaugh, host of a daily talk show: feminazis.

In such a climate, we should expect that some of Heilbrun's own criticism of this period has an edge. Her reviews of Carol Brightman's biography of Mary McCarthy and Sissela Bok's biography of her mother, Alva Myrdal, are probably the two most negative ones she has written. She attacks Brightman for not fully coming to grips with McCarthy's "nastiness" or her "virulent antifeminism" and describes Bok as an "unfeminist daughter" who fails to give an adequate account of her mother's accomplishments. The Heilbrun of the 1990s, whose feminism has taken her through so many battles, now has little patience with those who, in her view, fail to use its insights or its power for change. Published in the *Women's Review of Books,* both reviews, predictably, occasioned angry responses from readers.[25] Heilbrun's anger is stronger still in "The Thomas Confirmation Hearings or How Being a Humanist Prepares You for Right-Wing Politics," in which she recounts the battle of the Modern Language Association with Lynne Cheney, then head of the National Endowment for the Humanities, over the appointment of Carol Iannone to the council of the NEH. Venturing once more out of the academy and into the line of fire, Heilbrun denounces the tactics of those who defended Iannone and finds the experience of battling "the right wing" a preparatory lesson for the Anita Hill–Clarence Thomas hearings.[26] For Heilbrun, as for others, those hearings would constitute a critical moment of the decade. Given the polarizations and oppositions of these times, it is, perhaps, not surprising that Heilbrun marshals the resources of the detective-story genre to claim a power she might feel is slipping away as the 1990s unfold; in fiction, at least, she can make some things come out right. But she was also, of course, writing a biography about a real woman's life.

The Biography

In the preface to her 1995 biography, *The Education of a Woman: The Life of Gloria Steinem,* Carolyn Heilbrun reports that Gloria Steinem approached her to write the "authorized" biography. The two did not then know each other. What drew Steinem to Heilbrun, an academic who had not yet written a full-length biography, when, presumably, she could have had her pick of eminent feminist biographers? And what drew Heilbrun to Steinem when her primary interest had been in literary women and when her demonstrated strength had been not in writing the lives of women but in writing about the writing of those lives?

The woman who wrote *Writing a Woman's Life* might well have appealed to Gloria Steinem as a biographer. That book provided a new lens through which to view the accomplishments of women making deliberate choices to live a life devoted primarily to work, women who might previously have been seen as "failures," unable to find or keep husbands, deficient as mothers and daughters. Steinem would have seen in Heilbrun someone who could rescue her from those eager biographers who might poke their unauthorized noses into her affairs, seeking only sensationalism. Heilbrun would be able to see Steinem in the light of her achievements. Moreover, although Heilbrun had not yet written a full-length biography, she certainly knew how to write a story and, as a feminist, she knew the right questions to ask of a life devoted to activism. Finally, Heilbrun was an academic, albeit one whose work had moved out of the academy, and thus Steinem could be assured of a serious biography and a serious reception for that biography. The woman who had written *Writing a Woman's Life* was the biographer Gloria Steinem needed.

Writing Steinem's biography presented formal and thematic challenges. It is one thing to demand that we look differently at women's lives and ask different questions about them—as Heilbrun had done in *Writing a Woman's Life,* but it is quite another actually to write such a book. Steinem's life lacks the usual milestones: since she began taking care of her unstable mother while still young, she never, in effect, had a childhood and thus never "came of age"; she had many lovers but no marriage and, seemingly, no sustained, intimate relationship; she had no "divorces," and most of her lovers remain her friends; she had no children; she was always, and still remains, so attractive that at least some of the issues associated with women's aging do not seem relevant. How, then, could the story of such a life be structured?

In *Writing a Woman's Life,* Heilbrun teaches us to pay attention to women's work. But even so, Steinem presents problems: she came to feminism relatively early, and her moment of revelation occurred at a speak-out on abortion where the recognition was internal rather than dramatically external; she wrote hundreds of wonderfully witty and memorable essays but no substantial book; her struggles on behalf of the women's movement (the battle for ERA, the running of *Ms.* magazine, the endless campaigns for political candidates) were ongoing, unremitting, and grand in their way—but not in the same way as intellectual achievements. As a literary and cultural critic, Heilbrun knew how to make drama of the work of artists, but Steinem's has been the profession of a committed activist. Add to these challenges the fact that the ability to get close to the "real" Gloria Steinem is inhibited by the flux of countless media images about her and by her own practiced self-protectiveness. A final question surely remained for Heilbrun: she had never before focused a full-length work on one figure. Hers had been work of survey and synthesis, taut essays inquiring into the general patterns of women's lives and fictions. Would she, could she, concentrate on one woman—and one who had led a life very different from anything Heilbrun had known?

Heilbrun's words on the last page of *Writing a Woman's Life,* as she builds her vocabulary of risk, bear repeating: "we should make use of our security, our seniority, to take risks, to make noise, to be courageous, to become unpopular."[27] Writing a biography of the most visible living feminist would certainly qualify as a risk. So Heilbrun accepted Steinem's invitation, and the girl who had once stood before the biography shelves in the St. Agnes library was now, some half a century later, about to add her own book to the shelf.

There were undoubtedly attractions for Heilbrun in writing about Steinem. Steinem, after all, unparented, and with unpromising beginnings in Toledo, Ohio, was a perfect example of a reinvented woman. Talented, beautiful, she had already carved an enviable niche for herself in journalism when she turned to feminism. Often defined as the sum of her looks (even more true of a beautiful feminist Steinem who embodied an obvious contradiction in terms for many), she was especially eager to prove herself as journalist and as political activist. Heilbrun would have been intrigued by the possibilities of learning about a life involved with groups, people, travel, and politics. And the forces that had formed Steinem's public self would have fascinated Heilbrun; the book, after all, is about "the education of a woman." The fact that Steinem is a radical was important, too; at this point in her life, when Heilbrun was more radical herself, she would not have been interested in a woman whose life was not shaped by risk.

Moreover, as a woman without husband or children, Steinem was free in ways that many women are not, to claim a new pattern for her life. All of this, I would suggest, was appealing to Heilbrun, with one significant addition. Gloria Steinem is, in effect, the embodiment of the fantasy figure Carolyn Heilbrun herself had invented thirty years before; like Steinem, Kate Fansler is tall, willowy, blond, beautiful, professionally successful, sexual, childless, and a deliberate feminist.

What did Heilbrun set out to achieve in this biography? She said, at one point, that Steinem's "life must be the text because she offers no extensive texts for analysis."[28] This is ultimately both the biography's strength and its weakness. Reviewers, in general, have complained that Heilbrun fails to bring Steinem to life and that she idealizes her.[29] Steinem emerges as too good to be true, too iconic—a conclusion deriving, in part, perhaps, from the jacket illustration, a stylized portrait of Steinem with head raised to the future, looking like saint and visionary. To some extent, the criticism is just; we are not permitted to know the inner Steinem, and that, of course, may be because Steinem herself did not permit such access. "Steinem is a remarkably open person, yet beyond this openness there is something that is accessible to no one, probably not even to herself," writes Heilbrun; Steinem's therapist and her closest friends "recognize this apparent wall beyond which no one can look." Ultimately, Steinem is "elusive."[30] But Heilbrun herself is, arguably, not particularly interested in the *personal,* in the kinds of detail that make for an intimate portrait.

Let me illustrate this obliquely by turning to *The Players Come Again,* the novel published in 1990, the year Heilbrun began work on the Steinem biography, and the novel in which Kate Fansler herself is invited to write a biography of a woman, Gabrielle Foxx. During the course of her research, Fansler discovers a secret from Gabrielle's past; when pressed not to reveal this secret and not even to write the biography, but to publish instead an edition of Gabrielle's newly discovered novel, she, unpredictably, agrees. Yet there are some clues that explain her response. Throughout this novel, and elsewhere, too, Heilbrun herself—or Heilbrun through Cross and Fansler—has expressed a certain kind of ambivalence about biography. When Gabrielle's granddaughter Nellie announces that she has burned her grandmother's letters, Kate Fansler sympathizes: the personal life must be protected. Biography is important, Heilbrun's work seems to say, because it can show women possible models for the achieving life; it is not important, however, for revealing personal secrets. This is not, perhaps, surprising from a woman who has cherished "secret" selves and "psychic space." Heilbrun also seems to suggest, as does Janet Malcolm in her recent work on Sylvia Plath, that biography is impossible because one can never fully capture the life of another. There are multiple versions and interpretations of a life, but the life itself is elusive. *The Players Come Again* is at one level a meditation on biography; but it is also a book about the anxiety of writing biography, about not writing a biography, and about letting the work speak for itself. Certainly, in the book, Gabrielle, the potential subject of Fansler's biography, is a kind of disappearing center, met only in a narrative supplied by one character and in the reminiscences of others.

The reviewers are right, then, that Carolyn Heilbrun has not produced an inside picture of Gloria Steinem. And that brings us to the next criticism, that Steinem is idealized. Heilbrun admires Steinem, but she also takes her to task on a number of occasions, most notably describing her as "adolescent" in her relationships with men and sharply criticizing her book, *Revolution From Within* for its "familiar—or even tired" ideas.[31] Although Carolyn Heilbrun respects and honors Gloria Steinem, her reading of the life—and of the written work—is nuanced throughout. What Heilbrun is determined to value is the life Steinem has chosen because, in Heilbrun's terms, it is an exemplary, if not representative, life. As a critic of the culture, Heilbrun wants to claim Steinem's importance for that culture: that Gloria Steinem does important work in the world is enough. The question remains, of course, whether it is yet possible to write, and indeed to read, such a biography without the context of other models exploring a variety of unorthodox patterns for successful lives. Can we yet escape the kind of questions born from an earlier script that blame women for avoiding sustained relationships, for refusing motherhood, for defying our traditional tests for maturity? Indeed, I think this is one of the binds in which Heilbrun was caught: for it is as if Heilbrun were writing not the first but the second biography of Steinem. The first would have uncovered the scandals and taken Steinem to task for the compendium of her unconventional behaviors; Heilbrun wrote her biography, I believe, as a corrective against this phantom biography, just as she had rewritten the lives of chosen women in *Writing a Woman's Life*. In her eagerness to write against an as yet unwritten, but vividly imagined, conventional first biography of Steinem, she failed to provide both the illuminating detail and the tough criticism that such a biography would have offered.

Ultimately, readers will turn to this book, I suspect, for the pleasure of hearing Heilbrun think aloud about the many questions that arose as a result of her contemplation of Gloria Steinem's life. Heilbrun is at her best as moralist, at extracting the revelatory lesson from the particulars; at theorizing from the "text" of Steinem's life. In the mini-essays coursing through this biography, Heilbrun reflects on the women's movement, on beauty, on aging, and on the making of nonbiological families.[32] She produces an unconventional and contrary new theory on mothering, arguing that in Steinem's case the lack of mothering did not disable her but instead enabled her to resist socialization and thus choose an unorthodox life. (We may recall that Heilbrun's mother was not "overprotective," either.) It also becomes clear that, in the course of writing this biography, Heilbrun herself becomes more radical, deliberately removing herself from the more moderate wing of the feminist movement. Indeed, her investment in a more radical politics might have proved one of Heilbrun's greatest personal challenges in writing the biography: since she had been roundly criticized in the past for being too closely tied to the establishment, her more recent attraction to radical positions undoubtedly made it difficult to achieve the distance necessary for a cool evaluation of Steinem's political career. It remained to be seen what form Heilbrun's own radicalism would take next.

Thelma and Louise

Carolyn Heilbrun and I have a conversation about the film *Thelma and Louise*. She has seen it more than once and is very enthusiastic. I like the movie, too, but have a number of objections to what I see as unconvincing turns in the plot, such as Thelma's inviting a virtual stranger into her motel room not long after she has nearly been raped. "And what about the ending?" I ask, after Heilbrun has deftly defended against my other complaints, "I'm suspicious of the romantic treatment of death." She argues that this death is a choice. What matters is the quality of a life; death is not negative when it is a conscious and controlled choice. Patrice Umphelby makes much the same point in *Sweet Death, Kind Death*. Once a situation becomes impossible, you can choose to end it. I replayed this conversation over and over after I heard that Carolyn Heilbrun had resigned from Columbia University in May 1992.

Columbia University, May 1992

"Why don't you leave Columbia? You must have had lots of offers." I asked Carolyn Heilbrun this question in January 1992 after we had talked for some time about Heilbrun's resentment of Columbia's treatment of her. She said she did not want to leave Columbia, that two of her children and her husband work in New York City. She cannot imagine living anywhere but the city. In an afterword for *Changing Subjects: The Making of Feminist Literary Criticism,* written just about the time of our conversation, she remarks that "Columbia . . . is back in the hands of the men whose primary loyalty is to Columbia College and each other." She then makes a somewhat contradictory statement: "Columbia has stopped hurting me, but like someone who has escaped a battering marriage—and the analogy is, in many ways, not a far-fetched one for feminist women faculty—I cannot wipe out the terrible years. I cannot change the isolation of all my time at Columbia." Sometimes, then, the past does stick, does make a groove. Nevertheless, she speaks enthusiastically of the changes in her courses, of now teaching "great writers who are neither white nor upper class," and never hints that she might be thinking of leaving Columbia; after all, as she pointed out in a 1986 interview, "the revolution must take place within institutions."[33]

Certainly, anyone following the course of Heilbrun's career must be impressed by her dedication to working within the institution. On the face of it, Heilbrun's story is a classic one of personal and professional assimilation. All the ingredients are here. As a student, she excelled in academic institutions noted more than most for their anti-Semitism. A child of parents who had pulled up their roots, she was eager to find her roots, values, and traditions in the study of literature as that was practiced in an academic institution. Success in such an institution would, ideally, have nothing to do with accidents of gender, religion, and ethnic origin, but only with mind, merit, and accomplishment. The myth is a seductive one: if one is ambitious, learns the rules, plays by those rules, bends to the structures, assimilates the values, one can, in Norman Podhoretz's memorable words, "make it."

In this version of Heilbrun's history, we read her Wellesley story, "Thy People, My People," as one of painful but necessary assimilation, an expression of a desire to "pass"; we note her generally celebratory depictions of institutions in the early novels; and we applaud Kate Fansler's championship of "University College," the fictional counterpart of Columbia's School of General Studies, which can finally be integrated into the university as a whole in *Poetic Justice* and thus humanize the institution. Can we say that the picture we get of the academic institution in the early essays and novels is reasonably optimistic, that, in spite of everything, the institution is open to change, adaptation, improvement? "Educating Female People," written for *Columbia Forum* in 1962 and picked up by *Time,* shows that Heilbrun knew the institution did not meet women's needs but believed that reforms could make a difference. Recognizing that her own needs were too large to be contained in institutional form, she invented a pseudonym and wrote her novels. So one could make accommodations, find various expressions for one's identity, and still hope the institution would and could make changes. In any case, Heilbrun was prepared to struggle for an institutional identity; *Death in a Tenured Position* makes clear that those who opt out of the institution, the members of the women's commune, while certainly honorable, also opt out of power. The weight of the book opposes that choice; indeed, the only responsible option is to stay and work for reform. Even as late as *The Imperfect Spy* (1995), Heilbrun appears optimistic about the possibility of changing an institution, allowing four people—Kate Fansler, Reed, Harriet, and Blair—to make a difference at the benighted Schuyler Law School. And when she has not been writing novels under a pseudonym, novels that illuminate in dramatic and pointed ways the state of the academy, Heilbrun has been composing balanced, judicious essays, arguing for an academic acceptance of feminist criticism, for the importance of women's voices in the academy, against polarization of the sexes, and for a humanist ideal of wholeness. In this version of the Heilbrun narrative, her accession to the presidency of the Modern Language Association in 1984, her appointment to the Avalon Chair in the Humanities in 1986, and her selection as University Lecturer in 1986 are signal triumphs of her career. And she accomplished all this while raising three children and staying married to the same man for close to fifty years. She has succeeded both in what she would call the marriage plot and the quest plot.

So why did Carolyn Heilbrun resign from Columbia in 1992 in her sixty-sixth year when she had, by any standards, reached the pinnacle of professional success, and when she seemed, after a career spanning more than three decades, utterly secure in her chosen profession and institution, not an obscure provincial college but a renowned Ivy League university set in a major urban center? In 1992, to any casual observer, Heilbrun seemed anything but marginal; she had earned the credentials for a central role in her own institution and in the academy at large.

Just as important: why did Heilbrun choose to resign in such a public way? Was she saying that, unlike some of her fictional protagonists of this time, she would not simply disappear without a trace? Instead, she made a public occasion of her departure, speaking to the press, and making sure that all knew her reasons for leaving. Influenced, perhaps, by the activism of Gloria Steinem, she seized the opportunity to expose Columbia for its treatment of her and take a public stand on behalf of her students. I believe she had written herself into a position where she had to act, had to take risks, and she wanted, like the deliberate author of a fiction or a life, to take charge of her story and provide her own ending to the narrative of her experience at Columbia.

Dramatically announcing her determination to take early retirement, Heilbrun declared, according to the *Chronicle of Higher Education,* "I've lost the spirit to continue." Of her colleagues at Columbia she said, "The atmosphere became impossible. Quite literally, no one in the department spoke to me all year." [34] Columbia's failure to tenure a woman in Heilbrun's field and to admit several of her graduate students to the doctoral degree program precipitated Heilbrun's resignation. "I was a feminist front," she said to me. "They used me to pretend they would support feminist scholarship." The news reverberated in the academic world and beyond. Not only academic organs such as the *Chronicle of Higher Education* but also the *Los Angeles Times,* the *New York Observer,* and the *New York Times Magazine* ran stories on Heilbrun's confrontation with Columbia. [35] All the reporters wondered what it could mean when a woman of Heilbrun's stature and accomplishment believed herself to be, at best, an invisible member of her institution. Was she a crank? Was she justified? Does the resignation of one who is sixty-six count, anyway? And did she even resign—or did she merely take "early retirement"? Did her story of isolation and anger have more than personal resonance? In 1992, after more than two decades of the contemporary movement for women's liberation, what had changed?

There are no tidy answers to these complex questions. But we can try to tease out the connection between private pain and public circumstance and to understand the intersection of one life with others played out against the idiosyncratic structure of a particular institution during a particular passage of our cultural history. Some of Heilbrun's colleagues and students offer different pieces of the puzzle. [36] Her colleagues begin with a narrative about history and structure. I learn that

Columbia's central bureaucracy carefully guards its power, that administrators stay too long, that decisions tend to be made without enough public debate or faculty involvement, and that secrecy is the norm in policy-making. The result is inevitably an atmosphere of suspicion and distrust. Within the Department of English and Comparative Literature, the once tripartite structure of College, Graduate Faculty, and General Studies has been unified, but some long-term members of the department still look back with nostalgia to the old idea of Columbia, with the College as its intellectual center, while others summon back the inequities and rebuffs produced by that hierarchical arrangement. I am told, even by those unsympathetic to Heilbrun's choice to resign, that they acknowledge the historical pattern of Columbia's neglect of women.

Rachel Blau DuPlessis reports that even as late as 1966 she was "one of the first three women ever" to be appointed as a preceptor in the Columbia College English Department; she recalls, "apparently the decision to appoint women was one highly contested and debated, very rancorous." DuPlessis also lists the astonishing number of other feminists who passed through the Columbia English and French departments: Nina Auerbach, Louise Bernikow, Carolyn Burke, Barbara Christian, Kate Ellis, Judith Kegan Gardiner, Sandra M. Gilbert, Alice Jardine, Myra Jehlen, Nancy Milford, Nancy K. Miller, Kate Millett, Lillian Robinson, Naomi Schor, Catharine Stimpson, and Louise Yelin.[37] Heilbrun would add Gayle Greene, Constance Jordan, Alice Kaplan, and Susan Suleiman and point out that "*Columbia kept not a single one of them.*"[38] Barbara Christian, a student at Columbia in the late 1960s, recalls that she was the only black woman in the literature program. "I don't know how we women could have imagined that we really were going to get our Ph.D.'s and be professors," she said, "because there was no indication that there was anybody like us there on the faculty."[39] Erica Jong, in a letter to the *New York Times* responding to Heilbrun's departure from Columbia, stated that, in her experience as a graduate student at Columbia, "the graduate English department seemed designed to crush female talent and harass women into leaving."[40]

Some current faculty members declare, however, that this is old news and that, by 1992, attitudes toward women had changed for the better and that Heilbrun had influenced those changes; in resigning when she did, Heilbrun had simply allowed the old legitimate grievances to color a much rosier present. Was it true that Heilbrun, a person who hates to be cornered by the past, simply could not, in this case, fight her way out from under its shadow? In part, perhaps. But, after digging in Columbia files and asking more questions, I find that Columbia is not quite so easily let off the hook. Focusing now, only on the recent past, from 1980 onward, I discover in the papers for the Commission on the Status of Women, a letter written in 1980 to the chair of the Trustees Committee on Educational Policy by then chair of the Commission on the Status of Women, Joan Ferrante. Some would call 1980 the high point of feminism in the academy, but things were still moving slowly at Columbia. The letter calls attention to the fact that, since 1974, only twenty-five women but a total of 142 men were proposed for tenure in the university (the figures include tenure decisions at Barnard and in the Health Sciences). Moreover, in the eight years since Columbia established its Commission on the Status of Women and proposed its new plan for affirmative action, only five women had received tenure in the Graduate School of Arts and Sciences. Some offer an economic justification for this situation: after the events of 1968, alumni giving plummeted, and the subsequent loss of revenue, combined with government cutbacks on spending in higher education, meant that little hiring was done.

But the grievances of women did not only have to do with hiring; by 1982, seven faculty members, male and female, sufficiently concerned about conditions for women, set about forming the larger Ad Hoc Committee on Women at Columbia to draw attention to the concerns of all the women of the Columbia campus, especially in light of the decision finally to admit undergraduate women to the College the following year. In due course, a proposal for an Institute for Research on Women and Gender was produced; that recommendation made its way, with some opposition, through various committees, but it was finally approved, and Heilbrun became the institute's first director, serving from 1986 to 1989.

At last, change seemed possible. The economic boom of the 1980s, improved alumni giving, optimistic demographic data about potential increases in student numbers enabled a burst of new hiring. Under the enlightened leadership of Steven Marcus, the Department of English and Comparative Literature recruited a number of first-rate scholars with new ideas; the composition of the department was shifting. Marcus also successfully recommended Carolyn Heilbrun for the newly vacant Avalon Foundation Chair in the Humanities. In the mid-1980s, the period of Heilbrun's MLA presidency, Columbia seemed to be moving into a new era, and Heilbrun acknowledges as much.

But by the end of the 1980s, the mood—economic and intellectual—had changed again. Almost everyone I spoke with, faculty and students, noted that something had happened at Columbia in the late 1980s and the effect was to freeze out feminism. People offered various explanations for this situation. Several of those who were hired in the mid-1980s and who had changed the intellectual life of the department left for personal reasons. Budgets were shrinking again, especially, as always, for the humanities, and so new hiring was curtailed for the moment. Economics affected the poorly funded new Institute for Research on Women and Gender, too; the Center for American Culture, also founded in the 1980s and indicative of a new acceptance on Columbia's part of interdisciplinary approaches to literature and culture, folded by the end of the decade. Hardening attitudes signaled the backlash: those Columbia faculty who had been receptive to feminist approaches in the early 1980s were dismissing them by the end of the decade; many students, both undergraduate and graduate, regarded themselves as "post-feminist," perceiving feminist work as no longer relevant. By 1988, the Graduate Women's Association had fallen apart. Finally, even within academic feminism, as I noted earlier, important changes had occurred, the recognition that feminism was feminisms. Nancy K. Miller bravely dates the breakdown: "By 1985 . . . that interlocking sense of personal conviction and political solidarity . . . had already begun to erode seriously within the feminist community. This was the moment when white mainstream feminists finally began to pay attention to internal divisions that of course had been there from the beginning."[41] By the end of the decade, then, historical, cultural, and local forces had converged to halt a movement at Columbia that had seemed finally to be gathering momentum. Nor should we leave out of this account the personal. Heilbrun, now practiced in public bravery, was becoming increasingly outspoken. Called "strident," a "trouble-maker," an "extremist," she would not be compliant or deferential, she would not swallow anger.

"Were you surprised when Carolyn Heilbrun resigned?" I ask her colleagues and students. Her students, apparently, had no inkling of her imminent resignation. Even those closest to her said they were shocked. They had assumed all was well: "I thought she was powerful, central, esteemed, and respected," said Susan Nerheim, summing up the impressions of others. Her colleagues also did not expect a resignation, though they pointed to a history of battles. Indeed, that history illuminates the evolution of a particular feminist in the contemporary period as well as the relationship of women in general—even the most successful ones— to powerful institutions.

I have reported that Heilbrun was initially deeply committed to the academy; that she valued acceptance and inclusion, not disruption and revolution; that, as this version of her career suggests, she consistently chose to fight her battles from the inside; and that her subsequent severance from the institution seemed the least likely result, given the depth of her commitment and attachment. But in the light of her resignation, the narrative of her connection with Columbia yields different emphases, a story of neglect and isolation.

The seeds of struggle are there from the beginning, of course; let us return for the last time to the matter of assimilation. To be assimilated is to be absorbed, to become "like" (from the root Latin *similis*), to be incorporated into the substance of the larger whole. But was becoming part of the "we" that assimilation represents even attainable? "It was as a secret outsider that I operated, as Jew, as female. I pretended to be a part of two worlds, the gentile, the male, to neither of which I belonged," says Heilbrun in *Reinventing Womanhood*.[42] It is the "secret" and the "pretence" that I want to dwell on here, emphasizing the impossibility of belonging rather than the desire to belong. Reading "Thy People, My People" from this point of view, we pay less attention to the little girl's desperate need to "pass" and more to the narrator's implicit judgment of her weakness in wanting to pass. In any case, passing would not prove to be so easy. If it was hard enough for Lionel Trilling and Irving Howe to find places for themselves in the academy, how would women fare—especially when scholars of stature such as Trilling did not welcome their presence? Assimilation simply could not be an option.

In this narrative, Carolyn Heilbrun's breaks with the institution take center stage: her alliance with the students in 1968, her decision (with Joan Ferrante) to call a meeting of Columbia's tenured women in 1971, her attack on Lionel Trilling in the *Saturday Review* in 1972, and her decision to speak out on all manner of public occasions about the shortcomings of her institution and some of its more prominent faculty members. This version of the story records Heilbrun's long history of isolation, reads *Death in a Tenured Position* and *Trap for Fools,* with their ominous titles and their bleak vision of the contemporary institution, as central documents, and reveals the long history behind Heilbrun's decision to leave Columbia.

A Teacher

At her retirement from Columbia, Heilbrun had taught for over thirty years. The pedagogical impulse is strong in her, the work sounding an insistent moral refrain that women must take charge of the terms of their lives. Such acts can be inspired by the study of literature, through the medium of critical question and interpretation. For Heilbrun, the classroom walls are permeable; her emphasis is always on a larger context, a larger world. Victoria Rosner, one of her students, offers an anecdote that, for her, defines Heilbrun's essential quality as a teacher: "It was early in the semester, and we were all saying what we thought were these incredibly impressive things about [Joseph Conrad's] *Heart of Darkness* . . . and then Carolyn stopped the conversation dead by saying, 'All right class, these comments are all very interesting, but tell me' (and this is an exact quote) 'how would you teach this text to undergraduates?' And there was total silence."[43] To the ordinary reader, this remark may not seem especially startling; but to Rosner, used to the theory-driven classes of graduate education, Heilbrun's question demanded that the students not merely indulge themselves in spinning ideas but imagine those ideas put to service. Rosner's story is echoed in many of the comments made by Heilbrun's students: that she is practical, sensible, alive to the connections between ideal and action.[44]

Heilbrun had been publicly contemplating questions of pedagogy since the early 1970s. *The Theban Mysteries* (1971), in which Kate Fansler is invited back to her old private girls' high school to teach a seminar on *Antigone,* is a book about how and what, after Vietnam, after 1968, it is possible to teach. One could not simply go back to teaching the old texts in the old ways. Texts now had to be "relevant." That notion is now, at best, gently derided, and at worst, blamed for opening the door to most of the "ills" that beset modern education: ill-prepared students, science fiction, feminist perspectives, and falling standards. *Relevance,* in concert with other suspect terms, such as *character, literature,* and *moral vision* would in due course set theorists to grinding their teeth, but, for Heilbrun, thinking against the grain of fashion once again, relevance was, and would remain, a guiding principle that carried with it the charge to use literature in the work of cultural change. As for pedagogical method, we can find it expounded by a character in *The Theban Mysteries:* "Perhaps teaching is really a mutual experience between the younger and older, perhaps all there is to be learned is what they can discover between them."[45] Teaching is not, then, delivery of information, not lecture, but a "mutual experience" of discovery.

From some of the students who have worked most closely with Heilbrun, I get a picture of Heilbrun's seminars. They were carefully orchestrated, and for many years the structure almost never varied: Heilbrun took the first twenty minutes to set contexts and provide resources; then two students made presentations for twenty minutes each; general discussion filled the remaining forty minutes. But in Heilbrun's final years at Columbia, the nature of the student presentation changed: she asked the students to prepare questions rather than formal presentations. She wanted to avoid "graduate student grandstanding," to find a mode that would provoke discussion, what she called "intellectual fertilization."[46] She was more interested in the process of question and exploration than the set piece of finished thinking.

Yet discussion is not always comfortable in the Heilbrun classroom; students do not swap personal experiences (with the one exception of the seminar entitled "Biography and Autobiography"), nor does Heilbrun encourage intimacy. There is a grittiness to Heilbrun's classroom persona; she might look like a grandmother, she would say, but she was certainly not going to behave like one. Forceful, demanding, passionate, she can ask tough, even adversarial, questions. Says Susan Heath, a former student, who has taught with Heilbrun as her assistant and also served as her research assistant, "If she thought you were talking nonsense, she said so." She is "definite" in her views, "unafraid of having an idea or a point of view," reports Judith Resnik, a law professor who has team-taught with Heilbrun.[47] A few students are put off because she can be intimidating; one student I encountered did not find Heilbrun's classroom at all congenial, and one or two thought Heilbrun had learned too much from the distanced style of her own Columbia teachers.

Heilbrun agrees she is "emphatic" and warns the students about her directness, but says she also welcomes disagreement. "For how else can I learn?" she asks. That invitation to challenge is corroborated by almost all the students with whom I spoke; several told me that she had initially argued against a reading they had presented or an approach they had taken in an essay, but that they were able to win her over to their point of view. Said Miranda Sherwin, "She is very willing to have her original impression modified." Perhaps she is willing to change her mind because she pays such close attention. "She really listens," I am told by Jonathan Gill, who also remarked that she was exceptionally generous in opening her seminars to large numbers of students because, in his opinion, "she wanted to hear a range of different voices."[48]

Indeed, Heilbrun was a sought-after teacher at Columbia. Students lined up to take her courses; in her last semester, seventy-three people applied for a dozen places in her seminar, according to Susan Heath. I asked the students about Heilbrun's sense, expressed at the time of her resignation, that she was a "feminist front" at Columbia. They said, independently, that it was not so much that she was the only feminist, but that, in *her* classes, feminism came first. All her classes were feminist. "That was her primary discipline," said Margaret Vandenburg, another former graduate student. That statement might have made some of her colleagues shake their heads in dismay; yet I also heard that she was "non-doctrinaire about gender," and one of the "least rigid" professors when it came to politics.[49]

Heilbrun's supervision of her graduate students was careful and conscientious. She "took infinite pains with her students' essays," said Susan Heath, and people brought in several drafts of their master's essays. Susan Nerheim sent me her papers, marked up by Heilbrun, in order to show me how Heilbrun had taught her how to write, to cut the flab and make her points with precision and trenchancy. Susan Nerheim's first master's essay had apparently generated some controversy, and she was surprised when Heilbrun "went to bat" for her. "She didn't know me from Adam," said Nerheim.[50] Other students tell of institutional battles fought on their behalf, to allow them to study a special field for their oral examinations or to pursue a particular topic for an essay.

That Heilbrun welcomes the commerce of different voices in the classroom, the give-and-take of intellectual sparring, is demonstrated by her choice of team-teaching partners. The first was Tom Driver, then professor at Union Theological Seminary, in spring 1970. They decided to teach a course, capaciously entitled "Drama, Fiction, and the Modern World," with the emphasis on "the way women's lives are portrayed in certain major works of fiction." Few people were thinking at that time about women's lives in academic curricula, and Tom Driver admits that the topic was a surprise to him, too. But, he reports, "Carol knew that something was in the air." As always, Heilbrun relished the idea of collaboration with a mind that would challenge hers. In the early 1970s, Heilbrun and Catharine Stimpson had given their talk, "Theories of Feminist Criticism: A Dialogue," with its theme of oppositional and complementary feminist locations, but the two, though intrigued by the "genre of collaboration," never actually taught together.[51]

Then, in 1979, Heilbrun invited Nancy K. Miller, who was teaching in Columbia's French Department, to teach the first of three versions of a course they would call "The Heroine's Text." They, and others I spoke with, delight in the catalog of oppositions Heilbrun and Miller brought to the classroom: Heilbrun was fifty-three and Miller thirty-eight; Heilbrun was trained in English departments, Miller in French; Heilbrun argued for literature's moral and ethical reach, Miller for the power of a feminism wed to theory; Heilbrun was interested in the interactions of male and female literary traditions, Miller was bent on charting the "specificity" of women's writing; Heilbrun was drawn to the writer's moment in history, to the literary imagination, and to the stories embodied in literature, while Miller focused on close readings, the structure of texts, and linguistic idiosyncrasies. Both describe this early teaching experience as exhilarating: for Miller, it was a "formative moment"; for Heilbrun, "a vitality entered the classroom."[52] Their students felt the excitement, too. Susan Fraiman, now teaching at the University of Virginia, describes the sense of urgency she felt, the experience of "breaking new ground."[53] If Miller was impressed by Heilbrun's inside-out knowledge of literature and literary figures, Heilbrun was introduced to the arcane maneuvers of high theory and to a more intense focus on women's literary traditions. A lover of elegant, lucid prose, Heilbrun was dismayed by the turgid language of theory, but she was open to its possibilities, especially the potential of deconstruction, for unlocking texts. She was also convinced that feminist critics from different ideological locations needed to work not against but in concert with one another. Miller was and is an important influence in Heilbrun's life; Heilbrun's 1979 team-teaching invitation to Miller dates a desire for a more radical perspective, and, just as important, it signals the opening gesture of friendship, of access to a feminist community that would mitigate the social and intellectual isolation of Heilbrun's life at Columbia.

In the mid-1980s, Carolyn Heilbrun participated in a law school workshop, an experience that led to the development of a course in law and literature with Judith Resnik, a course Heilbrun taught first with Resnik at Yale Law School, and then with Subah Narasimhan of Columbia Law School. Heilbrun and Resnik also collaborated on an article, "Convergences: Law, Literature, and Feminism." It is not surprising that Heilbrun was attracted to this field, that, indeed, she saw it as yet another way "to bring the spirit back"[54] to the classroom, for, as she reports in the "Convergences" article, "here was a context in which real changes in the language and stories of women might be enacted." Declining to dismiss the theory that has taken over academic feminism, she nevertheless says, "I sometimes felt that we were just talking to ourselves when we should have been working in the public realm. . . . These women lawyers were out there fighting where it mattered and might even make an immediate and palpable difference (an extraordinary idea to one in literature)."[55]

But the difference was not likely to be quite so immediate. Heilbrun and Resnik encountered a field in which the voices of women were largely absent and in which literature was subordinate to law. "The idea that law and literature can be reciprocal, that literature has something to teach law, comes from Heilbrun," Resnik told me.[56] The course included literary texts as well as legal cases, proposing that the law, like fiction, rests as much on what a culture's available stories permit as on what are called objective facts and hard evidence; it matters, therefore, who controls and tells the stories. With this subject matter, Heilbrun was sure of her ground. When a character in *An Imperfect Spy* ponders her relation to Thomas Hardy's Tess of *Tess of the d'Urbervilles,* she asks, "Do you suppose I'm crazy at a time like this to be thinking about a character in a novel a hundred years old?" Theorists would shake their heads over her textual innocence, but we sense the weight of Heilbrun's authority behind Kate Fansler's reply: "If I thought you were crazy to think of Tess, I would have to think my whole life was crazy and worthless into the bargain."[57]

What Heilbrun writes and what she teaches is of a piece. Still, how to teach is quite a different matter from what to teach. In "Convergences," Heilbrun speaks frankly of the difficulties she encountered while teaching for the first time in a law school: the "angry response" of students "who feel themselves and their secure positions in the society threatened by studies of gender arrangements" and "the ambivalence of all students, but especially women students, toward female authority figures." At one point, she reflects on the difficulty for the woman teacher of finding "a place from which to speak."[58] Heilbrun has faced that difficulty as a public feminist intellectual, too, and it is certainly one that female teachers know well. Gail Griffin, recounting her own experiences as a young faculty member, defines the problem: "I was spending a great deal of time, and I saw my female colleagues spending a great deal of time, wrestling with the pressure from their students and sometimes their colleagues to play Academic Mommy. . . . women know only too well how near impossible it is to enact Mother but elicit the respect accorded to Father."[59] From the testimony of her students, Heilbrun clearly chose a classroom persona that defied gender stereotyping and rejected a maternal presence; "she was not the one to hand you the Kleenex," I learned. But it was impossible to pretend that gender did not matter, especially if that was the very subject under scrutiny. If one refuses to be mother—or grandmother—and one cannot be father, then where to look for professional models and how to claim the space from which to speak?

One solution Heilbrun found should not be surprising: collaborative teaching is, after all, another model of the split self. Paired teaching proposes not a single figure of authority but a model of interrogation and self-interrogation. Each member of the team has an acknowledged field of expertise, each has something to learn and something to teach. It is a new way of returning to the principle first set forth in *The Theban Mysteries,* that teaching is a "mutual experience between younger and older." During her last years of teaching, Heilbrun invited Susan Heath, her former graduate student, to teach with her. I suspect that the invitation stemmed, at least in part, from Heilbrun's sense that the collaborative classroom was the one she found most congenial.

For Heilbrun, until her resignation, teaching was a primary aspect of her professional identity. She says she loved to learn from her bright students and try out her own ideas. But, along with the characteristic optimism and unflagging commitment to change comes, at last, a certain discouragement: "Teaching as a feminist is not easy, either in early days or today. To the extent that colleagues say the problems will simply abate with time, twenty years has not proved them right."[60] Whatever now might bring the spirit back, she seems no longer to have the heart for it; Heilbrun continues her work now outside the academy. Indeed, now that she has retired, she does not "miss" teaching. As we have learned, after all, she does not look back.

Kate's Body

Most of the bodies that turn up or disappear in Heilbrun's fiction belong to women. Women's bodies do not have an easy time of it in this world, suffering death or banishment because they threaten to subvert a man's world or his work (*In the Last Analysis, The James Joyce Murder, A Question of Max, Sweet Death, Kind Death, No Word from Winifred*) or because they are too much the conventional woman, whether mother or scholar.[61] But bodies are also, to a remarkable degree, absent in this fictional world. For example, Kate's own body has virtually disappeared; we know she is beautiful, tall, and willowy, has her hair tidily controlled in a French twist, and has the effortless elegance born of expensively cut clothes. But her body is always discreetly kept out of sight—and not just by her clothes. Bulletins from high and low culture report that women are excessively burdened by their bodies, but Kate is remarkably free of hers. Even as she ages, she has no aches or twinges, no hormonal lapses, no blemishes, no sag, no unsightly pucker. This is indeed compelling fantasy: imagine a body that requires so little maintenance. There are oblique references to the satisfactory sex life of Kate and Reed, and she is occasionally tempted by desire (for Moon in *Death in a Tenured Position* and Blair in *An Imperfect Spy*), but for the most part her appetites are nicely limited. The body has, unlike the mind, decided to behave itself and not cause trouble.

Let us return to the disappearing self one last time; but note that what is disappearing this time is the body. In numerous articles and in conversation, Heilbrun has spoken of her bracing attitude toward aging. At about the age of fifty, she made the considered choice to simplify her life so as to devote more time to the work she loves. She would not give dinner parties; she would pay only minimum attention to the maintenance of her apartment. But the most interesting choices she made have to do with the body. According to Nancy K. Miller, soon after they met in the mid-1970s, Heilbrun "deliberately aged herself." She let her hair grow, stuffed it into a bun, and made herself into a grandmother about twenty years before she actually became one. The new hairstyle meant that she never again had to go to the hairdresser. Heilbrun tells me of other, similar decisions: she buys her clothes from catalogs, refusing to waste time shopping; she will not diet; she wears neither dresses nor panty hose; she does not have her teeth bleached; she does not go to a doctor for routine checkups. Most of us drop our jaws when we hear this catalog of refusals; we are inspired and exhilarated, but we are not quite sure, as we puff on the treadmill and make an appointment to tint the grey in our hair, that we can emulate her example. In a culture where what counts is a youthful appearance wrestled from starvation diets, cosmetic surgery, rigorous exercise, and careful dressing, Heilbrun has decided to celebrate the freedom that aging can bring. Not that these decisions have been easy ones; she still, in print and in conversation, will talk of weight, of clothes, about her "rumpled" look, about the chicness of others; but this is part of what we have been seeing all along: the conflicts attending the visible struggle to change. The makeover that interests Heilbrun is not of the body but of the self. The mind/body split is not a problem but another solution. So she has, in effect, disappeared out of her body, banished it from consciousness, eluded photographs, and embodied herself in prose.

A Self in Progress

I know of no other feminist who has provided us with such a detailed record of her intellectual journey as Carolyn Heilbrun. From "Hamlet's Mother" to "The New Story of Mother and Daughter"; from Constance Garnett to Gloria Steinem; from *The James Joyce Murder* to *The Players Come Again,* we have watched Heilbrun write herself through the last four decades and the various stages of the women's movement and feminist literary theory. She begins with mothers, with wanting women to be more than mothers, with a large question about identity; she is cautious to start with, taking moderate positions, appealing to reason, and working her way toward androgyny, her ideal realization of a full self for both men and women. In asking prominent feminist critics how they would evaluate Heilbrun's achievement, I learn that many of them have great respect for her 1973 book on androgyny. For Sandra M. Gilbert and Susan Gubar, *Toward a Recognition of Androgyny* was influential in their own work on modernism, an "enthralling" book, and one of the first to open a new conversation about gender and point to "the crucial role Bloomsbury played."[62] For Rachel Blau DuPlessis, "it made one see, in a flash, that feminist cultural work meant the reseeing of everything from gender-laden perspectives."[63] Catharine Stimpson, who publicly opposed androgyny as a possible feminist model, still pays tribute to Heilbrun for making androgyny "a literary subject."[64] This praise is particularly significant in light of the fact that androgyny seemed a dead idea by the end of the 1970s; indeed, even the recent *Oxford Companion to Women's Writing in the United States* dismisses the term in a terse paragraph.[65] But, like the return of the repressed, androgyny seems to be rearing its double head again: cropping up in graduate school dissertations; in the second thoughts of critics like Phyllis Rose;[66] and reappearing in contemporary theory, often masked or cross-dressed, and always under an alias.

Reinventing Womanhood proposed a reworking of the androgyny ideal with an emphasis on how women could learn from male models without becoming "honorary males." Heilbrun set forth a brave argument, albeit beset with tough contradictions, but with the rise of theory and the emphasis on "difference" in the academy, it did not find a receptive audience. Nevertheless, that book is still in print, and it is still the book through which many nonacademic women find their way to feminism. By the time *Reinventing Womanhood* was published, Heilbrun was becoming identified not as a literary critic but as a public critic of the culture, and it is there, I would suggest, that she has made her major contributions. From the beginning of her writing life, with the 1962 essay on "Educating Female People," Heilbrun had been arguing for social change. That article had an effect, touched a nerve, and was carried out of its academic home in *Columbia Forum* and into the pages of *Time* and other national magazines and newspapers. Heilbrun had something to say—and she had a knack for saying it with style.

She wrote with the dedicated discipline of the young girl who, long ago, read her alphabetical way through biographies, and she published widely, wisely placing parts of her books-in-progress in a variety of journals, wasting nothing, reiterating her ideas, driving them home. She sought multiple audiences, publishing in scholarly journals, law journals, the *New York Times Book Review, Opera News, Ms.* magazine, *Harper's Bazaar, Armchair Detective,* and even the *Bulletin of the American Association of Retired Persons.* By the time she published *Writing a Woman's Life,* theory had cordoned off the academic world: a tight circle of scholars were speaking only to the initiated few, and so an audience was ready for a book that would return attention to the subject of women's lives. In *Writing a Woman's Life,* Heilbrun devised a brilliant solution to the problem she had tackled in *Reinventing Womanhood,* that of finding models for female achievement. She would not now look to men; she would not even look to literature; she would convert the lives of successful women to texts and read those texts in such a way as to offer new stories about the structure of women's lives. Indeed, the book's compelling thesis is that stories determine lives and that new ways of living can only be wrought from new stories. Feminist critics speak of the "inspirational" and "visionary" quality of *Writing a Woman's Life,* and most important, of Heilbrun's ability to crystallize the new ideas about biography in language that a broad, general audience could appreciate.[67]

The popular Amanda Cross novels attracted an even larger audience for the ongoing story of a woman academic negotiating the culture wars in professional and institutional settings. They do not satisfy everyone's taste: some find the settings too insular, the dialogue too precious, and the characters too comfortable with their upper class; besides, there is not enough action, and scarcely even a dead body. But others delight in the literate and literary Kate, find resonance in her deepening anxieties, and admire the quality of her battles. Feminist critics credit Heilbrun as Cross with "the revival of the feminist crime novel . . . moribund since . . . Dorothy Sayers's *Gaudy Night*" and overturning the conventions of a form that ordinarily affirms the established social arrangements.[68] As Heilbrun herself put it, "with the momentum of a mystery and the trajectory of a good story with a solution, the author is left free to dabble in a little profound revolutionary thought."[69]

As her reputation grew, Heilbrun would write forewords and afterwords, introducing and commenting on the works of others. A generous and receptive reader, she wrote enthusiastic reviews of Ellmann's *Thinking about Women,* Millett's *Sexual Politics,* and of Gilbert and Gubar's *Madwoman in the Attic,* recognizing them to be landmark

texts. She declared that Nancy Milford's 1970 biography of Zelda Fitz-
gerald inaugurated the new biography for women and that May Sarton's
rewritten autobiography, *Journal of a Solitude* (1973), set a standard for
a new kind of honesty in women's autobiography;[70] indeed, she was the
first important critic to draw serious attention to Sarton's work. The
once solitary Wellesley student now has an intellectual community of
women writers and scholars. For some colleagues and students, she is
the mentor she never had, though she never comforts at the expense
of honest criticism. In demand as a speaker, she has given keynote addresses, commencement speeches, and, of course, her presidential address for the Modern Language Association. In this context, her public
resignation from Columbia has added resonance, the act of a person
who will claim public space for the cultural implications of her actions:
a representative stand against still implacable institutions.

Following the lessons Heilbrun has taught in *Writing a Woman's
Life,* we can say that the making of a career like Heilbrun's is not an
accident; it is the product of ambition and will and courage. Heilbrun
deliberately and consciously made a reputation, constructed a public
self. This does not mean that every act was the product of calculation;
indeed, this book has made clear that Heilbrun has "made up" her self
as she went along—for scarcely any models were at hand. Moreover,
since she is a reserved person, these public steps could not be taken without anxiety and, sometimes, anguish. But the large ambition, the reach,
was always there.

In talking about teaching, Heilbrun recounted that in the "Biography and Autobiography" seminar she wanted to "get the class to understand what [she], of course, had learned through dire experience, how
hard it is to find a voice to speak in." With this book, I have tried to
show how Heilbrun has constructed her voice and forged her public self,
what she chose to hide at first, what she later revealed. Heilbrun has
created over the years an unmistakable voice: confident, emphatic, deliberate, audacious. It talks her into new positions. But it does not always
disguise the struggle, the vulnerabilities behind the clarity, the cost of a
developing range of risk. It does not flinch from challenge or from rage.
Wit is its weapon—to pry open a controversial topic, to skewer some
piece of pomposity or pretension, to control and direct the anger. Wit
also serves to protect: to keep the writer at a distance from the subject,
to preserve the private self.

If it is hard to find a voice to speak in, it is perhaps even harder to claim a place from which to speak. Heilbrun's characteristic location is best seen not from within the terms of the women's movement or academic feminism but from a vantage point outside those circles. Here we can find Heilbrun often choosing to address the unconvinced—those who have no sympathy with her positions, those who are fully entrenched in their own. From this point of view, *Reinventing Womanhood* exhorts and persuades those women who have not yet found their way to feminism rather than those who are already there. In the joint talk she gave with Catharine Stimpson, "Theories of Feminist Criticism: A Dialogue," in which they split the feminist critic into opposing selves within feminism, Heilbrun (as X) reveals her program as follows: "I am ready to use the literature of the world to train men to read themselves, rather than only to train women to notice how unheard or exploited they have been."[71] Her mission, then, was to change the minds of men. She opened a 1976 essay in the *Chronicle* with the statement: "The power to change the frightful imbalance of the sexes in the faculties of our institutions of higher education rests, I believe, with the two groups least likely, at first blush, to offer hopes for that change: men over and women under 40."[72] If those were the two groups least likely to change, then those were the two groups Heilbrun would address. In her many articles and important public addresses directed to the profession, she has argued to those presently in positions of power for the place of both feminism and women in the classroom. Her tone is tempered at first but becomes sharper as the years go by, the stakes become higher, and the audiences become more daunting. From time to time she turns to address those who most fire her anger and who, she thinks, are least likely to change, the Janet Mandelbaums, those "older academic women [who] appear to exist in an irreversible state of fear in the presence of their male colleagues."[73] A visual image for the locus I have been describing is Heilbrun's stand on the steps of Low Library, her back to the students, her face to those (the police, the institutional administration) who would threaten them. From this perspective, the places from which she has chosen to speak do not look quite so safe.

For the costs of choosing a public self are high, as we have seen: to be a public force is also to be a target; to have a public presence is also to suffer the unruly projections and distortions of an audience. A feminist public intellectual is particularly at risk: depending on her audience, she will be seen as too feminist or not feminist enough; she will be attacked for not speaking for everyone or she will be attacked as presuming to speak for everyone. Indeed, Heilbrun does not speak for everyone: she speaks primarily for those with education, with access to meaningful work, and with the means to make choice possible. Yet, in the places she has staked out for herself, she has spoken with force and with fortitude, and she has been speaking for four decades. Her grand subject is the formation of an achieving self and the ways of enlarging the possibilities for that self. Sometimes in the background, sometimes in the foreground is the accompanying story of her own evolving self: split, divided, reinvented, angry, yearning, lacking, achieving, risking, playing, disappearing—and always writing and rewriting. Heilbrun often walks a different path, writes against the grain of prevailing ideas, or travels a little out of step with them. She now has a community of women friends, her family, grandchildren—but at her core is isolation.

As I am faced with the difficulty of concluding this book and writing a final paragraph, I am heartened by the thought of Heilbrun's own resistance to endings: "We women have lived too much with closure," she says in the final pages of *Writing a Woman's Life*, "this is the delusion of a passive life." Heilbrun ends a book or an essay without presuming she has said the last word and without presuming she will never change her mind. Says the redoubtable Grace Knole from *The James Joyce Murder*, "You've got to keep going, and changing, or die."[74] The changes of Heilbrun's mind have been the theme of this book; its subject, a continuing intellectual journey.

Epilogue

The journey is over.
Love to all,

— CAROLYN

Death sets a Thing significant
The Eye had hurried by

— EMILY DICKINSON

And to think, we supposed we knew her. . . . We never know it all; we only make up stories about it, and sometimes our characters seem fully developed; but they have only fooled us again.

— CAROLYN G. HEILBRUN,
Sweet Death, Kind Death

When I wrote the last lines of what was the last chapter of this book sometime in April 1997, I was not sure if my acquaintance with Carolyn Heilbrun would survive beyond the book's publication. I knew that I would continue to be fascinated by what I had then described as Carolyn's "continuing intellectual journey," but our professional relationship was at an end—and I did not doubt that Carolyn would disagree with some of my conclusions. Unexpectedly, however, our acquaintance turned into a friendship that continued and deepened. We kept in touch over the years, increasingly so as time passed. I visited her many times in New York City; she visited me when I was living in Alexandria, Virginia, and we spent a sweltering summer day walking through the Vietnam and Roosevelt memorials. She also invited me on several occasions to her country house in Staatsburg, New York, a place where she closely guarded her solitude. Mostly, we kept in touch by frequent e-mails or telephone, talking about work, friends, family, politics, our passing states of mind, the seasons: she dreaded summer and its "dangers," welcoming the chilly dark of winter. We met for the last time during the Virginia Woolf Conference held at Smith College in June 2003. We walked the campus, lunched, and sat for an hour or two overlooking Paradise Pond. "Do you believe in destiny?" she asked. This was an old conversation with us, one in which I always came up blank, and she was always mystifying. She believed in chance, she said on this occasion, though, paradoxically, also in "pattern"; she did not know where the pattern came from, but believed that "in certain lives, things do happen when they must."

In July, Carolyn wrote to say that she had been invited to submit an essay to the Modern Language Association's journal, *PMLA*, "something non-lit-crit," different from the usual scholarly *PMLA* essay. In September, she asked if I would be willing to read the manuscript in progress; while she had often talked about showing me work before, this was the first time she actually did. During our telephone conversation about the manuscript, I proposed the title for that essay, "From Rereading to Reading"; the title reflected my hope, against the evidence, that the essay promised an intellectual move forward, another change of mind.[1] Six days later, a book arrived from Carolyn, Azar Nafisi's *Reading Lolita in Tehran,* a book affirming that reading matters in the world and that life and lives can be read against books. Later, I thought I recognized this gift as both a message and a gesture of goodbye.

The week beginning Sunday, 5 October 2003, seemed, on the face of it, to be a week like any other. Carolyn was in New York City while her husband, Jim, had gone to their Staatsburg house, taking Lucy the dog. On Tuesday, Carolyn took her customary walk with her old friend Mary Ann Caws.[2] I received several e-mails from Carolyn early that week; one, on Sunday, asked when I next planned to visit the city. On Thursday, 9 October, Carolyn's close friend Susan Heath arrived at her apartment by appointment for their weekly dinner. Just one week before, Carolyn had attended a book party given to celebrate the publication of her son Robert's first detective novel, *Offer of Proof.* At one point during the event, Jim had become ill—from what later turned out to be an allergy to wine—and Carolyn took him home, slipping away from the party without a word of goodbye.

When Susan Heath entered the apartment building, the elevator man remarked that he thought "Mrs. Heilbrun" was away because the mail had not been picked up from the doormat. Susan rang the doorbell but there was no answer—and then still no answer when she called from the phone downstairs as well. Susan insisted that the superintendent take her up in the freight elevator, which allowed access through the kitchen. She found Carolyn stretched out in the bed, dead, a plastic bag around her head. An autopsy revealed Carolyn had also taken a powerful concoction of alcohol and barbiturates, sedatives that could be relied on for their hypnotic, soporific effects. Carolyn was not leaving this outcome to chance.

On a bureau in the foyer, under a Don Bachardy drawing of Christopher Isherwood that Carolyn said her children always described as "a man holding his own severed head in his hands,"[3] an enigmatic note offered her final words: "The journey is over. Love to all, Carolyn." The suicide stunned, but the note shocked, too, by its brevity, by the fact that it was written on her formal headed notepaper, and by its closing sentiment: Carolyn, with her small circle of family and friends, was most unlikely to send her love to "all." Next to the reading chair in her study lay the detective novel she had published in 2000, *Honest Doubt*. On her desk a calendar, which displayed only one day at a time, was stopped at Tuesday, 7 October.

In her 1997 book, *The Last Gift of Time: Life beyond Sixty,* which appeared just after my book went to press, Carolyn had published her letter to the world that she would commit suicide—indeed, had planned to do so at the age of seventy: "Having supposed the sixties would be downhill all the way, I had long held a determination to commit suicide at seventy." With a jarring jauntiness she added, "Quit while you're ahead was, and is, my motto." While death itself was "welcome," she said, the prospect of long illness or living too long filled her with "deep anxiety and dread."[4] But seventy came and went, and because she was still productive and healthy, she had postponed the date with death; but lest we be lulled into believing she had rethought her plan, she cautioned: "Each day one can say to oneself: I can always die; do I choose death or life? I daily choose life the more earnestly because it is a choice."[5]

On that October day, Carolyn chose death.[6] She had done what she had insisted she would do, but somehow friends and family could not accept the news. Why now? She was healthy, as far as anyone knew. True, she was seventy-seven—aging, but surely not aged; and she had given no immediate warning. And why did she not send letters to her family and to her friends, all of whom anxiously watched the mail in the days following her death in the hope of some final message, some expression of farewell? She had time; she knew what she was planning. So why did she just leave a generic note on impersonal headed notepaper? Any death hauls its unwieldy baggage to the door of survivors, but suicide delivers a special mix of grief, anger, guilt, remorse, sorrow—and, of course, impenetrable mystery. As the days passed, the questions multiplied. Was Carolyn depressed, despondent, troubled, afraid? What could anyone have done or said to make her stay?

And yet—she had clearly spelled out her intention to kill herself. In *The Last Gift of Time,* she had written herself into a place where she must commit suicide. When I said to her once that she had carried the rhetoric of risk too far, written herself into a corner that eradicated rather than enabled choice, she looked at me and said: "You know, I do plan to commit suicide."

What made that day in October 2003 the right moment? We can speculate about some possible reasons. Carolyn had faced several professional disappointments in recent years: her last three detective novels had gone more or less unnoticed, and, for the first time, she was not able to persuade a publisher to issue in paperback her latest nonfiction book, *When Men Were the Only Models We Had: My Teachers Barzun, Fadiman, Trilling.* She believed she was losing her readership, falling into invisibility. And then came the thing she dreaded most: the lack of the next writing subject. She had made considerable headway on a book about female detectives but had been discouraged by her editor. She had also made several attempts to write about female poets of her generation—especially Adrienne Rich and Maxine Kumin—but, for a variety of reasons (including the noncooperation of the subjects), the projects fizzled out. The next book was simply not happening. On 28 November 2002, just about a year before her death and shortly after the publication of her last detective novel, *The Edge of Doom,* she wrote me an e-mail saying, "No, I'm not working on anything and am determined not to sink into despair at least until the new year."

Epilogue

Then, driving in the country in early May 2003, Jim had a car accident. While he was unharmed, it became clear that he would no longer feel confident about driving, and that marked a dramatic change in their lives and routines. One friend had suffered a stroke; another, undergoing a scheduled check-up, discovered she had a serious lung ailment. The political situation, especially the war in Iraq, added its weight. Carolyn took to speaking of last things: this would be her last detective story; her last speaking engagement. Anticipating, and as ever dreading, her scheduled appearance for a public interview at the Virginia Woolf Conference in June, she wrote to me on 23 April of that looming event: "My last venture forth," then, on 29 April: "I'm already thinking about dying so I don't have to go." But she had often made such vows, and the sentence about dying seemed a theatrical flourish, bracketed between her delight in reading Meg Wolitzer's *Wife* (we had bought copies in the local bookstore when I visited her in Staatsburg shortly before) and her pleasure both at her daughter Emily's visit and at the memory of accompanying her daughter Margaret and granddaughter Penelope on a three-generation "Take Your Daughter to Work" day.

Was she depressed, people asked? I can imagine the quizzical look with which Carolyn might have greeted that question, might have thrown up her hands that this one word, depression, was asked to cover so many forms and nuances of sadness. Certainly, she would not have taken antidepressant pills to blur the edges of her contact with the world. Yet, as she often acknowledged, a strain of melancholy haunted Carolyn. Perhaps sadness ran in her family. In *Reinventing Womanhood*, she writes: "Even now, I cannot think of the emptiness and futility of my mother's life without pain"; and, while she skims over it in less than a paragraph, she also writes in that book of her father's nervous breakdown and his subsequent psychoanalysis, which, she tells us, with an odd and notable exactness, lasted two and a quarter years. Her mother married her father, she relates, "against the advice of her doctor cousin, who said my father's mother was crazy."[7] In *The Last Gift of Time*, she reports that she reconnected to her father's family late in life and learned that some of her cousins "suffered deeply from depression and despair; one had committed suicide."[8] She herself steered clear of psychoanalysis, and perhaps she had the writer's fear that if she gave up her secrets, her writing life would dry up.[9] In *The Last Gift of Time,* she devotes a whole chapter to sadness; she ranges broadly over many kinds of sadness, personal and political, but dwells particularly on the sadness of her own death: "The idea of death, of one's disappearance from the stage, evokes the regret that these eyes, this appreciation, this particular apperception, will be gone from the world." Later, thinking of her children, she says, "I find myself reflecting that I shall miss them, all three, all differently when I am dead— even as I recognize this to be sentimental nonsense. What I mean is that I hope they will miss me, and such a hope inevitably contains a melancholy element."[10]

In 2000, Carolyn published an essay in a collection devoted to Christopher Isherwood. She lamented that not many people read this brief memoir of Isherwood—and she never reissued it elsewhere. The memoir, entitled "My Isherwood, My Bachardy," includes the account of a meeting she and Jim had with Isherwood and his partner, Don Bachardy, in Santa Monica in 1970, shortly after she had published a monograph on Isherwood for Columbia University Press—and it reveals as much about Carolyn as it does about Isherwood. In recalling what was, she admits, an "uncharacteristic" wish to meet the writer, she concludes that she was drawn to "Isherwood's search for a spiritual life." Then comes a surprising confession: "When I think back at how I dropped my spiritual angst, like an unwanted female Chinese baby, at their feet, to have that bundle returned to me with grace and something close to understanding I, even at my advanced age, squirm with embarrassment." In 1973, or so she recalls the date, she saw Isherwood and Bachardy again, at the December Modern Language Association Convention in New York City, and "they kindly went with me to an empty meeting room and tried to comfort me as I explained my sense of emptiness and purposelessness."[11] But Isherwood appeared at the MLA convention in 1974, not 1973. No doubt this is just a faulty recollection, yet it is worth noting that Carolyn's mother, Estelle, had died in March 1973, and "emptiness" is a word Carolyn has associated with her even as she, the accomplished daughter, has seemed to dissociate herself from her mother's lack of purpose (*"Even now, I cannot think of the emptiness and futility of my mother's life without pain"*).

We cannot know if her mother's life or her mother's death was linked in memory with these feelings of emptiness, though it is perhaps more than coincidence that her mother died at age seventy-seven, the same age at which Carolyn took her own life. More remarkably, as she looks back at this strange series of connections with Isherwood and Bachardy, Carolyn hits upon the startling image of an unwanted female Chinese baby to embody her angst. Of all unwanted babies, these are perhaps wanted least. Did she herself feel like an unwanted baby? In *Reinventing Womanhood*, Carolyn writes that her mother "had not planned to have children" and that she, Carolyn, was "left largely to care for [her]self," but she goes no further.[12] Yet, in e-mail correspondence with me in March 2005, Emily and Margaret, Carolyn's daughters, recalled that Carolyn had "often" said she was "specifically told that she was unwanted by her mother" and that her conception had resulted from a failure of birth control. Her mother had terminated at least one previous pregnancy, but this time, Archie, Carolyn's father, urged Estelle to have the child.

It was always difficult to get Carolyn to talk about her mother, but she acknowledged that Estelle was not attentive or demonstrative, though she invariably claimed that her mother's lack of attention allowed her the independence she craved. Carolyn did repeat one story several times: one summer, after sending Carolyn off to camp for several weeks, Estelle set sail for Europe, therefore missing all the visiting days at the camp. This memory of being the lone and lonely child without visitors seemed to shape Carolyn's memory of her relation to her mother. While I am not proposing an easy equation between Estelle's emotional unavailability and Carolyn's angst, we surely cannot ignore Carolyn's haunting repetition of an "emptiness" that connects her with Estelle and her image of an unwanted baby that resolutely disconnects them.

Unpredictably, the very private Carolyn trusted Isherwood and Bachardy with a confession that exposed her vulnerability. She was touched by their gracious responses, and visited, at their direction, a monk in a California monastery and a man who led a Vedanta group in New York; but, despite the genial receptions from Isherwood and Bachardy, something was wrong. She tells us, "Isherwood did not like women, certainly not women who were neither young nor outstandingly attractive; that distaste was early evident in our meeting and was never to become less so."[13] How telling that Carolyn describes Isherwood, her spiritual mentor, in almost the same terms she used in the 1970s to describe her relation to her unwilling intellectual mentor, Lionel Trilling: "Most women for whom male teachers become mentors turn to them with a devotion either daughterly or loverlike. I was neither attractive nor submissive enough to have made either role possible."[14] At the monastery, the monk, pointing to a hummingbird, directs attention away from "just a plain female" to the beautiful male.[15] Even in her seventies, when Carolyn wrote this essay, what strikes us is her overwhelming memory of rejection, the connection of angst with being female, the dogged attempts to seek acceptance from those least able or willing to give it.

When Carolyn saw Isherwood and Bachardy again in 1983, she says she "had outgrown [her] need for Isherwood's spiritual counsel," but perhaps that was simply a way of closing the topic and putting an end to the essay.[16] For in 1983, she was putting the finishing touches to *Sweet Death, Kind Death,* a novel whose central character, Patrice Umphelby, has a plan to commit suicide. At the time, a full two decades before Carolyn's own death, the novel seemed (to me, at least) to be about the threat posed by revolutionary theories about women's middle years, about the puzzling antifeminism of women's colleges, and about the complexities of writing a woman's life (two biographers are writing Patrice's life). Patrice's eccentric attitude toward death certainly seemed provocative, but, especially since she is, in fact, murdered, hers was a view readers were freed from seriously confronting.

In retrospect, however, we see that *Sweet Death, Kind Death* anticipates many of the themes of *The Last Gift of Time,* including Carolyn's theory of suicide. Patrice, who is dead when the novel opens, has many close similarities to Carolyn; perhaps, indeed, in her name, Umphelby, Carolyn slyly planted a split and secret "m--e." We learn that, before her death, Patrice was a professor of history, wore serviceable clothes, spoke her mind, was a thorn in the institution's side, and wrote successful fiction as well as scholarly books on the newfound power of middle-aged women. Like Carolyn, Patrice believed the idea of death invested the present with intensity and determined to commit suicide. Patrice was indeed "in love with death," but she believed "the proper span of human life [was] three score years and ten" and would not hasten death, though she feared living past "the proper moment" when she had the mental and physical ability to make the choice. In the only encounter between Kate Fansler and Patrice in a fog-bound airport, they discuss subjects Carolyn herself continued to worry at: destiny and the nonexistence of God.[17] In as late a novel as *The Puzzled Heart* (1998), Kate dwells on "the purposelessness of existence, . . . the lack of reason for so much that occurred. It was a sin of the spirit, she knew; a failure of faith in the rightness of the universe—of God, in short. Yet she doubted that acedia was limited to agnostics or to those who had lost their faith. Indeed, she knew it was not."[18]

The matter of a spiritual quest returns again in the last essays Carolyn wrote. One, a contribution to the special issue "Women Aging," was published in the *Women's Review of Books* in July 2003; the other, "From Rereading to Reading" (mentioned earlier), was issued posthumously in the March 2004 *PMLA*. In the essay on aging, "Taking a U-turn: The Aging Woman as Explorer of New Territory," the title baffles by its seeming contradiction: how does one who is reversing direction explore new territory? Is the new territory simply old territory seen from a new (reversed) perspective? Or is a U-turn merely another way of going round in circles? The essay leaks exhaustion: "I had . . . grown weary . . . ; I had grown weary," Carolyn says, speaking of the failures of feminism. To reignite her "capacity for attention," she turns to, for her, the new territory of science, to the men of science, whose achievements have lasting significance and who offer a model of life in which work is primary, domestic life and relationships secondary.[19] What is the psychic drama played out here? If the achievements of feminism are rolled back, if women are still to be judged primarily as wives and mothers, what will Carolyn's life and work have meant? But if men's lives are the only models, what more can she say of that?[20] Indeed, she will not write about this new territory of science even as she, who has defined her life by work, fears "living with the certainty that there is no further work demanding to be done." Asking "what part has God in [the universe]?" she affirms her agnosticism, finding truth in Wallace Stevens's "Sunday Morning": "We live in an old chaos of the sun."[21]

I have written elsewhere of "From Rereading to Reading," in which Carolyn returns once again to the possibility of exploring a new universe: she knows that if she is to stay mentally alive, she must find new subjects, must stop repeating and circling back.[22] But the new universe, in its old chaos, offers little comfort, no answers, a dead end. If the spiritual struggles of Wallace Stevens stand behind "Taking a U-turn," the *Rubáiyát*—with its questions about meaning, about faith, and its focus on living intensely in the present moment—shadows "From Rereading to Reading."[23] Carolyn's own book, *Honest Doubt,* left at her death next to her reading chair, draws its title from Alfred Lord Tennyson's *In Memoriam,* an elegy for his friend Arthur Henry Hallam, in which Tennyson, too, wrestles with faith and doubt.[24] Carolyn seems to resolve her struggle in favor of doubt, but such a resolution paradoxically provokes its own persistent questions. Toward the end of "Taking a U-turn," Carolyn reflects on her decision, recorded in *The Last Gift of Time,* to take her own life; in this essay, she does not make a declaration but asks a final question: "Is the end of the journey now near?"[25]

And so we point to some possible reasons that add up to that October decision: the intellectual and emotional exhaustion, the lack of inspiriting work, the spiritual angst, the questions about her life's work, the sense of things running down. We study Carolyn's given reasons and we list some other possible reasons, but we are still not satisfied. The suicide of a friend or a public figure disrupts our own assumptions about the value and meaning of life and its proper span— and so, challenged and threatened, we search for the reasons behind the reasons. Toward the end of *A Trap for Fools,* Kate remarks of literature professors, "We deal in subtexts, in the hidden story."[26] At one point, when we talked about that last *PMLA* essay, Carolyn told me she worked in "layers." And so we reread Carolyn's work, the fiction against the nonfiction, and wonder about the layers, the hidden story.

Hunting for clues, I find myself dwelling on several passages from *Writing a Woman's Life,* all of them having to do with Carolyn's relationship to her fictional character Kate Fansler. The first comes from chapter 6, the chapter devoted to Amanda Cross:

> And it is [Kate Fansler], rather than the persona "Amanda Cross," who has come to be a presence in my life. . . . I remember reading once that Simenon, when he had ignored Maigret for many months,

would find him waiting around corners, silently confronting his creator, demanding incarnation, or at least attention. So it has been with Kate. And when I recently promised not to begin a new detective novel until I had finished another, different kind of book, she would not let me be. So for the first time I wrote short stories about her, told by her niece Leighton Fansler as a kind of Watson. Though I have often thought in the past that I would write no more detective novels, I now think that I shall probably be forced to write them as long as Kate is there to nudge me.[27]

The second passage, the quotation with which I began this book, is from the introduction, where Carolyn famously sets forth her declaration that there are four ways to write a woman's life:

the woman herself may tell it, in what she chooses to call an autobiography; she may tell it in what she chooses to call fiction; a biographer, woman or man, may write the woman's life in what is called a biography; or the woman may write her own life in advance of living it, *unconsciously,* and without recognizing or naming the process. (my italics)[28]

Again in chapter 6, Carolyn is recording her reasons for having become a writer of detective stories—and then comes this:

All the conscious reasons for writing were good ones; they operated, they were sufficient to explain my actions. Yet the real reasons [for writing fiction] permitted me . . . *to write my own life on a level far below consciousness,* making it possible for me to experience what I would not have had the courage to undertake in full awareness. (my italics)[29]

"A level far below consciousness." What did she mean by this mysterious phrase? It becomes even more mysterious when we recall that Carolyn claimed not to have much truck with the unconscious. She invariably dismissed what she called psychobabble and claimed no acquaintance with unruly introspection. How then did she know consciously she was writing her life unconsciously? Were there subjects she

knew she was consciously avoiding but yet approaching in her fiction? The first quotation I have offered here suggests a recurring dream: the ghosts of Kate and Leighton beckoning her to write even though she had determined not to. Rereading Carolyn's work, I find myself contemplating the ways in which the detective fiction might have recorded Carolyn's life on a level far below consciousness.

Carolyn wrote these words about the importance of Kate in her life and about the unconscious sometime around 1987. She had turned sixty in 1986; Carolyn had always paid careful attention to the decades of her life, and sixty was a crucial birthday, as she was to record in *The Last Gift of Time*. Despite the fact that sixty seems relatively young these days, Carolyn was beginning to think of herself, and to describe herself, as old. What were the fictions she was writing at that time? In 1986, she had published a novel with the enigmatic title *No Word from Winifred*. In the introduction to her *Collected Stories,* Carolyn tells us that the story that beckoned in 1987 was "Tania's Nowhere,"[30] one of a trio of stories dating from that time narrated by Leighton Fansler. A later story, "The Disappearance of Great Aunt Flavia," was also told by Leighton. In chapter 6 of this book, "Stepping Out of the Circle," I wrote about the disappearing/invisible woman, including as well in this category a story called "Murder without a Text." I puzzled over the women in Carolyn's fiction who disappear without a word and whose disappearances are never fully accounted for in the logical terms that the detective story conventionally demands. A thread was left dangling; and so I find myself coming back to that mystery here, a mystery that has, of course, become even more poignant in the wake of Carolyn's own disappearance.

No Word from Winifred and "Tania's Nowhere" emerge from the same imaginative moment: in both, a woman slips out of her life without a word to anyone and simply disappears. As I remarked in that earlier chapter, Carolyn once told me that she regarded *No Word from Winifred* as one of her best novels, and so it obviously had particular significance for her. As a way of focusing on this wish to disappear, I return now to the little-known "Tania's Nowhere," the short story that begged to be written when Carolyn had promised her publisher that she would not write a story until *Writing a Woman's Life* was finished, the story that raised so many questions for me when I first wrote about it in these pages. What follows is a kind of meditation on that story, one thought opening to another.[31]

The barest bones of the story are these: at the age of sixty-two, Tania Finship disappears, without a word or a sign, from her life in New York as a professor of Russian literature, as a wife, and as a mother of grown children.[32] Kate Fansler, called in to solve the case, discovers Tania driving a horse-drawn carriage around Central Park, cross-dressed in the costume of an Edwardian cabbie. At the end, Tania returns to her job and her family.

In the introduction to *The Collected Stories*, recalling the origin of "Tania's Nowhere," Carolyn writes: "the thought of a story about Kate Fansler came to me."[33] So is this not so much a story about Tania Finship (whose name suggests kinship) as it is a story about Kate herself—a story of kinship with Kate? Of the mystery of Tania's disappearance, Leighton the narrator says, "only Kate could have solved it." Indeed, after Kate hears Tania's story of escape, Kate tells her, "I understand more than you'll ever know about how you felt."[34] With respect to kinship, we note that Carolyn herself was just over sixty and was a professor in New York with a husband and grown children. She had lived in the same apartment on Central Park West for more than three decades, taught at the same university for close to three decades, stayed married to the same husband for more than four decades—though, not too long after writing "Tania's Nowhere," she would purchase a lithograph, called *Departure*, depicting three variations of a woman, with suitcase in hand, in the act of walking away from the viewer. (I reflected on this lithograph in chapter 7 of this book, "A Rhetoric of Risk.") In telephone and e-mail conversations with the artist, Ruth Weisberg, in June 2005, I learned that Carolyn had made a special visit to her Venice, California, studio. "Carolyn admired several [prints and drawings]," recalled Weisberg, "but her response to *Departure* was of a different order. There seemed to be an immediate visceral reaction and what I would call a sense of recognition. She seemed riveted and quite sure that this was the one she wanted to have." Margaret Heilbrun, in an e-mail to me on 29 June 2005, "clearly" remembers Carolyn explaining the image to her: "She said to me, 'You see, the woman has decided to leave and she starts to leave and then there's that moment when she stops and looks back, and then she does leave.'" According to Margaret, Carolyn viewed the picture as three phases of one process of departure, "with the middle clearly understood by [Carolyn] to be a moment of uneasiness about the decision." Indeed, now the lithograph takes on added freight, as surely do the conversations Carolyn and I had about the film *Thelma and Louise*.[35]

Perhaps, given its literal closeness to home, Tania's story needed to be told at several removes. In the story, Tania describes her escape as a "dream." We have Tania's dream within Carolyn's dream of a summons from Kate via Leighton; and we have narrations within narrations: from Tania to Kate to Leighton, to the silenced (disappearing) Amanda Cross, to the Carolyn supposedly preoccupied with something else when Kate and Leighton came knocking. And all the narrations have gaps and silences: "But if you decide to go back, . . . 'Never apologize, never explain,'" says Kate to Tania of a story that surely requires some explanation.[36]

I teach an introductory writing course called, as it happens, "Leaving Home," and this past semester I gave the students two stories to read side by side: "Tania's Nowhere" and Nathaniel Hawthorne's "Wakefield." I offered no background information about the authors; the students simply read and discussed the texts—the one about a woman, the other about a man—and then wrote papers about why these characters had left their homes. Some students condemned Tania for her "selfish" desertion; others admired her choice to depart her humdrum life; and one student read her exit as an attempt to escape her fear of death. Fear of death, I wondered silently, or possession by it? And so my student opened the door, and death (which I had been thinking about all along) made its entrance.

Leighton introduces Tania's story thus: "What was clear to Kate at the very beginning of the case was that, by the time Tania Finship was sixty-two and almost the oldest member of the faculty in her department, or anywhere else, she had become beloved. After her disappearance, it became clear that, in the opinion of her colleagues and students, she had not known this." Would she not have left had she thought she was loved? At the end of the story, when Tania returns to her familiar world, her family and colleagues are "glad" to see her, "so she found out she was loved."[37] In *Writing a Woman's Life*, in a passage about Virginia Woolf that follows hard upon the admission that Carolyn was writing the Fansler stories on a level far below consciousness, Carolyn writes: "[Woolf] needed to be loved, and she knew it. Most of us women, I think, transform our need to be loved into a need to love, expecting, therefore, of men and of children, more than they, caught in their own lives, can give us."[38]

Hawthorne's Wakefield also leaves home in part with the intent of finding out whether he is loved. Having settled in the next street to spy upon his wife, he wants to know that she misses him, really misses him: "He will not go back until she be frightened half to death." Roused to an unfamiliar intensity, some "energy of feeling" when he witnesses a doctor's visit to his grieving wife, he still fails to return to relieve his wife of her suffering; perhaps she will even die of her sorrow. But she recovers, and the years pass, and she grows plump and content again. After twenty years, he inexplicably finds himself in front of his old house, ready to mount the steps. The narrator intervenes to cry, "Stay, Wakefield! Would you go to the sole home that is left you? Then step into your grave!"[39] As Wakefield crosses the threshold, the narrator offers this ominous pronouncement: "Amid the seeming confusion of our mysterious world, individuals are so nicely adjusted to a system, and systems to one another, and to a whole, that by stepping aside for a moment a man exposes himself to a fearful risk of losing his place for ever. Like Wakefield, he may become, as it were, the outcast of the universe."[40]

For Hawthorne, Wakefield's desertion of his family, his utter coldness of heart, is a death sentence, a suicide. In freeing himself from systems and obligations, in attempting perhaps to live with more intensity, he has exiled himself from life; he is the outcast of the universe. "Outcast" is also the word that Virginia Woolf uses in a journal entry written about an occasion when she wanted to escape Richmond for London but Leonard intercepted her, fearing for the balance of her mind if she went to the busy, chaotic city: "I felt it was intolerable to sit about, & must do the final thing, which was to go to London. . . . Saw men & women walking together; thought, you're safe and happy[,] I'm an outcast."[41] Tania, too, wishes to escape obligations and systems, the sheer dailiness that robs life of its edge: "Mine has been such an orderly life," she says, and she imagines that her disappearance will be good for her husband, Tom, as well: "He's been worried," she says, "but I bet he's also felt alive." Tom, however, seems to value their routine. He tells Kate: "It was a good life. Regular. . . . Every day was just like every other."[42]

Later, when Tania asks Kate how she solved the mystery, she responds that light began to dawn when Tom quoted a line from *Macbeth* but attributed it to *Hamlet*. Kate says, "Hamlet may really have been closer: 'I could be bounded in a nutshell, and count myself a king of infinite space, were it not that I have bad dreams.'" Then she asks Tania, "Was that it, or was it Macbeth: 'cabined, cribbed, confined?'"[43]

We might meditate on what it means that Tania feels cabined, cribbed, and confined—or that she has bad dreams. We might even ask why it is significant that Tom has confused *Hamlet* with *Macbeth*. Yet, when I Googled the quotation from *Macbeth* to review the context, I found myself on a Web page composed by Bill Peschel on Dorothy Sayers. There I discovered that Miss Climpson, a character in Sayers's *Unnatural Death,* makes Tom's mistake of misattributing the same quotation to *Hamlet.*[44] Is Carolyn paying a kind of insider's homage to Sayers? Or is she thinking, below consciousness, perhaps, of the book's title—*Unnatural Death*—or of the old lady, dying of cancer, whose death at the beginning of that novel nevertheless seems "sudden, unexpected, . . . mysterious"?[45]

Tania's adventure takes an unusual form. She does not flee to some exotic isle, make off with a new partner, learn to fly or paint, buy a Porsche, or ferret out rare orchids—but, having shed the commitments and requirements of her former life, she drives a carriage in Central Park just a few blocks from where she lives. On the face of it, on the literal level, a very odd choice. What fantasy, what need *below consciousness,* does the act of driving a carriage seem to satisfy? And so, perhaps, we come to the heart of the story. In the final chapter of *The Last Gift of Time,* called "On Mortality," Carolyn says, "As I have admitted, I was, at the end of my sixties, 'half in love with easeful death'—to borrow Keats's lovely phrase—turning every consciously considered moment of life into a balance: life or death." And then she quotes Emily Dickinson:

> Because I could not stop for Death—
> He kindly stopped for me—
> The Carriage held but just Ourselves—
> And Immortality.[46]

When Carolyn via Amanda via Leighton via Kate sent Tania off to be a carriage driver, was she thinking of Dickinson's carriage ride, perhaps the most famous carriage ride in literature?

> Because I could not stop for Death—

Or should it be:

> Because Death would not stop for me—
> I kindly stopped for Him—

Tania becomes Death; Death becomes her: she is the most civil of the carriage drivers; the most elegant in her spiffy suit; the most knowledgeable about the park. She is he. And we note that Kate, not Tania, is Death's passenger.

Dickinson's poem continues:

> We passed the School, where Children strove
> At Recess—in the Ring—[47]

Tania and Kate pass the carousel, where the painted horses circle round and round in a deadly dance without choice or point.

Dickinson's carriage is destined for the "House that seemed / A Swelling of the Ground—." Is Tania's carriage on its way to "Room Nineteen," to a "Room of One's Own"?[48] The drive is the letting go, the wrenching free from commitments, from the old pull of relationships, from the obligations of womanhood that men of science cannot know. In "Tulips," Sylvia Plath captures this liminal moment, the tug of war between life and death: from her hospital bed, wanting only to let go, she sees the photograph of her husband and child: "Their smiles catch on to my skin, little smiling hooks."[49]

And so to the title: "Tania's Nowhere." Almost at the end of the elegiac last chapter of *The Last Gift of Time,* Carolyn quotes Stevie Smith:

> Why do I think of Death
> As a friend?
> It is because he is a scatterer,
> He scatters the human frame
> The nerviness and the great pain,
> Throws it on the fresh fresh air
> And now it is nowhere.
> Only sweet death does this,
> Sweet Death, kind Death,
> Of all the gods you are the best.[50]

This poem became the epigraph to *Sweet Death, Kind Death,* the novel whose main character intends to commit suicide (though she does not take her own life), the novel that takes on a new significance after Carolyn's own death. Does this image of death scattering the human frame, which is now in some utopian "nowhere," explain the enigmatic title and the inspiration for "Tania's Nowhere"?

I am suggesting, of course, that the dream that beckoned Carolyn while she was writing about life in *Writing a Woman's Life* was a dream about death; indeed, the story works as a dream in ways that it fails as a story, for Tania's motivations, Tania's relationships are never really explored. It is a dream of being sixty, of a struggle with being loved and slipping free, of connection and disconnection—and perhaps of immortality, that other figure in Dickinson's carriage. It is a dream of controlling death, for Tania is the driver; and so perhaps my student, who spoke of Tania's fear of death, was right after all.

But it is also, significantly—in 1987—the dream of a return. In the end, Tania comes back to her old life, called, it seems, by the sight of Kate grading papers: the old summons back to work. Kate rescues Tania from the brink even as she nudges Carolyn to write Kate's stories. And so Tania returns with the secret knowledge earned by all those questing heroes who travel to the underworld, knowledge that, however, cannot be shared (as Kate had instructed: "Never apologize, never explain"). Indeed, "no one ever knew where she'd been."[51]

Ten years later, in 1997, Carolyn published *The Last Gift of Time*. The first essay following the preface, in which she reveals her decision to commit suicide, is called "The Small House." Carolyn recounts how, as her grown children and their families and friends make increasing use of the family's long-owned country house (in Alford, Massachusetts), she determines "secretly" to buy a house of her own, where she can enjoy weekend solitude without disturbance. Before too long, she finds her "dream retreat" in Staatsburg:

> It had been hopefully built twenty years ago as a barn destined to be turned by someone into a dwelling. A perfectly square building with a large window evoking a hayloft, this new, cowless barn stood for some time, like a beached and deserted ship, on a windy hill. The builder camped out in the back of his unsold barn, waiting; then, in the 1980s, a couple, enraptured and challenged, bought the barn and designed an inside. They left a huge living room, with a neat kitchen attached; above, with balconies that looked down on the living room, was an only slightly smaller bedroom with a cathedral ceiling.[52]

This dream house bears a startling resemblance to the retreat she had imagined some ten years before for Winifred in *No Word from Winifred,* the book that had special meaning for Carolyn. When Winifred disappears from her life and takes up a solitary existence milking cows and writing, the house she escapes to is described by Winifred as follows: "It was an A-frame, built for some family reason. . . . A-frames were a big thing in the late '60's. They were easily put up, had high 'cathedral' ceilings, a bath and kitchen. The sleeping area was a loft built over the back half of the main room, and this detracted from the appeal of the place for all but the young and active. . . . I like heights and space; I liked the pointed ceiling."[53] Winifred relates that the cabin she "had [previously] been occupying was cramped, and cheap";[54]

she, too, then, had been "cabined, cribbed, confined." Writing "in advance of living," Carolyn creates a solitary refuge for Winifred that, some ten years later, she translates into reality for herself. The gap between fiction and nonfiction, dream and reality is closing; indeed, we need to look more closely at this house. Of her plans for the house, Carolyn says: "I intended to put no pictures on the walls; I wanted it like this: stark, unadorned, comfortable."[55] The last adjective surprises in its context—comfortable?—unless we take it as meaning the offer of consolation against grief and sadness. Carolyn tells us she wants this house to separate her from family, a house where she will enjoy solitude. We are reminded, perhaps, of the chilling portrait recounted in *Honest Doubt* of Dean Kimberly, who has chosen solitude and abandoned her domestic life, having divorced her husband and arranged to see her grown children and grandchildren only rarely.[56] Dean Kimberly describes her "contentment" in a home that is "quiet, tidy . . . with no thought of anyone else in my space."[57] At the end of Carolyn's essay about her house, however, she describes her husband knocking at the door; he has arrived to keep her company, and she is pleased to see him. He stays, and, as time goes on, they take up their old weekend togetherness. She muses, "I wanted to prove I could be a woman alone, and I had failed": the essay that began with "I" ends with "we."[58]

But this was not the way the real story ended. Carolyn unilaterally decided that she and Jim should take turns visiting the Staatsburg house—she one weekend, he the next. She did indeed succeed in being a woman alone there and allowed few visitors. Invited to the house on several occasions, I was struck by the bareness, the sheer emptiness of the space.[59] Looking back now on that house and Carolyn in it, I see her as deliberately emptying her life, flattening out the emotions, erasing memory—practicing solitude, preparing for the long silence. In choosing her house, she says she wanted no old trees: "We had magnificent ancient sugar maples at the other house; they died, they lost limbs, they collapsed in unexpected storms. I loved them and they threatened to break my heart." This house, immune from emotion ("I didn't . . . want to love this new house"), and significantly evoked as a "stark wooden rectangle on a windy hill,"[60] recalls again the house in Dickinson's poem:

Epilogue

We paused before a House that seemed
A Swelling of the Ground—
The Roof was scarcely visible—
The Cornice—in the Ground—

In this respect, Carolyn's epigraph to her essay on the "small house," from W. H. Auden's "Thanksgiving for a Habitat," is especially telling, for it seems to deny while acknowledging the fantasy behind the fantasy of the house:

> a toft-and-croft
> where I needn't, ever, be at home *to*
>
> those I am not at home *with* . . .
> . . . .
> and not a windowless grave, but a place
> I may go both in and out of.[61]

Had Carolyn ever come close to death? Where did the fear, the love, the need to control come from? Thinking of Plath's poem "Tulips" again, I reflect that, shortly after this book was published, Carolyn told me that, at the age of forty, she had been diagnosed with breast cancer. Very few people knew of this—either at the time or since: her husband, of course; her oldest friend, Tom Driver; a few other close friends; and in due course her son and her daughters, who needed to know to protect their own health. But despite the fact that she had written about many personal aspects of her life, indeed, had published in 1997 *The Last Gift of Time,* the closest she had come to a full-length memoir, she had never written about her breast cancer. Or, at least, she had not written about it directly. Interestingly enough, Patrice in *Sweet Death, Kind Death* also had suffered from breast cancer; she, too, had kept it secret. Patrice's daughter says, "She didn't choose to talk about it— I think hugging secrets to oneself was a hallmark of her generation, at least its women, perhaps because all the struggles were so hard."[62] Over a period of years, I asked Carolyn many times why she had not

written about her cancer. "What's the point? No one would be interested," she repeated, refusing to recognize how significant, for many
women, this news would be.

Carolyn had turned forty in 1966. Despite the openness of the
era, there was not much frank discussion of breast cancer at that time.
Of all diseases that attack women, it was—and perhaps is—the most
feared, striking at sexuality, femininity, and possibly life itself. And
Carolyn was young, with three children under the age of eleven. In
those days, the typical treatment was a radical mastectomy followed
by cobalt radiation, which often left burn scars. A few years later, in
the midseventies, Betty Ford and Happy Rockefeller, two prominent
women of Carolyn's generation (Ford was born in 1918, Rockefeller
in 1926), would reveal their battles with breast cancer, opening the
subject to public discussion and, in the process, saving many women's
lives. But Carolyn kept her secret. She saw herself as a feminist pioneer—as a fearless confronter of aging and its attendant discontents—
but this she could not discuss.

But what was it she could not discuss? Did she fear the diminu-
tion of attraction, questions about her sexuality? Was she ashamed of
her body? Did her sense of being "mutilated" explain her avoidance
of mirrors and photographs, the frequent self-deprecatory remarks
about her appearance? When we first talked about the cancer, I asked
if she had thought she would die. "Not really," she responded; after
the operation she just got on with her life. But each time she told me
the story, she would add new details. Usually, when Carolyn recounted
stories of the past, they tended to be the same each time, as if the telling of them had shaped how they would always be told. This was particularly true of stories about Columbia, say, or about her family. But
the breast cancer was different. In September 2001, she telephoned me,
ostensibly to talk about a new biography of Edna St. Vincent Millay.
But somehow the conversation turned to illness: the illness of a friend
and then her own past illness. On this occasion, she told me that the
operation had taken place barely a month after her fortieth birthday,
on 9 February 1966; she who was vague about most dates clearly had
this one wedged in her brain. She had been aware of a lump in her
breast for years, but the doctors had dismissed it. By the time the lump
was deemed cancerous, it was a "mass" that filled her whole breast.

She had a radical mastectomy, which included removal of the muscle in the chest wall and lymph nodes; cobalt treatment followed. The operation was "utterly deforming," she revealed, "horribly disfiguring."

"No one expected me to live," she said, and so I asked her again if *she* thought she would die. I cannot say whether by this time she trusted me more or was more prepared to remember, but she offered: "I assumed I would die." From that operation, she said, dated her decision to live her life intensely, wasting no time, making every moment precious. "It changed my life," she said. "It was then that I gave up dinner parties"—"dinner parties" being the code, I understood, for the sort of superficial, social behaviors that kill time rather than making the most of it. She would only do "what mattered to [her]," by which she meant work and spending time with people she prized. "That judgment of intensity," she concluded, "I really have stuck by it."[63] In *Sweet Death, Kind Death,* one of Patrice's biographers points out that Patrice, too, changed fundamentally after her husband was killed: "It [the death] marks a change in her life; after her period of grief and mourning a profound switch, such as one finds often in those who have been close to death. One's whole scale of what is important seems to shift: social niceties fade, those conversations and events which offer intensity matter more. Life becomes both more and less valuable."[64]

Subsequently, Carolyn avoided doctors whenever possible, though she did have some cancerous moles removed from her face; nevertheless, it was clear that if disease struck again, she would be prepared. I am suggesting that her mental preparation was long, that she imagined herself (wrote herself) into the place where her own death, her own "disappearance from the stage," was possible. She staged, if you like, elaborate rehearsals, though whether below consciousness or not we have no way of knowing. Signs of her preoccupation appear even as early as 1970, when she introduces, in *Poetic Justice,* a character (like Patrice, a surrogate for herself) named Emilia Airhart, an unmistakable reference to Amelia Earhart, famous both for her pioneering aviation and for her mysterious disappearance.

Carolyn's catalog of refusals lengthened in the last years: the list of things she would no longer do. Finally, as she announces in her last two essays, that catalog would include writing for publication. Even the acquisition of a dog—the dog (as she writes in *The Last Gift of*

Time) that would encourage her out of the house into daily exercise—strikes me now rather as a way of withdrawing from professional obligations: "I do not think I go out during the day as often as I used to. . . . Perhaps if I did not have [the dog], I would accept more speaking engagements."[65] E-mail, too, which she also extols in *The Last Gift of Time,* was a way of replacing calls and visits. She was busy emptying her life, purging desire, learning not to miss things, disciplining her imagination, disconnecting from family and friends. The emptiness she once dreaded was now the object of her desire. Perhaps this is why she could not write those last letters of farewell we all wanted; to have done so would have been to undo her slow process of making a solitude.

This preparation, both in Carolyn's life and in her work, was in the service of performing her idea of the good death. For in taking her life, what she also refused was disease, endless medications, mutilation by surgeries, frailty, failing faculties, caretaking, and—most of all—dependency: the intolerable burdening of, and the relinquishment of control to, others. She did not, after all, commit suicide at sixty or even at seventy. She practiced a long restraint; she waited until she believed she had written herself out and had no more work to do, until she had decided, as Patrice had concluded, "life was not worth living."[66] She waited until seventy-seven, the age at which her own mother had died. Did she consider the effect of this chosen death on others, especially on those close to her? In "Tania's Nowhere," Tania thinks her disappearance has made her husband feel "alive";[67] in *Sweet Death, Kind Death,* Patrice's daughter says of her mother, "There was more space for me when she was gone."[68] But nowhere does Carolyn seem to imagine the darker drift of suicide, the circles spreading out from a private choice made in solitude.[69]

Inevitably, feminists must ask whether Carolyn intended her choice of death to serve as a model. Throughout her writing life, and especially in *Writing a Woman's Life,* she had offered new ways to envision the plots of women's lives. In particular, she had focused on the middle and later years, traditionally periods when women felt their powers fading, as opportunities for new directions and beginnings. But a beginning also requires an ending—and clearly Carolyn had thought long and hard about the ending of her own story. The decision to end her life at a moment of her choosing grew logically out of her belief that women should reinvent their selves, write their own texts, and take charge of their own destinies. Yet I hope this book has also suggested that Carolyn's striving toward selfhood was never easy, that self-realization involved a struggle with self-doubt and sometimes self-disdain; indeed, her final choice came from a particular set of experiences, from a particular intellectual, emotional, and psychological constellation. In *Sweet Death, Kind Death,* Patrice's biographers, thinking that she has indeed committed suicide, worry about how to treat her choice in their biography:

> [Archer and Herbert] were also deeply troubled that, in speaking honestly of Patrice's love of death, of her knowledge of how death gave intensity to middle age as passion and hope gave intensity to youth, they might mislead the young. [They] were afraid that every discouraged young person would take Patrice's welcome of the idea of death as an invitation to youthful suicide, and that would be a terrible thing indeed. For suicide in youth and at seventy are as different as are a youthful woman and a woman of seventy.[70]

Writing of what I have described as Carolyn's preparation for death, I am aware of the distortion that comes from focusing too entirely on the subtext. The text recedes and all we see is subtext. In *The Last Gift of Time,* Carolyn memorably describes her life as "borrowed time." "Each day," she writes, "one can say to oneself: I can always die; do I choose death or life? I daily choose life the more earnestly because it is a choice."[71] For if she was "in love" with death, and if she disciplined herself for death, she was also in love with life: she lit up when there was talk of more work to do, thrilled by the requests for essays from *Women's Review of Books* and *PMLA* in the last months before her death. The impulse toward life and the impulse toward a death that would happen only "at the proper moment" constituted an ongoing struggle. On 14 August 2003, she wrote to me: "All my good friends are social people, devoted to their extended families. The friends I have like me seem to vanish into utter solitude. I hope I don't. Right now I'm feeling a bit on top of things." *"I hope I don't."* Carolyn wanted to be wooed by life even as she was seduced by death. Despite her valiant efforts, it is possible she did not escape the romance plot in the end.

I do not believe she planned the day of her death long in advance. The conditions had to obtain: an empty apartment, the assurance that she would be found by her friend Susan Heath. But ultimately, I think she let chance pick the day. The pattern, after all, was set.

Summoning her up, I am walking with her on New York streets. She stops often to look at me while she makes or takes a point. Like a crazy New York politician, she meets and greets every single dog, noting out loud its approximate age, its pedigree, and its temperament. She has a strange special voice for dogs, high-pitched and girlish. In a restaurant, she orders heartily: lamb chops or some thick cut of beef. "You will think I'm conventional," she says (no chance), though she assures me that with her friend Nancy Miller she has now taken to eating sushi and feels most adventurous. We sit for hours and drink a whole bottle of wine. While we savor our good food, she always asks me how my spiritual life is.

I close with a final return to that haunting matter of the disappearing woman. My friend Judith Fetterley calls me as I am finishing this epilogue and tells me to read a story recounted in Carol Lee Flinders's book *At the Root of This Longing: Reconciling a Spiritual Hunger and a Feminist Thirst.* The story concerns the selkie, "the creature ubiquitous in North Sea legend who is a woman on land and seal at sea." I offer it now as a coda:

> When a selkie removes her sealskin to rest on a beach, says the tradition, she can be captured and kept as a woman by whoever seizes the sealskin. The story has many tellings, but in most the selkie lives on land and bears a child, maybe several, and has entirely forgotten who she really is. But one day she finds the sealskin, and, overwhelmed by longing for the sea and the liberty she'd known there, she slips it on and disappears, leaving a grieving family behind.[72]

Notes

Abbreviations

ARNWBC   *Annual Reports Number of the Wellesley College Bulletin*
CDS   *Columbia Daily Spectator*
CNWCB   *Catalogue Number of the Wellesley College Bulletin*
NYT   *New York Times*

Introduction

1. Carolyn G. Heilbrun, *Writing a Woman's Life* (New York: Norton, 1988), 26.

2. Carolyn G. Heilbrun, *Reinventing Womanhood* (New York: Norton, 1979), 16.

3. See Betty Friedan, "The Forfeited Self," in *The Feminine Mystique* (New York: Norton, 1963; reprint, New York: Dell, 1964), 299–325 (citations are to the reprint edition).

4. Carolyn G. Heilbrun [Amanda Cross, pseud.], *The Players Come Again* (New York: Random House, 1990), 216.

1. "Thy People, My People"

1. See Heilbrun, *Reinventing Womanhood,* 19, 52–53, 55, 57, 58, 59, and chapters 1 and 2 generally.

2. I conducted interviews with Carolyn Heilbrun from 1992 to 1996. These interviews are the source of all information about, and quotations from, Heilbrun not otherwise attributed.

3. See Phyllis Méras (1953), "Carolyn Gold Heilbrun '47: Portrait of a Feminist English Scholar Who Writes Detective Stories," *Wellesley* 68, no. 3 (1984): 14.

4. See "The Deans' Report," *ARNWCB,* 30 Oct. 1943, 14–15.

5. Virginia Pope, "Campus Hits," *NYT Magazine,* 1 Aug. 1943, 20–21.

6. Reported on the front page of the *NYT,* 26 Aug. 1943.

7. See "Wellesley to House Male Supply Group," *NYT,* 20 Aug. 1943, 7.

8. "Historical Sketch," *CNWCB,* 25 Oct. 1943, 22.

9. Quoted in Helen Lefkowitz Horowitz, *Alma Mater: Design and Experi-*

ence in the Women's Colleges from Their Nineteenth-Century Beginnings to the 1930s, 2d ed. (Amherst: Massachusetts Univ. Press, 1993), 44. Horowitz provides an excellent history of the founding of Wellesley College.

10. Ibid., 54, 53. Horowitz does point out that the president's power was curtailed because Durant was really in charge, 53.

11. See Ella Keats Whiting, "The Faculty," in *Wellesley College 1875–1975: A Century of Women* (Wellesley MA: Wellesley College, 1975), 112.

12. "Historical Sketch," *CNWCB*, 25 Oct. 1943, 23–24.

13. See "Officers of Instruction and Administration," *CNWCB*, 25 Oct. 1943, 11, 12.

14. "President's Report," *ARNWCB*, 30 Oct. 1945, 15.

15. "Great Expectations," *Wellesley College News*, 2 Sept. 1943, 2.

16. See "Preparation for War Service," and "Historical Sketch," *CNWCB*, 25 Oct. 1943, 37–38, 24; "The Deans' Report," *ARNWCB*, 30 Oct. 1943, 12–14.

17. I conducted interviews with Carol Logan Barnes, Nancy Posmantur Golden, and Rose Wind Stone of the class of 1946, and with Helen Mary (Miggs) Ignatius Dlouhy, Sylvia Crane Eisenlohr, Ann Hartman, and Nan Weiser Ignatius of the class of 1947.

18. Interview with Carol Logan Barnes, 18 Mar. 1996.

19. *WE of Wellesley* ran an issue on the UNO, 3, no. 3, 1946. An article, "Women for Peace," by Mrs. Jan Paparek (U.S.-born wife of the minister from Czechoslovakia) argued: "The fact that there are so few women in the General Assembly of the United Nations Organizations seems to indicate that the women of the world have the great responsibility of producing women leaders for peace. What a challenge!" (23). An article by Ginny Beach 1947, "Women Must Assume Responsibility by Active Participation in Politics" (*Wellesley College News*, 5 Dec. 1946), reported that Wellesley students, canvassing for Martha Sharpe, candidate for the House of Representatives, found that many women would not vote for a woman: "This attitude seems to indicate two things: first, that women do not trust themselves in politics, and second, that they are not sufficiently aware of their political obligations" (2).

20. See "Officers of Administration," *CNWCB*, 25 Oct. 1943, 16–19.

21. See "English," *CNWCB*, 25 Oct. 1943, 75.

22. See "President's Report," *ARNWCB*, 25 Oct. 1944, 10. For the calendars of events, see "Lectures, Concerts, and Art Exhibitions," *ARNWCB*, 25 Oct. 1944, 26; "Lectures, Concerts, and Art Exhibitions," *ARNWCB*, Sept. 1947, 31.

23. This review was reprinted in the centennial edition of the *NYT Book Review*, 6 Oct. 1996, 72.

24. See "Purposeful Living," *Wellesley College News*, 27 Nov. 1943, 2;

"Liberal Arts Record?" *Wellesley College News,* 30 Sept. 1943, 2; and "Future or Failure?" *Wellesley College News,* 16 Sept. 1943, 2.

25. Interviews with Helen Mary (Miggs) Ignatius Dlouhy, 20 Mar. 1996; Nancy Posmantur Golden, 29 Feb. 1996; Rose Wind Stone, 6 Mar. 1996; Nancy Posmantur Golden, 29 Feb. 1996; Miggs Ignatius Dlouhy, 20 Mar. 1996; Nan Weiser Ignatius, 20 Mar. 1996; Carol Logan Barnes, 18 Mar. 1996.

26. See Carolyn G. Heilbrun, "Educating Female People," *Columbia University Forum* 5, no. 2 (1962). Heilbrun, speaking of the female undergraduate, says, "she strives, during the four college years, as much for the acquisition of a bachelor as for a bachelor's degree" (35).

27. "Historical Sketch," *CNWCB,* 25 Oct. 1943, 24; "The Fleet's In," *Wellesley College News,* 30 Sept. 1943, 2.

28. Betty Friedan, "The Way We Were—1949," in *"It Changed My Life": Writings on the Women's Movement* (New York: Norton, 1985), describes the confused experience of women at this time as "schizophrenic" (12). See also Friedan, *The Feminine Mystique,* 40.

29. Edith Christina Johnson, "The Vocational Liberal Art," *Wellesley Magazine* 25, no. 5 (1941): 410.

30. Biographical file on Elizabeth Manwaring, Wellesley College Archives.

31. Florence Howe, "Feminism and Literature," in *Images of Women in Fiction: Feminist Perspectives,* ed. Susan Koppelman Cornillon (Bowling Green OH: Bowling Green Univ. Popular Press, 1972), 256.

32. See especially Sandra M. Gilbert and Susan Gubar, "Soldier's Heart: Literary Men, Literary Women, and the Great War," in *No Man's Land: The Place of the Woman Writer in the Twentieth Century,* vol. 2, *Sexchanges* (New Haven: Yale Univ. Press, 1989), 258–323.

33. Ipsen and Cutler, "Phi Betes Marry, Sell Shoes, Collect Pins, Sometimes Study," *Wellesley College News,* 22 Feb. 1945, 1.

34. Nancy Forsythe, "The Story of Susan Chandler," *WE of Wellesley* 4, no. 3 (1947): 19.

35. "Reporters Reveal Reasons for Not Getting Engaged," *Wellesley College News,* 8 Dec. 1943, 8.

36. "Suggested Cheer for the Class of '48," *WE of Wellesley* 2, no. 2 (1945): 18.

37. Barbara Anne Sutton, "Flash!" *WE of Wellesley* 4, no. 2 (1946): 47.

38. *Legenda* (Wellesley yearbook), 1947, 86.

39. Friedan, *The Feminine Mystique,* 62; Friedan, *"It Changed My Life,"* 6; Friedan, *The Feminine Mystique,* 69.

40. Adrienne Rich, "Taking Women Students Seriously (1978)," in *On Lies, Secrets, and Silence: Selected Prose 1966–1978* (New York: Norton, 1979), 238.

41. See "Summary of Students," *CNWCB*, 25 Oct. 1943, 205; for information about numbers of applications for the class of 1947, see "The Deans' Report," in *ARNWCB*, 30 Oct. 1943, 17.

42. See Méras, "Carolyn Gold Heilbrun '47," 14.

43. Interviews with Helen Mary (Miggs) Ignatius Dlouhy, Sylvia Crane Eisenlohr, Ann Hartman, and Nan Weiser Ignatius; Miggs Ignatius Dlouhy, 20 Mar. 1996; Nan Weiser Ignatius, 20 Mar. 1996.

44. *Legenda* 1947, 91.

45. Details of Heilbrun's academic honors are included on her Wellesley College transcript.

46. See Méras, "Carolyn Gold Heilbrun '47," 13.

47. The *Wellesley Alumnae Census* was submitted to Wellesley College 1 November 1963 by Personnel and Marketing Research Division, The Psychological Corporation. Table 6, "Marital Status of Wellesley B.A.'s by Class," table 17, "Age at Marriage for Wellesley B.A.'s by Class," and table 33, "Number of Children for Wellesley B.A.'s by Class," appear in vol. 5, *Alumnae Family Profiles*. Table 4, "Wellesley Graduates Who Have Received Graduate Degrees from Colleges Other than Wellesley by Class," appears in vol. 2, *Educational Profiles of Wellesley B.A's by Class*.

48. Interview with Ann Hartman, 20 Mar. 1996.

49. Mairi N. Morrison 1983, "Heilbrun Says College 'Afraid of Feminism,'" *Wellesley College News,* 30 Apr. 1982, 1.

50. Nora Ephron, "Reunion," in *Crazy Salad: Some Things about Women* (New York: Knopf, 1975), 31, 32.

51. Interview with Ann Hartman, 20 Mar. 1996.

52. Heilbrun received the Alumnae Achievement Award in 1984. The other class member to receive that award was Gwendolyn Gunter Morgan.

53. See Carolyn G. Heilbrun, "Helen Hayes in *Happy Birthday,*" *Wellesley College News,* 10 Oct. 1946, 5. Heilbrun was drama critic for the *News* from 27 Sept. 1946 to 15 May 1947.

54. Ephron, "Reunion," 31–32.

55. Carolyn G. Heilbrun, "*Barefoot Boy with Cheek,*" *Wellesley College News,* 20 Mar. 1947, 5; "*Call Me Mister,*" *Wellesley College News,* 27 Feb. 1947, 5.

56. Katherine Balderston's *Thraliana: The Diary of Hester Lynch Thrale* was awarded the Rose Mary Crawshay Prize by the British Academy in 1944 (biographical file on Katherine Balderston, Wellesley College Archives).

57. Méras, "Carolyn Gold Heilbrun '47," 14.

58. Biographical files on Charles Kerby-Miller and Mary Curran, Wellesley College Archives.

59. Polly Platt 1948, "Receives Prize," *Wellesley College News,* 15 June 1946, 3.

60. Miriam Berkley, "Carolyn Heilbrun/Amanda Cross," *Publishers Weekly,* 14 Apr. 1989, 47.

61. See *"Atlantic* Prizes to College Students," *Atlantic Monthly,* June 1946, 35; I am grateful to Michael Curtis and Lucie Prinz of the *Atlantic Monthly* for help with my research. Michael Curtis says that the *Atlantic Monthly* would typically circulate supplements to colleges participating in the contests; however, since this supplement has not survived, he cannot verify its existence.

62. More typical of the kind of story one might have expected a student to write about Jews in the postwar years can be found in Josephine Livingston's "The Beethoven Five," *Quarto* (Columbia School of General Studies) 1, no. 1 (1949): 1–11. The story unequivocally condemns a society matron for her prejudice against admitting Holocaust survivors to her country club.

63. Carolyn G. Heilbrun, "Thy People, My People," *WE of Wellesley* 4, no. 1 (1946): 24. Subsequent references to this story appear in parentheses in the text.

64. Lionel Trilling uses strikingly similar terms in his short story, "Funeral at the Club, with Lunch," *Menorah Journal* 13 (Aug. 1927), 386. See Alexander Bloom, *Prodigal Sons: The New York Intellectuals and Their World* (Oxford: Oxford Univ. Press, 1986), for this reference: "In another of the stories of his year at Wisconsin, [Trilling] described his desire to find a 'cultivated' society in academe, 'men living pleasantly, well-mannered, civilized, among whom he could be one . . . there would be no confinement . . . here there was no crying of "Jew!"'" (23).

65. Heilbrun, *Reinventing Womanhood,* 53, 54.

66. Ibid., 52–53, 52.

67. Ibid., 58, 53.

68. Adrienne Rich, "Split at the Root: An Essay on Jewish Identity (1982)" in *Blood, Bread, and Poetry: Selected Prose 1979–1985* (New York: Norton, 1986), 110, 112.

69. Heilbrun, *Reinventing Womanhood,* 55, 56–57.

70. Ibid., 60, 58, 59.

71. Ibid., 60, 61, 60, 22, 23.

72. Ibid., 20, 62.

73. Ibid., 58, 57.

74. Rich, "Split at the Root," 110–11.

75. Heilbrun, *Reinventing Womanhood,* 60, 20.

76. Brett Harvey, *The Fifties: A Women's Oral History* (New York: HarperCollins, 1993), 162.

77. "Are We Proud?" *Wellesley College News*, 3 Feb. 1944, 2.

78. Maud Hazeltine Chaplin, "Students: In the Beginning and Now," *Wellesley College 1875–1977*, 168.

79. Interviews with Ann Hartman, 20 Mar. 1996; Miggs Ignatius Dlouhy, 20 Mar. 1996.

80. Berkley, "Carolyn Heilbrun/Amanda Cross," 48.

81. Heilbrun, *Reinventing Womanhood*, 18.

82. Harvey, *The Fifties*, 162.

83. Interview with Carol Logan Barnes, 18 Mar. 1996.

84. See Sheri Elissa Steisel 1985, "Jewish Life on Campus—A Current Perspective" and Molly Myerowitz Levine 1964, "Annals of an Orthodox Jew at Wellesley in the '60s," *Wellesley* 70, no. 1 (1985): 16, 14. In the next issue of the magazine, a letter from one of Heilbrun's classmates was published. Cynthia Colby Gabrielli 1947 writes: "The intellects and individuality of Jewish women at Wellesley impressed one 1947 classmate. Whether called a 'distribution' or 'quota' system, something was at work in the selection process in 1943 to bring only the brightest of big-city girls who were Jewish to campus, where a just moderately brainy WASP from New Hampshire had the intelligence to recognize and be grateful for their presence," *Wellesley* 70, no. 2 (1986): 40.

85. Heilbrun, *Reinventing Womanhood*, 61.

86. Florence Howe, "Literacy and Literature," *PMLA* 89 (May 1974): 438.

87. See Irving Howe, *World of Our Fathers* (New York: Harcourt Brace Jovanovich, 1976), 630.

88. See "Do Your Part," *Wellesley College News*, 11 Nov. 1943, 2; and "Stamp Out All Anti-Semitism Seminar Theme," *Wellesley College News*, 15 Feb. 1945, 2.

89. See Ann Jones, "The Bess Mess," reviews of two books about Bess Myerson, *Washington Post Book World*, 15 Apr. 1990, 3.

90. Rich, "Split at the Root," 110.

91. See Irving Howe, *World of Our Fathers*, 410, 412; Alexander Bloom, *Prodigal Sons*, 23; and Susanne Klingenstein, *Jews in the American Academy 1900–1940: The Dynamics of Intellectual Assimilation* (New Haven: Yale Univ. Press, 1991), 177–78.

92. Alexander Bloom, *Prodigal Sons*, 146–47, 142–46.

93. First published in *Menorah Journal* in 1925, "Impediments" was included in Lionel Trilling, *Of This Time, of That Place and Other Stories*, selected by Diana Trilling (New York: Harcourt Brace Jovanovich, 1979), 3–10.

94. Rich, "Split at the Root," 114.

95. See Méras, "Carolyn Gold Heilbrun '47," 14; Carolyn G. Heilbrun,

Hamlet's Mother and Other Women (New York: Columbia Univ. Press, 1990), 1.

96. Rich, "Split at the Root," 107.

97. Susan Gubar takes up the tangled and conflicted relationship of Judaism and feminism in "Eating the Bread of Affliction: Judaism and Feminist Criticism," *Tulsa Studies in Women's Literature* 13 (1994): 293–316. Susan Gubar also referred me to a recent essay by Susanne Klingenstein, "'But My Daughters Can Read the Torah': Careers of Jewish Women in Literary Academe," *American Jewish History* 83, no. 2 (1995): 247–86. Klingenstein follows the careers of a number of prominent Jewish feminists in the academy, including Gubar and Heilbrun.

98. Méras, "Carolyn Gold Heilbrun '47," 14.

2. The Unwilling Mentor

1. See, for example, Isobel Kneeland, "The Defiler," and D. Preston Boone, "The Story of a Lady," both in *Quarto* 4, no. 2 (1953): 51–59, 20–24; and V. Sheridan Fonda, "Moonlight on Glass," *Quarto* 5, no. 1 (1954): 51–71. These three stories paint portraits of neurotic, strange women who are without men for one reason or another.

2. Annette Landau, "Summer Session," *Quarto* 1, no. 3, (1950): 17, 19, 23.

3. See David Halberstam, *The Fifties* (New York: Villard, 1993), 12.

4. Interview with Lionel Trilling in *Columbia Alumni News* 43, no. 7 (1952): 21.

5. Dan Wakefield, *New York in the Fifties* (Boston: Houghton Mifflin, 1992), 2.

6. Susan Douglas, *Where the Girls Are: Growing Up Female with the Mass Media* (New York: Times Books, 1994), 50.

7. C. Wright Mills, *White Collar: The American Middle Classes* (New York: Oxford Univ. Press, 1953), 175, 176; David Riesman, in collaboration with Reuel Denney and Nathan Glazer, *The Lonely Crowd: A Study of the Changing American Character* (New Haven: Yale Univ. Press, 1950), 332.

8. Wakefield, *New York in the Fifties,* 141. He quotes Michael Harrington, *Fragments of the Century* (1973) who reported that one source of friction between the bohemians and the Irish and Italians was "that we were always in the company of good-looking and liberated women." "Liberated" in those days, of course, meant sexually unrestrained—not intellectually independent.

9. Both the Burroughs incident and the Ginsberg-Snyder encounters are

reported in Barry Miles, *Ginsberg: A Biography* (New York: Simon & Schuster, 1989; reprint, New York: Harper Perrenial, 1990), 137, 199 (citations are to the reprint edition).

10. Rich, "When We Dead Awaken: Writing as Re-Vision (1971)," in *On Lies, Secrets, and Silence*, 42; Friedan, *The Feminine Mystique*, 38.

11. Heilbrun, *Reinventing Womanhood*, 62–64.

12. Klingenstein, *Jews in the American Academy*, 7; Grayson Kirk, "Commencement Address," *Columbia University Bulletin of Information: Commencement Number 1953*, 6 June 1953, 10, 12.

13. Frank Vitiello 1953, "Doleful Students Fear Bleak Future," *CDS*, 14 Dec. 1950, 1; "Deans Plan for Student Draft," *CDS*, 5 Jan. 1951, 4; "Nothing to Lose," *CDS*, 12 Apr. 1951, 2. "The Word on Work," *CDS*, 16 Feb. 1950: "It has been stressed before in many places that job opportunities are getting fewer and rarer. While the outlook for the prospective job hunter cannot be said to be dim, it is not what it was in the great years just after the war" (2). "Pigeonholed Plans," *CDS*, 27 Nov. 1950, 2. The loyalty oath was discussed on numerous occasions: "Long Time A-Coming," *CDS*, 21 Oct. 1949, 2; "Loyalty Oaths," *CDS*, 28 Apr. 1950, 2; "'Not Now Nor Ever,'" *CDS*, 11 Apr. 1951, 2. Lawrence K. Grossman 1952, "Policy on Outside Speakers Filled with Inconsistencies," *CDS*, 22 Nov. 1950, 6; Martin Patchen 1953, "Faculty on Fast," *CDS*, 30 Nov. 1950, 1. The *Columbia Daily Spectator* discussed Columbia's acceptance of discriminatory gifts in "Paradox," 3 Nov. 1949, 2; and in Lawrence K. Grossman 1952, "Admissions Head Denies Discrimination Charges," 18 Nov. 1949, 1. The newspaper also reported that the Amateur Fencing League discriminated against Negroes, "Fencing and Bias," 1 Dec. 1949, 2. Many editorials and articles recounted pressure to end discrimination in fraternities and other campus organizations: "Missed Opportunity," 17 Jan. 1950, 2; Dan Greenberg 1953, "College Student Board Bias Views Sent to Administration," 22 Nov. 1950, 5; "Fraternity Deadline," 28 Nov. 1951, 2. Mel Ember 1953, "NAACP Ask Change in Commager Book," *CDS*, 14 Mar. 1951, 1. "Letters to the Editor," *CDS*, 24 Apr. 1950, 2.

14. Interview with Steven Marcus, 26 Sept. 1996. Subsequent references to comments by Steven Marcus are derived from this interview.

15. See, for example, *CDS*, "Undergraduation," 4 May 1951, 2; "The Role of G. S.," 31 Oct. 1951, 2; "As a Social Club . . . ," 1 Nov. 1951, 2; "G. S. and Extra-Currics," 30 Sept. 1952, 2.

16. Anna Campbell, "A History of the Women's Graduate Club of Columbia University 1895–1925," MS, 1, Women's Graduate Club Papers, Rare Book and Manuscript Library, Columbia University.

17. Women's Graduate Club Papers, Rare Book and Manuscript Library, Columbia University.

18. I. I. Rabi, "Science and the University," *Columbia University Bulletin of Information: Commencement Number 1954,* 26 June 1954, 7.

19. Aristide Zolberg 1953, "March *Jester* Jabs Women; Late Issue Found Feverish," *CDS,* 27 Apr. 1950, 4.

20. Interviews with Tom Driver, 8 Jan. 1992, and with Robert Pack, 18 Mar. 1996. Subsequent references to comments by Tom Driver and Robert Pack are derived from these interviews.

21. Carolyn G. Heilbrun, foreword to *The Poetics of Gender,* ed. Nancy K. Miller (New York: Columbia Univ. Press, 1986), vii.

22. Heilbrun, *Reinventing Womanhood,* 129.

23. Recounted in Diana Trilling, *The Beginning of the Journey: The Marriage of Diana and Lionel Trilling* (New York: Harcourt Brace, 1993), 265.

24. See Miles, *Ginsberg,* 37; Lyndall Gordon, *Shared Lives* (New York: Norton, 1992), 179; and Wakefield, *New York in the Fifties,* 29, 30, 31.

25. Wakefield, *New York in the Fifties,* 31. Miles, *Ginsberg,* reports that after Ginsberg wrote offensive graffiti on his dormitory-room window, Trilling interceded with the dean on his behalf (61). In another, more serious incident, Miles recounts that Trilling again offered help when Ginsberg was arrested for an alleged connection with burglaries (119).

26. See Wakefield, *New York in the Fifties,* who reports the sentiments of Ned O'Gorman and Sam Astrachan, 32; and Diana Trilling, *Beginning of the Journey,* 250.

27. Wakefield, *New York in the Fifties,* 31.

28. Gordon, *Shared Lives,* 178, 48, 223.

29. Wakefield, *New York in the Fifties,* 29.

30. See Mark Krupnick's excellent study, *Lionel Trilling and the Fate of Cultural Criticism* (Evanston IL: Northwestern Univ. Press, 1986), especially chapter 2, "The Gentleman and the Jew," 19–34. Diana Trilling, in *Beginning of the Journey,* reveals the private Lionel Trilling in ways no one had done before: we learn, for example, of his drinking and his psychoanalysis.

31. Diana Trilling, *Beginning of the Journey,* 266, 269, 267.

32. Ibid., 270, 271, 250, 251. Diana Trilling states that "there is evidence in Lionel's notebooks that anger was one of the roads by which his new set of mind was achieved" (271).

33. Ibid., 250.

34. Heilbrun, *Reinventing Womanhood,* 126, 127.

35. Carolyn G. Heilbrun, "The Politics of Mind: Women, Tradition, and the University," in *Hamlet's Mother,* 213.

36. Carolyn G. Heilbrun, "Women, Men, Theories, and Literature," first published in *Profession 81* (Modern Language Association of America); reprinted in *Hamlet's Mother,* 190.

37. Noted in Krupnick, *Lionel Trilling*, 102.

38. Lionel Trilling, "Freud and Literature," in *The Liberal Imagination: Essays on Literature and Society* (New York: Viking Press, 1950), 39, 49.

39. Lionel Trilling, "The Sense of the Past," in *Liberal Imagination*, 186.

40. Diana Trilling, *Beginning of the Journey*, 274, 277.

41. Krupnick, *Lionel Trilling*, 12, 16–18, 173, 142–43, 9, 171, 14.

42. Lionel Trilling, "The Lesson and the Secret," first published in *Harper's Bazaar*, 1945; reprinted in *Of This Time, of That Place*, 68, 69.

43. Lionel Trilling, *The Middle of the Journey* (New York: Viking, 1947; reprint, with an introduction by Lionel Trilling, New York: Avon, 1976). Lionel Trilling, "Of This Time, of That Place," first published in *Partisan Review*, 1943; reprinted in *Of This Time, of That Place*, 91.

44. Heilbrun, *Reinventing Womanhood*, 128.

45. Alice Jardine, "Death Sentences: Writing Couples and Ideology," in *The Female Body in Western Culture: Contemporary Perspectives*, ed. Susan Suleiman (Cambridge: Harvard Univ. Press, 1986), 86. Carolyn G. Heilbrun ends the quotation at "writing," in her "Presidential Address 1984," first published in *PMLA*, 1985; reprinted in *Hamlet's Mother*, 206.

46. Heilbrun, "Presidential Address," 206.

47. Interview with Columbia faculty member, Joan Ferrante, 8 Jan. 1992. Ferrante has known Heilbrun since 1963, when they both taught in the School of General Studies.

48. Heilbrun, foreword to *Poetics of Gender*, vii.

3. Split Selves: The Mother and the Writer

1. See Adrienne Rich, *Of Woman Born: Motherhood as Experience and Institution* (New York: Norton, 1976), 26, 28, and 175; and Rich, "Split at the Root," 114.

2. Friedan, *The Feminine Mystique*, 60; Rich, *Of Woman Born*, 31–32.

3. See Heilbrun, *Reinventing Womanhood*, 17.

4. Rich, "Split at the Root," 117.

5. Carolyn G. Heilbrun, "The Character of Hamlet's Mother," first published in *Shakespeare Quarterly*, 1957; reprinted in *Hamlet's Mother*, 10.

6. See Friedan, *The Feminine Mystique*, 11–27; and Rich, *Of Woman Born*, 21–22, 28–29.

7. Carolyn G. Heilbrun, *The Garnett Family* (New York: Macmillan, 1961), 15. "In the Garnett family, genius did not cluster in a generation; rather the peculiar family talent for literary service was handed down from generation to generation, with such continuity that each son completed or edited some of his father's work" (16).

8. Richard Hoggart, "Chosen Tasks," review of *The Garnett Family* by Carolyn G. Heilbrun, *New Statesman*, 7 July 1961, 22.

9. Heilbrun, *The Garnett Family*, 167, 100 (quoting David Garnett), 101, 175, 170, 163, 172.

10. The letter from Erik Wensberg, referring to the lunch and inviting the article is dated 23 Oct. 1961; Heilbrun's letter accompanying the article is dated 16 Nov. 1961. *Columbia Forum* Papers, Rare Book and Manuscript Library, Columbia University.

11. Heilbrun, "Educating Female People," 36, 33, 37, 34.

12. See "Marry Early, Learn Later," *Time*, 25 May 1962, 51.

13. Letter to Carolyn Heilbrun, 22 May 1962, *Columbia Forum* Papers, Rare Book and Manuscript Library, Columbia University.

14. Carolyn G. Heilbrun, "I've Been Reading: A Course of Mistaken Identity," *Columbia University Forum* 7, no. 3 (1964): 40.

15. Letter, Peter Spackman to Carolyn Heilbrun, 8 July 1964; letter, Carolyn Heilbrun to Anne Horan, managing editor of the *Forum*, 3 Aug. 1964. *Columbia Forum* Papers, Rare Book and Manuscript Library, Columbia University.

16. James Gold, "Lionel Trilling, 1905–1975," *CDS*, 12 Nov. 1975, 5.

17. In the day-long conference organized on 30 Oct. 1992 to celebrate Heilbrun's retirement from Columbia, "Out of the Academy and into the World with Carolyn G. Heilbrun," Rachel Blau DuPlessis spoke eloquently of Heilbrun's achievements as an essayist. In a 24 Sept. 1966 letter to the author, Du-Plessis wrote, "I think Heilbrun, in a Wolfean tradition, has all the virtues of the essay—the antiauthoritarian authority, the interrogation of cultural assumptions, the agnosticism, the humane passion."

18. Carolyn G. Heilbrun, "The Woman as Hero," *Texas Quarterly* 8, no. 4 (1965): 132, 133, 138, 134, 133, 135, 134.

19. I am grateful to my colleague, Frances Hoffmann, for this insight. See also Hester Eisenstein, *Contemporary Feminist Thought* (Boston: G. K. Hall, 1983), xix–xx, for useful definitions of radical feminism, socialist feminism, and liberal feminism.

20. Carolyn G. Heilbrun, "The Bloomsbury Group," *Midway* 9 (autumn 1968): 75, 74. However, Heilbrun does revise some of her opinions later. Reviewing Phyllis Rose's biography of Virginia Woolf, *Woman of Letters: A Life of Virginia Woolf*, she seems to accept Rose's view of Woolf's male friends: "Woolf, Rose shows us, saw herself rejected not only by the male patriarchy of her Victorian childhood but by the homosexuality of the young men who surrounded her in her youth. . . . she discovered, as do all women whose male friends are homosexual, their profound distaste for womanhood," "Women's Biographies of Women: A New Genre," *Review* (Blacksburg VA) 2 (1980): 343.

21. Heilbrun, "The Bloomsbury Group," 73. These sentences do not appear in the version included in Carolyn G. Heilbrun, *Toward a Recognition of Androgyny* (New York: Knopf, 1973; reprint, New York: Harper Colophon, 1974), 126 (citations are to the reprint edition).

22. See Robin Morgan, "Introduction: The Women's Revolution," in *Sisterhood Is Powerful: An Anthology of Writings from the Women's Liberation Movement,* ed. Robin Morgan (New York: Vintage, 1970), xiii–xiv, where she elaborates on some of the costs for women of expressing their feminism.

23. Carolyn G. Heilbrun, "Virginia Woolf in Her Fifties," first published in *Twentieth-Century Literature,* 1981; reprinted in *Hamlet's Mother,* 82.

24. Carolyn G. Heilbrun, "Amanda Cross," in *Twentieth-Century Crime and Mystery Writers,* ed. John M. Reilly (London: Macmillan, 1980), 339, 400; Carolyn G. Heilbrun, "Sayers, Lord Peter, and God," *American Scholar* 37 (1968): 326.

25. Heilbrun, *Writing a Woman's Life,* 51.

26. For this and other information about Dorothy L. Sayers, see James Brabazon, *Dorothy L. Sayers: A Biography* (New York: Scribner's, 1981).

27. Heilbrun, "Women, Men, Theories, and Literature," 184.

28. See Doris Grumbach, "A Mysterious Faculty for Murder: The Professor Did It," *Columbia* 7, no. 3 (1981): 36. She also makes the point that "Heilbrun's double identity is convenient. In her mysteries, Amanda Cross is able to make frequent observations about academic life that are far more candid than any that Carolyn Heilbrun might be willing to incorporate into her scholarly writing" (36). Heilbrun herself points out that "it could definitely interfere with getting tenure if you wrote novels or detective stories," interview with Jane Merrill Filstrup, "The Professor Who Writes Detective Stories," *Graduate Woman,* AAUW 74, no. 4 (1980): 16.

29. Heilbrun, *Writing a Woman's Life,* 114, 117.

30. In "'To Create a Space for Myself': Carolyn Heilbrun a.k.a. Amanda Cross and the Detective Novel," *Amerikastudien/American Studies* 39 (1994): 525–35, Carmen Birkle argues that "Heilbrun is able to create a new space for herself by moving between the fictional self in the text and the real self in academia" (526); the fictional self empowers the "real" self "to affirm her position in professional life" (525). This is a valuable insight, and in subsequent chapters I clarify the ways Heilbrun and Cross exchange lessons.

31. Heilbrun, "Sayers, Lord Peter, and God," 334.

32. Maureen T. Reddy, "She Done It," *Women's Review of Books,* Dec. 1986: "There seem to have been few feminist mysteries between 1935 [Dorothy Sayers's *Gaudy Night* was published in 1934] and 1964, the year that . . . *In the Last Analysis* appeared" (8).

33. Heilbrun, *Writing a Woman's Life,* 114. She later adds, "Creating Kate Fansler and her quests, I was re-creating myself" (117). But see the earlier interview with Diana Cooper-Clark in *Designs of Darkness: Interviews with Detective Novelists* (Bowling Green OH: Bowling Green State Univ. Popular Press, 1983). When asked how much of herself is in Kate, Heilbrun then responded ambiguously, "Obviously a good bit. But still, not too much" (191).

34. Heilbrun, *Writing a Woman's Life,* 115.

35. Ibid., 123, 81.

36. A number of critics have noticed Kate Fansler's lack of friends. See, for example, Maureen T. Reddy, *Sisters in Crime: Feminism and the Crime Novel* New York: Continuum, 1988), 65; and Trisha Yarbrough, "The Achievement of Amanda Cross," *Clues* 15, no. 1 (1994): 98.

37. See, for example, Carolyn G. Heilbrun, "Marriage Perceived: English Literature 1873–1944," first published in *What Manner of Woman: Essays on English and American Life and Letters,* ed. Marlene Springer, 1977; reprinted in *Hamlet's Mother,* 112–33.

38. See the interview with Diana Cooper-Clark, 191–92. Kathleen Gregory Klein is one of several critics to make this point, noting that Reed even has to explain the mysteries in *The James Joyce Murder* and *Poetic Justice.* See Kathleen Gregory Klein, "Feminists as Detectives: Harriet Vane, Kate Fansler, and Sarah Chayse," *The Armchair Detective* 13, no. 1 (1980): 35.

39. Steven Carter has produced an excellent analysis of the Amanda Cross novels up to and including *Death in a Tenured Position* in "Amanda Cross," in *Ten Women of Mystery,* ed. Earl F. Bargainnier (Bowling Green OH: Bowling Green State Univ. Popular Press, 1981). Carter also notes the development of Cross's social vision and, as I do, sees Cross as "eventually becoming a strong advocate of social change." He also makes the point, which I develop in chapter 5 that "the further [Cross] has moved from traditional stances, the further she has moved from the traditional forms" (270).

40. Heilbrun, "Amanda Cross," 400.

41. Other possible hints include a reference to an article Fansler has written on "James's use of the American heroine," (perhaps a veiled allusion to Heilbrun's "The Woman As Hero,"); and an aside about a "Professor Anderson" who shocks Kate Fansler by quoting Edna St. Vincent Millay even though he is "an eighteenth century man with a strong distaste for all female writers since Jane Austen." (In 1961, Quentin Anderson had succeeded Charles Everett as administrative head of the Columbia College English Department.) See Carolyn G. Heilbrun [Amanda Cross, pseud.], *In the Last Analysis* (New York: Macmillan, 1964; reprint, New York: Avon, 1966), 107, 7 (citations are to the reprint edition).

42. Heilbrun, *In the Last Analysis,* 55; Carolyn G. Heilbrun [Amanda Cross, pseud.], *The James Joyce Murder* (New York: Macmillan, 1967; reprint, New York: Ballantine, 1982), 52 (citations are to the reprint edition).

43. Heilbrun, *James Joyce Murder,* 169, 112.

44. At one point in *James Joyce Murder,* Kate Fansler remarks, "Are you suggesting that I have not only exposed my nephew to murder, but have placed him in a camp filled with queers?" (109).

45. Heilbrun, *In the Last Analysis,* 63, 147–48.

46. The point about Fansler's feminist independence is made by Klein, "Feminists as Detectives," 31–35.

47. Heilbrun, *Reinventing Womanhood,* 64.

48. Heilbrun, *Writing a Woman's Life,* 120.

49. In "Speaking of Books: A Modern among Contemporaries," *NYT Book Review,* 30 Jan. 1966, Heilbrun notes a distinction between contemporary and modern writers in the latter's favor. Quoting Stephen Spender, she tells us that contemporary writers write of "how the world may be changed," whereas modern writers "reform nothing" (2). In "For Children: Reform the Reformers," *NYT Book Review,* 26 Feb. 1967, Heilbrun is frustrated by reading bad children's books that strive for relevance: "What we need, not to put too fine a point on it, is a little less social significance, and a little more . . . family" (26).

50. Carolyn G. Heilbrun, review of *Feminism and Art: A Study of Virginia Woolf* by Herbert Marder, *Journal of English and Germanic Philology* 68 (1969): 310.

51. Sylvia Plath, *The Bell Jar* (London: William Heinemann, 1963; reprint, London: Faber & Faber, 1966), 194 (citations are to the reprint edition); Rich, "When We Dead Awaken," 40; Diane Wood Middlebrook, *Anne Sexton: A Biography* (Boston: Houghton Mifflin, 1991), 55, 64.

52. At the summer institute organized by the National Council of Teachers of English, Myrtle Beach, 1988, Sandra M. Gilbert and Susan Gubar spoke of their collaboration as a way of easing the anxiety of authorship.

53. Heilbrun, *Reinventing Womanhood:* "That I managed to keep my personal and professional lives so separated permitted me to survive" (22).

4. The Androgyny Model

1. Diana Trilling, "On the Steps of Low Library," in *We Must March My Darlings: A Critical Decade* (New York: Harcourt Brace Jovanovich, 1977), 101–2.

2. Carolyn G. Heilbrun [Amanda Cross, pseud.], *Poetic Justice* (New York: Knopf, 1970; reprint, New York: Avon, 1979): Kate Fansler wonders that "a

bunch of half-baked, foul-mouthed Maoist students ... could be followed in their illegal acts by nearly a thousand moderate, thoughtful students" (47, citations are to the reprint edition).

3. Tom Driver calls Heilbrun "Carol," as do other friends who knew her in the 1950s.

4. Reddy, in her perceptive reading of the Amanda Cross novels in *Sisters in Crime,* has also noted that "the center of interest in *Poetic Justice* is ... Kate's increasing involvement with University College" (58).

5. See Dean M. Schmitter, "Lewisohn during the Crisis: A Faculty Viewpoint," *Focus,* no. 3 (1968): 13, 15. This issue of *Focus,* a publication of the School of General Studies, contains several articles about the uprising under the general title "Crisis at Columbia."

6. Heilbrun, *Poetic Justice,* 48, 88, 92, 131.

7. Amanda Cross contributed "Spinster Detectives" to *Murderess Ink: The Better Half of the Mystery,* perpetrated by Dilys Winn (New York: Workman, 1979). This article suggests that Cross originally intended to make Kate Fansler totally independent in the tradition of spinster detectives, whom she describes as turning "their solitude into power and their superfluity into freedom"; such women will never "revolve in some male-centered orbit" (96, 97).

8. Heilbrun, *Poetic Justice,* 156. For Steven Carter's discussion of balance in this novel, see "Amanda Cross," 277–78. Carter draws similar conclusions with respect to Kate's attitude to the institution, but sees her marriage as a positive sign of "change." For his notion of balance as a "dynamic" rather than static concept, see 284. Reddy, *Sisters in Crime,* 59–60, also has a useful discussion of balance in *Poetic Justice.*

9. Heilbrun, *Poetic Justice,* 104.

10. See Heilbrun, *Reinventing Womanhood:* "Women, even if they choose the men ... choose only to be chosen" (66). Still, the marriage of Reed and Kate is intended to be a union of equals.

11. For one account of this process, see Marge Piercy's "The Grand Coolie Damn," in *Sisterhood Is Powerful,* 421–38.

12. Morgan, "Introduction: The Women's Revolution," in *Sisterhood Is Powerful,* xvii–xviii.

13. For the "NOW Bill of Rights," see *Sisterhood Is Powerful,* 512.

14. From "Redstockings Manifesto," in *Sisterhood Is Powerful,* 535.

15. Valerie Solanis, "Excerpts From the SCUM (Society for Cutting Up Men) Manifesto," in *Sisterhood Is Powerful,* 514.

16. Kate Millett, *Sexual Politics* (New York: Doubleday, 1970; reprint, New York: Ballantine, 1978), 33 (citations are to the reprint edition).

17. Phyllis Chesler, "Patient and Patriarch: Women in the Psychotherapeutic Relationship," in *Woman in Sexist Society: Studies in Power and Power-*

lessness, ed. Vivian Gornick and Barbara K. Moran (New York: Basic Books, 1971; reprint, New York: NAL, 1972), 384 (citations are to the reprint edition).

18. George Winchester Stone Jr., "Brief Remembrance of Things Past and Hopes for Things to Come," *PMLA* 99 (1984): 322.

19. "Conventions and Membership, 1883–1983," *PMLA* 99 (1984): 455–56.

20. Paul Lauter, "Society and the Profession, 1958–83," *PMLA* 99 (1984), points out that "speaking at the MLA convention once meant advancement in the hierarchical structure of the profession" (416).

21. Ibid., 418.

22. John Hurt Fisher, "Report of the Executive Secretary," *PMLA* 85 (1970): 535.

23. Germaine Brée, "Presidential Address 1975," *PMLA* 91 (1976): 362.

24. Several presidents have used these watchwords. Germaine Brée spoke of "solidarity," in "Presidential Address 1975," *PMLA* 91 (1976): 364; Maynard Mack of "outreach," in "To See It Feelingly," *PMLA* 86 (1971): 370; Walter J. Ong of "professionalism," in "Presidential Address 1978: The Human Nature of Professionalism," *PMLA* 94 (1979): 388; and Jean Perkins of "historical examples," in "Presidential Address 1979: *E Pluribus Unum*," *PMLA* 95 (1980): 312.

25. Louis Kampf, "'It's Alright, Ma (I'm Only Bleeding)': Literature and Language in the Academy," *PMLA* 87 (1972): 382, 378, 380, 378, 381.

26. Florence Howe, Laura Morlock, and Richard Berk, "The Status of Women in Modern Language Departments: A Report of the Modern Language Association Commission on the Status of Women in the Profession," *PMLA* 86 (1971): 465.

27. See Laura Morlock et al., "Affirmative Action for Women in 1971: A Report of the Modern Language Association Commission on the Status of Women in the Profession," *PMLA* 87 (1972): 530–40.

28. Florence Howe, "Literacy and Literature," 436, 434. 441.

29. William Schaeffer, "Editor's Column," *PMLA* 93 (1978): 355. The other essay was Paul Sherwin's "Dying into Life: Keats's Struggle with Milton in *Hyperion*."

30. See "Report of the Subcommittee of the Senate Executive Committee on the Status of Women at Columbia," May 1971; and "Statement of Columbia Women's Liberation Curriculum Committee Before the Columbia Senate Hearings on the Status of Women in the University," 11 Mar. 1970, Commission on the Status of Women Papers, Senate Office, Columbia University.

31. "Report of the Commission on the Status of Women/Columbia University," March 1975, 1, 3–4, 4, 5, 6, Commission on the Status of Women Papers, Senate Office, Columbia University.

32. Ibid., 5.

33. Nan Robertson, "Trilling Cites Education Crisis," *NYT,* 27 Apr. 1972, 45.

34. Interview with Robert Hanning, 9 Sept. 1996.

35. Heilbrun, *Reinventing Womanhood,* 46.

36. Carolyn G. Heilbrun, *Christopher Isherwood* (New York: Columbia Univ. Press, 1970), 34, 38, 44.

37. Ibid., 19, 5–8.

38. Carolyn G. Heilbrun, "Millett's Sexual Politics: A Year Later," *Aphra* 2 (summer 1971): 39, 43.

39. "American Scholar Forum: Women on Women," *American Scholar* 41 (1972): 599.

40. Ibid., 623.

41. Ibid., 605.

42. Ibid., 618. See also Heilbrun, *Reinventing Womanhood:* "In the past those women who have made their way successfully into the male-dominated worlds of business, the arts, or the professions have done so as honorary men, neither admiring nor bonding with other women, offering no encouragement to those who might come after them, preserving the socially required 'femininity,' but sacrificing their womanhood" (29).

43. Heilbrun, *Poetic Justice,* 106.

44. Heilbrun, *Reinventing Womanhood,* 154.

45. Jeanne Addison Roberts, "Feminist Murder: Amanda Cross Reinvents Womanhood," *Clues* 6, no 1 (1985): 6, 5, 6. Roberts sees the death of Janet Mandelbaum in *Death in a Tenured Position* as problematic, too.

46. See Rich, *Of Woman Born,* 274–80.

47. Deborah Kelly Kloepfer, *The Unspeakable Mother: Forbidden Discourse in Jean Rhys and H. D.* (Ithaca: Cornell Univ. Press, 1989), 49.

48. Rich, *Of Woman Born,* 236.

49. Heilbrun, *Poetic Justice,* 43, 44.

50. Susanne Klingenstein makes an excellent point in "'But My Daughters Can Read the Torah'": "the solution to *Poetic Justice,* in which Trilling turns out to be the one who killed the Dean in order to preserve General Studies . . . has the quality of a dream since it fulfills Heilbrun's wish that just once Trilling would show himself enlightened and actively support her side" (268).

51. Heilbrun, *Reinventing Womanhood,* 126. The unmasking is described in Filstrup, "The Professor Who Writes Detective Stories," 16.

52. Quoted in Carolyn G. Heilbrun, "The Masculine Wilderness of the American Novel," *Saturday Review,* 29 Jan. 1972, 43.

53. Ibid., 41.

54. Quoted in ibid., 43.

55. Ibid., 43.

56. Heilbrun, *Toward a Recognition of Androgyny*, x–xi, 57.

57. Virginia Woolf, *A Room of One's Own* (1929; reprint, New York: Harcourt, Brace & World, 1957), 102, 108 (citations are to the reprint edition).

58. See Lionel Trilling, preface to *The Opposing Self: Nine Essays in Criticism* (1955; reprint, New York: Harcourt Brace Jovanovich/A Harvest Book, 1979), x (citations are to the reprint edition).

59. Heilbrun, *Toward a Recognition of Androgyny*, ix–x.

60. See Lionel Trilling, preface to *Opposing Self*, xiii, xiv.

61. Heilbrun, *Toward a Recognition of Androgyny*, x.

62. See Heilbrun, *Toward a Recognition of Androgyny*, 58, 91–92, 101; and Carolyn G. Heilbrun, "Further Notes toward a Recognition of Androgyny," *Women's Studies* 2 (1974): 144.

63. Carolyn G. Heilbrun, review of Mary Ellmann's *Thinking about Women*, *NYT Book Review*, 17 Nov. 1968, 42, 4.

64. Heilbrun would use the same terms of emigration to another "country" in her 1984 "Presidential Address," 206; but by 1984 that "country" had become a "women's space."

65. Joyce Carol Oates, review of Heilbrun's *Toward a Recognition of Androgyny*, *NYT Book Review*, 15 Apr. 1973, 7, 12.

66. Nancy Topping Bazin and Alma Freeman, "The Androgynous Vision," *Women's Studies* 2 (1974): 185–215.

67. See Barbara Charlesworth Gelpi, "The Politics of Androgyny," *Women's Studies* 2 (1974): 151–60, esp. 151–52.

68. Cynthia Secor, "Androgyny: An Early Reappraisal," *Women's Studies* 2 (1974): 163, 164, 167, 165. On the ways in which androgyny fosters rather than defeats polarization, see also Daniel Harris, "Androgyny: The Sexist Myth in Disguise," *Women's Studies* 2 (1974): 171–72.

69. Elaine Showalter, "Virginia Woolf and the Flight into Androgyny," in *A Literature of Their Own* (Princeton: Princeton Univ. Press, 1977), 264.

70. Hester Eisenstein, in *Contemporary Feminist Thought*, 58–68, makes many of these arguments against androgyny. In addition, she points out that the "androgynous concept embodied an uncritical vision of maleness and of masculinity: the qualities of aggression, competitiveness, leadership, and so on were taken to be good in themselves, and therefore important for all people to acquire" (63).

71. Elsa Greene, review of Heilbrun's *Toward a Recognition of Androgyny*, *Women's Studies* 2 (1974): 261. Sandra L. Bem, "Probing the Promise of Androgyny," in *Beyond Sex-Role Stereotypes: Readings toward a Psychology of Androgyny*, ed. Alexandra G. Kaplan and Joan P. Bean (Boston: Little, Brown, 1976), 48–62, esp. 48.

72. Interview with Susan Stanford Friedman, 13 Sept. 1996. In 1979,

Friedman planned to offer a paper on androgyny at the Simone de Beauvoir Conference in New York City, but, having arrived at her session, she was prevented from reading her paper by a democratic vote of the audience.

73. Carolyn G. Heilbrun and Catharine Stimpson, "Theories of Feminist Criticism: A Dialogue," in *Feminist Literary Criticism: Explorations in Theory,* ed. Josephine Campbell Donovan (Lexington: Univ. Press of Kentucky, 1975), 61, 72.

74. Accordingly, I henceforth refer to Heilbrun as the author of the detective novels.

75. Carolyn G. Heilbrun [Amanda Cross, pseud.], *The Question of Max* (New York: Knopf, 1976; reprint, New York: Avon, 1977), 86, 112 (citations are to the reprint edition).

76. Several critics make this complaint. See, for example, Mary Cantwell, "The Mystery of Women Mystery Writers," review of *Death in a Tenured Position, NYT Book Review,* 22 Mar. 1981, 22; and J. M. Purcell, "The 'Amanda Cross' Case: Sociologizing the U.S. Academic Mystery," *The Armchair Detective* 13, no. 1 (1980). Purcell regards this fault as an aspect of elitism: "Cross adopts the technical convention that each important *speaker* . . . shares the same conversational style; by implication, the same background; and . . . basically the same social views" (38).

77. Heilbrun, *The Question of Max,* 137, 146.

78. Heilbrun, *Reinventing Womanhood,* 177–78. Heilbrun, *The Question of Max,* 23.

79. Heilbrun, introductory note to part 5, "Detective Fiction," in *Hamlet's Mother,* 229.

80. Reddy, *Sisters in Crime,* 49, 14.

81. See Cooper-Clark, "Interview with Amanda Cross," 195–96.

82. Heilbrun, *Reinventing Womanhood,* 130.

83. Carolyn G. Heilbrun [Amanda Cross, pseud.], *The Theban Mysteries* (New York: Knopf, 1971; reprint, New York: Avon, 1979), 53 (citations are to the reprint edition).

84. In *Poetic Justice,* Kate Fansler declares, "I also realize that superficial good manners may cover the most appalling nastiness and hostility" (57).

85. Nancy K. Miller, "Decades," in *Changing Subjects: The Making of Feminist Literary Criticism,* ed. Gayle Greene and Coppélia Kahn (London: Routledge, 1993), 35.

86. George Stade, *Confessions of a Lady-Killer* (New York: Norton, 1979), 11, 14, 30.

87. See reports of meetings of the MLA Executive Council and the MLA Delegate Assembly in *PMLA* 93 (1978): 310; *PMLA* 95 (1980): 432; and *PMLA* 93 (1978): 502, 500.

88. In *Toward a Recognition of Androgyny,* Heilbrun had said, "Perhaps

in writing of the Bloomsbury group here I may discover myself to be at the watershed of opinion about them, so that appreciation of their accomplishments and original way of life will become but another reasonable critical position" (116).

89. This is exactly the kind of power Birkle attributes to Heilbrun's fictional self in "'To Create a Space for Myself,'" 525.

90. See Heilbrun's foreword to *Poetics of Gender,* vii.

5. Feminism in a Tenured Position

1. See Susan Faludi's trenchant analysis of Friedan's book in *Backlash: The Undeclared War against American Women* (New York: Crown, 1991), 318–25.

2. Betty Friedan, *The Second Stage* (1981; rev. ed. with introduction and afterword by the author, New York: Summit Books, 1986), 31, 318–19, 28, 110, 83–123, 319–20, 41, 45.

3. Deirdre Bair, *Simone de Beauvoir: A Biography* (New York: Summit Books, 1990), 609.

4. Friedan, *Second Stage,* 319. Adrienne Rich, "Compulsory Heterosexuality and Lesbian Existence," *Signs* 5, no. 4 (1980): 648, 648–49.

5. Rich, "Compulsory Heterosexuality": "The lie of compulsory female heterosexuality today afflicts not just feminist scholarship, but every profession, every reference work, every curriculum, every organizing attempt, every relationship or conversation over which it hovers" (657).

6. See Ann Ferguson, "Patriarchy, Sexual Identity, and the Sexual Revolution," in "On 'Compulsory Heterosexuality and Lesbian Existence': Defining the Issues," by Ann Ferguson, Jacqueline N. Zita, and Kathryn Pyne Addelson, *Signs* 7, no. 1 (1981): 158–99. Ferguson points out that Rich romanticizes lesbianism and ignores other kinds of resistance, and she interrogates Rich's use of the word "coercive," 160, 170–72.

7. Carolyn G. Heilbrun, "A Response to *Writing and Sexual Difference,*" in *Writing and Sexual Difference,* ed. Elizabeth Abel (Chicago: Univ. of Chicago Press, 1982): "The failure of the ideal community of feminism to come into existence is, to judge from her prolix admonitions in *The Second Stage,* what has driven Betty Friedan to embrace the language and phallocentrism of feminism's opponents" (292).

8. Heilbrun, "Virginia Woolf in Her Fifties," in *Hamlet's Mother,* 80. Lynda Koolish, review of books about Virginia Woolf, including *Virginia Woolf: A Feminist Slant,* ed. Jane Marcus, *Signs* 11 (1986): 559. Heilbrun, "Virginia Woolf in Her Fifties," 87, 84. Heilbrun, *Reinventing Womanhood,* 15.

9. Jane Gallop, *Around 1981: Academic Feminist Literary Theory* (New York: Routledge, 1992), 4.

10. Heilbrun, "Virginia Woolf in Her Fifties," 85.

11. Carolyn G. Heilbrun, "Hers," *NYT,* 5 Feb. 1981, sec. C, 2.

12. Heilbrun, "Virginia Woolf in Her Fifties," 88.

13. Heilbrun, *Reinventing Womanhood,* 16, 31, 32, 140.

14. Ibid., 22.

15. See, for example, Heilbrun, *Writing a Woman's Life,* 20.

16. Elaine Showalter, "Feminist Criticism in the Wilderness," in *Writing and Sexual Difference,* 13.

17. Ibid., 14, 15.

18. Carol Gilligan, *In a Different Voice: Psychological Theory and Women's Development* (Cambridge: Harvard Univ. Press, 1982), 2. Faludi, *Backlash,* points out that, in the 1980s, "it became easy to appropriate Gilligan's theories on behalf of discriminatory arguments that could cause real harm to women" (331).

19. Mary Daly, *Gyn/Ecology: The Metaethics of Radical Feminism* (Boston: Beacon Press, 1978), 39.

20. Elaine Showalter, "Feminist Criticism in the Wilderness," 15.

21. Heilbrun, "A Response to *Writing and Sexual Difference,*" 294, 297.

22. Heilbrun, *Reinventing Womanhood,* 19.

23. In *No Man's Land,* vol.3 *Letters from the Front* (New Haven: Yale Univ. Press, 1994), 371, Sandra M. Gilbert and Susan Gubar also note Chodorow's influence on Heilbrun in *Reinventing Womanhood.*

24. Nancy Chodorow, *The Reproduction of Mothering: Psychoanalysis and the Sociology of Gender* (Berkeley: Univ. of California Press, 1978), 7, 218.

25. The phrase is reminiscent of Trilling's in describing Yeats's "long quarrel with the culture," from the preface to Lionel Trilling, *Opposing Self,* xiv.

26. Heilbrun, *Reinventing Womanhood,* 127.

27. A note is worth adding here: when Diana Trilling was interviewed in *Publishers Weekly,* 1 Nov. 1993, and asked her response to reviews of *The Beginning of the Journey,* she acknowledged, "the best was Carolyn Heilbrun in the *Boston Globe*—a very generous-spirited piece" (54).

28. Heilbrun, *Reinventing Womanhood,* 129, 136, 129, 131, 132.

29. Ibid., 16.

30. See Heilbrun, *Reinventing Womanhood,* 123, and also "Women's Biographies of Women," where Heilbrun notes, "Women have long declined, or have been unable, to make individual fictions of their lives, to ignore the general fiction inscribed for them, to contrive distinctive stories of which they, as individual females, are the protagonists. The reason is not far to seek: woman's destiny, an erotic one leading to marriage, depended wholly upon another's activity, another's pursuit, another's *speaking*" (338).

31. Heilbrun, *Reinventing Womanhood,* 26.

32. See, for example, Reddy, *Sisters in Crime:* "From my perspective, the real problems with [the notion of adopting male models] are its unexamined assumptions about the nature of achievement and the goals of feminism. Heilbrun here accepts both the masculinist definition of achievement as outward success in the existing hierarchy and the popularized, liberal reduction of feminism to merely a process of adding women in to preexisting institutions; she also assumes that female bonding has to do mostly with women helping other women in this process of adding in" (51–52). Margo Jefferson's review, "The Lives of Women," in the *NYT Book Review,* 13 May 1979, is an extended denouncement, challenging Heilbrun's authority on all the topics she takes up in the book ("she falsifies and reduces," 31). Refusing to see that Heilbrun's feminism sets her apart from most women of her generation, Jefferson claims she is "no different from any number of women who became feminists" (7).

33. Toril Moi, *Sexual/Textual Politics: Feminist Literary Theory* (London: Methuen, 1985), 66–67.

34. Heilbrun, *Reinventing Womanhood,* 22.

35. I am grateful to Susan Gubar for pointing out that feminist secular Jews in the academy were, for the most part, not ready to contemplate the matter of Jewish identity until the 1980s, interview, 23 Sept. 1996.

36. Reddy, *Sisters in Crime,* argues that *Death in a Tenured Position, Sweet Death, Kind Death,* and *No Word from Winifred* "raise questions about the idea of the university, especially the prestigious university, but offer the optimistic hope that such universities are capable of change" (145). My sense is that, by the time of *Death in a Tenured Position,* Heilbrun has begun to lose her optimism about the possibility of institutional change.

37. Carolyn G. Heilbrun [Amanda Cross, pseud.], *Death in a Tenured Position* (New York: Dutton, 1981), 3. Subsequent references to this novel appear in parentheses in the text.

38. Sally R. Munt, *Murder by the Book: Feminism and the Crime Novel* (London: Routledge, 1994), has little patience for Kate's attitudes here: "Kate casts lesbian lifestyle as an exotic diversion to be indulged and tolerated, rather as one would a persistently yapping puppy." Munt sees this novel as "firmly maintaining bourgeois security" (36).

39. See Heilbrun, "Marriage Perceived," 112–33, and Carolyn G. Heilbrun, "Marriage and Contemporary Fiction," *Critical Inquiry* 5 (1978): 309–21. The latter article was revised as part of chapter 6, "Marriage and Family," in *Reinventing Womanhood.*

40. See Reddy, *Sisters in Crime,* "Some crime novels teach us how to read as women. . . . This is true of many of the Amanda Cross books, but most strikingly and effectively so in *Death in a Tenured Position*" (13).

41. See "Her Jewishness," in Robert Coles, *Simone Weil: A Modern Pilgrimage,* Radcliffe Biography Series (Reading MA: Addison-Wesley, 1987), 43–62.

42. Helena Michie, in "Murder in the Canon: The Dual Personality of Carolyn Heilbrun," *Massachusetts Studies in English* 9, no. 3 (1984), develops the theory that while Heilbrun as critic "focusses primarily on rereadings of the canon," as Cross she moves "away from the center of the canon" (2). Further, Michie argues that *Death in a Tenured Position* is a "deliberate investigation into the fatal consequences of a woman looking to the canon for guidance" (9); for the consequence of "the internalization of patriarchal values and patriarchal texts is moral, intellectual and political suicide" (10).

43. Carter, "Amanda Cross," puts this well: "The crime here is not the act of an individual driven by personal motives; it is the spiritual harm done by ingrained social attitudes that need to be changed" (294).

44. Marty S. Knepper in "Who Killed Janet Mandelbaum and India Wonder? A Look at the Suicides of the Token Women in Amanda Cross's *Death in a Tenured Position* and Dorothy Bryant's *Killing Wonder,*" *Clues* 13, no. 1 (1992), notes that "it is the limitations of the feminists, . . . not just the obvious problems with the patriarchy, and its fear of female power, that cause the tragic deaths of the token women" (57–58). Michie, "Murder in the Canon," also has an important discussion of Kate's complicity in the death (10).

45. Carter, "Amanda Cross," observes that Cross "has skillfully remolded the classical mystery form into a near perfect vehicle for her strong feminist vision" (292). In her witty essay, "Feminism Meets the Detective Novel," *Clues* 3, no. 2 (1982), Judith Wilt also considers the ways Heilbrun takes feminist liberties with the detective-story form (47–48).

46. Heilbrun, "Hers," 2.

47. Ibid., 2.

6. Stepping Out of the Circle

1. Susan Bolotin, "Voices from the Post-Feminist Generation," *NYT Magazine,* 17 Oct. 1982, 117.

2. Anne Taylor Fleming, "The American Wife," *NYT Magazine,* 26 Oct. 1986, 31, 39.

3. See Karen Greenspan, *The Timetables of Women's History* (Simon & Schuster, 1994), 393, 395, 397, 401; and *Feminist Chronicles 1953–1993,* ed. Toni Carabillo, Judith Meuli, and June Bundy Csida (Los Angeles: Women's Graphics, 1993), 108.

4. Vivian Gornick, "Who Says We Haven't Made A Revolution? A Feminist Takes Stock," *NYT Magazine*, 15 Apr. 1990, 27, 52.

5. *Feminist Chronicles*, ed. Carabillo et al., 118. Faludi, *Backlash*, 401.

6. The seven pro-choice Democrats were Barbara Mikulski, Maryland; Bob Graham, Florida; Wyche Fowler Jr., Georgia; Tom Daschle, South Dakota; Kent Conrad, North Dakota; Timothy Worth, Colorado; and Brock Adams, Washington. The pro-life Democrats elected were John Breaux, Louisiana; Harry Reid, Nevada; and Richard Shelby, Alabama. (Shelby switched to the Republican Party in 1994.)

7. Faludi, *Backlash*, 316.

8. Douglas, *Where the Girls Are*, 232–33, 222.

9. Faludi tells the story at length, *Backlash*, 378–88.

10. Miriam Schneir, "Andrea Dworkin," in *Feminism in Our Time: The Essential Writings, World War II to the Present*, ed. Miriam Schneir (New York: Vintage, 1994), 420–21.

11. In *The Education of a Woman: The Life of Gloria Steinem* (New York: Dial, 1995), 293, Carolyn Heilbrun writes about trashing in the feminist movement, quoting from "Trashing," an essay by "Joreen" [Jo Freeman], published in *Ms.*, Apr. 1976.

12. *Feminist Chronicles*, ed. Carabillo et al., 119.

13. A number of Columbia faculty and staff members reported to me that prolonged negotiations with Barnard caused the delay.

14. See, for example, Roberta M. Hall with Bernice R. Sandler, "The Classroom Climate: A Chilly One for Women?" Project on the Status and Education of Women, Association of American Colleges, Washington, D.C., 1982; and Bernice R. Sandler with Roberta M. Hall, "The Campus Climate Revisited: Chilly for Women Faculty, Administrators, and Graduate Students," Project on the Status and Education of Women, Association of American Colleges, Washington, D.C., 1986.

15. Interview with Catharine Stimpson, 1 Apr. 1996.

16. Paul Lauter, "Society and the Profession," 417.

17. Interview with Joel Conarroe, 21 Mar. 1996.

18. "1981 MLA Elections—Candidate Information," *PMLA* 96 (1981): 914.

19. See reports of meetings of the MLA Executive Council and the MLA Delegate Assembly in *PMLA* 98 (1983): 280; *PMLA* 99 (1984): 482; *PMLA* 98 (1983): 438; and *PMLA* 99 (1984): 264.

20. English Showalter, "Report of the Executive Director," *PMLA* 100 (1985): 359, 360. Interview with English Showalter, 16 Sept. 1996.

21. Interviews with Joel Conarroe, 21 Mar. 1996, and Phyllis Franklin, 19 Mar. 1996.

22. Carolyn G. Heilbrun [Amanda Cross, pseud.], *No Word from Winifred* (New York: Dutton, 1986), 94.

23. Heilbrun, introductory note to part 4, "Feminism and the Profession of Literature," in *Hamlet's Mother*, 174.

24. Heilbrun, "Presidential Address," 203.

25. I take the phrase from Heilbrun herself; in "The Politics of Mind: Women, Tradition, and the University," *Hamlet's Mother*, she says, "Women within the University need not only to pass from the margin to the center of intellectual life, they need help from the University in confronting the problems of being female in our culture, and especially in the culture of the University at this time" (221).

26. Heilbrun, introductory note to part 4, in *Hamlet's Mother*, 174. And see the letter from Evelyn Birge Vitz in "Forum," *PMLA* 101 (1986): 247–48.

27. Heilbrun, "Presidential Address," 205, 204.

28. Ibid., 202, 204.

29. See Heilbrun, "A Response to *Writing and Sexual Difference*," 291–97.

30. Heilbrun, "Presidential Address," 208.

31. Ibid., 211.

32. Heilbrun, foreword to *Poetics of Gender*, viii.

33. Carolyn Heilbrun kindly provided me with a copy of the original speech. In the published version, Heilbrun says, "often the most sophisticated male readers of cultural texts, even those who in their own work underscore the material and symbolic conditions that produce a politics of mind, resist the broader implications of feminist theory. Thus we discover these words from a prominent male scholar, my colleague, Edward Said: 'Nearly everyone producing literary or cultural studies makes no allowance for the truth that all intellectual or cultural work occurs somewhere, at some time, on some very precisely mapped-out and permissible terrain, which is ultimately contained by the State. Feminist critics have opened this question part of the way, but they have not gone the whole distance.' Women, it seems, are likely to be condemned both if they do go all the way, and if they don't" ("Politics of Mind," *Hamlet's Mother*, 215–16). In the speech, Heilbrun does not identify Said.

34. Heilbrun, "Politics of Mind," MS, 1, 2, Carolyn G. Heilbrun's personal papers.

35. Jessica Raimi, "Not Carved in Stone," *Columbia College Today* 17, no. 1 (1990): 15.

36. Lionel Trilling, "Mind in the Modern World," *The Last Decade: Essays and Reviews, 1965–1975*, ed. Diana Trilling (New York: Harcourt, Brace, Jovanovich, 1979), 105, 110, 117–18.

37. Heilbrun, "Politics of Mind," 213.

38. Ibid., 215.

39. Ibid., 214, 217, 216. Not included in the published version of the speech is the reference to the Columbia humanities course (Heilbrun, "Politics of Mind, MS, 9–10).

40. Heilbrun, "Politics of Mind," 221, 222.

41. Heilbrun, "Women's Biographies of Women," 343.

42. As Nancy K. Miller points out in her foreword to Heilbrun's *Hamlet's Mother*, "the margin of distance is always marked in Heilbrun's thinking"; while her many "visible signs of public recognition . . . make her seem an insider to the institution she addresses, her language and its resistance to the stereotypes of privilege and comfort keep alive the difference of view that defines the outsider" (xiii).

43. Heilbrun, "Presidential Address," 204, 206.

44. Carolyn G. Heilbrun [Amanda Cross, pseud.], *Sweet Death, Kind Death* (New York: Dutton, 1984; reprint, New York: Ballantine, 1985), 147 (citations are to the reprint edition).

45. Ibid., 174. Heilbrun acknowledges her own similar lack of nostalgia for the past in "Three Changes," "Hers" column, *NYT,* 19 Feb. 1981; reprinted in *The Norton Reader,* ed. Arthur M. Eastman et al., 6th ed. (New York: Norton, 1984), 425–27.

46. In *Writing a Woman's Life,* Heilbrun refers to black women writers but says that they are, for the most part, beyond the scope of her study (60–61, 74–75).

47. From *In the Last Analysis,* we learn that Kate Fansler met Reed Amhearst through her temporary involvement in reform politics, but there is no mention of marches or activism.

48. Carolyn G. Heilbrun [Amanda Cross, pseud.], *A Trap for Fools* (New York: Dutton, 1989), 93.

49. Ibid., 60.

50. Ibid., 57.

51. Heilbrun, *In the Last Analysis,* 35.

52. Heilbrun, *A Trap for Fools,* 144.

53. Ibid., 152, 30, 69, 82, 15.

54. Heilbrun, *Writing a Woman's Life,* 65.

55. Ibid., 50.

56. Ibid., 53.

57. Ibid., 31.

58. Ibid., 117, 48.

59. From a talk at Skidmore College, Saratoga Springs, NY, 30 Sept. 1992. This theme also emerges in several of her essays, for example, Cynthia Ozick, "Portrait of the Artist as a Bad Character," in *Metaphor and Memory: Essays* (New York: Vintage International, 1991), 97–100.

60. In a short story published at about this period, "Once upon a Time," *Ellery Queen's Mystery Magazine,* Aug. 1987, Heilbrun writes of "a gesture of love" offered by a female graduate student to a female associate professor. The professor, "rigid with terror," cannot respond (17).

61. Heilbrun, *No Word from Winifred,* 212.

62. Carolyn G. Heilbrun [Amanda Cross, pseud.], "Tania's No Where," in *Women of Mystery,* ed. Cynthia Manson (New York: Carroll & Graf, 1992), 108, 116.

63. Ibid., 116, 105, 115, 116.

64. Ibid., 116.

65. Carolyn G. Heilbrun [Amanda Cross, pseud.], "Murder without a Text," in *A Woman's Eye,* ed. Sara Paretsky (New York: Delacorte, 1991), 114–35.

66. This is precisely the point in yet another story about a disappearing woman, Carolyn G. Heilbrun [Amanda Cross, pseud.], "The Disappearance of Great Aunt Flavia," in *Reader, I Murdered Him: Original Crime Stories by Women,* ed. Jen Green (New York: St. Martin's, 1989). A middle-aged woman first disappears and then, because of her invisibility, is able to expose the hypocrisy of the corrupt Minister of the Divine Church of the Airwaves.

67. Heilbrun, *Writing a Woman's Life,* 130–31.

68. *Feminist Chronicles,* ed. Carabillo et al., 131.

69. Heilbrun, "The Politics of Mind," 222.

70. Heilbrun, *Writing A Woman's Life,* 114.

71. Ibid., 131.

72. Susan L. Clark, "Review of *No Word from Winifred,*" *Armchair Detective* 21, no. 1 (1988): 92.

73. Marina Angel, "Women in Legal Education: What It's Like To Be Part of a Perpetual First Wave or the Case of the Disappearing Woman," 61 *Temple Law Rev* 799 (1988).

74. Nancy K. Miller, "Representing Others: Gender and the Subjects of Autobiography," *Differences* 6, no. 1 (1994): 17.

75. The words are Adrienne Rich's from *What Is Found There: Notebooks on Poetry and Politics* (New York: Norton, 1993), 181; Rich's context is not feminism but "white hate crimes, white hate speech."

76. Heilbrun, *Writing a Woman's Life,* 120.

7. A Rhetoric of Risk

1. Carolyn G. Heilbrun [Amanda Cross, pseud.], *An Imperfect Spy* (New York: Ballantine, 1995), 13.

2. Anne Matthews, "Rage in a Tenured Position," *NYT Magazine,* 8 Nov. 1992, 72.

3. Heilbrun, *The Players Come Again,* 228, 116. In "Second Chances: Amanda Cross's Dorinda," *The Ellen Glasgow Newsletter* 28 (spring 1992), Pamela R. Matthews notes the source for Dorinda in Ellen Glasgow's *Barren Ground* and argues that Glasgow, Glasgow's Dorinda, and the women characters in *The Players Come Again,* "become part of a web of female connection that questions a patriarchal status quo and reinterprets the past in order to re-imagine a present and future in which women occupy central rather than peripheral positions" (3).

4. Sandra M. Gilbert, "'That Great Sanity, That Sun, the Feminine Power': May Sarton and the (New) Female Poetic Tradition," in *A Celebration for May Sarton: Essays,* ed. Constance Hunting (Orono ME: Puckerbrush Press, 1994), 272–73.

5. Carolyn G. Heilbrun, "Virginia Woolf and James Joyce," in *Hamlet's Mother,* 74, 60, 66.

6. Carolyn G. Heilbrun, "Sacrificed to Art," review of *Nora: The Real Life of Molly Bloom* by Brenda Maddox, *Women's Review of Books,* Sept. 1988, 5. Heilbrun, "Virginia Woolf and James Joyce," 65, 73.

7. Heilbrun, "Virginia Woolf and James Joyce, 71."

8. Carolyn Heilbrun mentions all these sources, except for the Maddox biography (which she implicitly intends us to see as a source), in *The Players Come Again.*

9. According to Brenda Maddox, *Nora: The Real Life of Molly Bloom* (Boston: Houghton Mifflin, 1988), 330, Nora provided Joyce with the language and experience on which he could build the characters of Molly and Anna Livia Plurabelle.

10. Ibid., 294.

11. Heilbrun, "Sacrificed to Art," 5.

12. Heilbrun, *The Players Come Again,* 215.

13. Heilbrun, "Virginia Woolf and James Joyce," 67, 69.

14. Heilbrun, *The Players Come Again,* 208, 216.

15. Ibid., 159.

16. Carolyn G. Heilbrun, "*To the Lighthouse:* The New Story of Mother and Daughter," in *Hamlet's Mother,* 135, 137, 138. Carolyn G. Heilbrun, "Method in Madness," *Opera News,* 22 Jan. 1994, 19, 45.

17. Heilbrun, *Reinventing Womanhood,* 160.

18. Heilbrun, *Writing a Woman's Life,* 131.

19. Carolyn G. Heilbrun, "Meet Richard III, a Contemporary in All That's Evil," *NYT,* 12 Aug. 1990, sec. 2, 6. A fistful of letters attacked her "one-dimensional feminist reading" of the play, "Letters," *NYT,* 2 Sept. 1990, sec. 2, 3, 9.

20. See, for example, Nancy K. Miller, "Representing Others," 1–27.

21. Karen Lehrman, "Off Course," *Mother Jones,* Sept./Oct. 1993; see, especially, Elizabeth Fox Genovese's letter to the editor in response to Lehrman's article, *Mother Jones,* Nov./Dec. 1993, 7.

22. Daphne Patai and Noretta Koertge, *Professing Feminism: Cautionary Tales from the Strange World of Women's Studies* (New York, Basic, 1994), xviii–xix.

23. Christina Hoff Sommers, *Who Stole Feminism: How Women Have Betrayed Women* (New York: Simon & Schuster, 1994), 16.

24. Helen Vendler, "Feminism and Literature," *New York Review of Books,* 31 May 1990, 23.

25. See "A Man's Woman," Heilbrun's review of *Writing Dangerously: Mary McCarthy and Her World* by Carol Brightman, *Women's Review of Books,* Feb. 1993, 17, 18, and the letters in *Women's Review of Books,* Mar. 1993, 5, and Apr. 1993, 4; and also "Exceptions and Rules," Heilbrun's review of several biographies, including *Alva Myrdal: A Daughter's Memoir,* by Sissela Bok, *Women's Review of Books,* Nov. 1991, 16, and the letters in *Women's Review of Books,* Mar. 1992, 4–5.

26. Carolyn G. Heilbrun, "The Thomas Confirmation Hearings or How Being a Humanist Prepares You for Right-Wing Politics," 65 *Southern California Law Rev* 1569, 1569 (1992).

27. Heilbrun, *Writing a Woman's Life,* 131.

28. Carolyn G. Heilbrun, afterword to *Changing Subjects,* 271.

29. Greg Johnson, in the *Atlanta Journal-Constitution,* 1 Oct. 1995, deplores the "sketchy portrayal of [Steinem's] character and personality" (10); Alice Echols in *Newsday,* 10 Sept. 1995, sums up the biography as "hagiography" (46); and Wendy Kaminer in the *NYT Book Review,* 10 Sept. 1995, declares that "Heilbrun describes her subject as godlike . . . she is consistently apologetic about whatever might be perceived by feminists as Ms. Steinem's shortcomings" (36).

30. Heilbrun, *The Education of a Woman,* 408.

31. Ibid., 382, 396.

32. Patricia Holt, *San Francisco Chronicle Book Review,* 24 Sept. 1995, makes a similar point: "The details are fascinating enough, but even better is the way Heilbrun cuts into the narrative from time to time to ponder the larger picture" (6).

33. Heilbrun, afterword to *Changing Subjects,* 270; Mark Lussier and Peggy McCormack, "Heilbrun: An Interview," *New Orleans Review* 13, no. 4 (1986): 71.

34. Scott Heller, "A Leading Feminist Literary Critic Quits Post at Columbia, Citing 'Impossible' Atmosphere," *Chronicle of Higher Education,* 20 May 1992, A13.

35. See, especially, A. Matthews, "Rage in a Tenured Position," and Kay Mills, "Life after a Tenured Position," *Los Angeles Times Magazine,* 19 July 1992.

36. I have constructed the following narrative from conversations with Carolyn Heilbrun; Betty Jemmott, former Secretary of Columbia University; Joan Ferrante, David Kastan, Steven Marcus, Robert Hanning, and Jean Franco, all faculty members at Columbia; and Susan Heath, Susan Nerheim, and Margaret Vandenburg, all former or present graduate students at Columbia. It is likely that no one of them would agree with everything I say here.

37. Rachel Blau DuPlessis, "Reader, I Married Me: A Polygynous Memoir," in *Changing Subjects,* 100, 109.

38. Heilbrun, afterword to *Changing Subjects,* 269.

39. Interview with Barbara Christian, 18 Sept. 1996.

40. Erica Jong, letter to the editor, *NYT Magazine,* 29 Nov. 1992, 12.

41. Nancy K. Miller, "Decades," in *Changing Subjects,* 40.

42. Heilbrun, *Reinventing Womanhood,* 61.

43. Interview with Victoria Rosner, 6 Aug. 1996.

44. During the course of writing this book, I spoke with the following former and present graduate students at Columbia University: Alicia Carroll, Susan Fraiman, Jonathan Gill, Beth Harrison, Susan Heath, Susan Nerheim, Victoria Rosner, Miranda Sherwin, and Margaret Vandenburg.

45. Heilbrun, *The Theban Mysteries,* 24.

46. Interview with Miranda Sherwin, 8 Aug. 1996.

47. Interviews with Susan Heath, 9 Mar. 1996; Judith Resnik, 22 Apr. 1996.

48. Interviews with Miranda Sherwin, 8 Aug. 1996; Jonathan Gill, 29 Aug. 1996.

49. Interviews with Margaret Vandenburg, 14 Mar. 1996; Jonathan Gill, 29 Aug. 1996.

50. Interviews with Susan Heath, 9 Mar. 1996; Susan Nerheim, 13 Mar. 1996.

51. Interview with Catharine Stimpson, 27 Mar. 1996.

52. Interview with Nancy K. Miller, 12 May 1996; Carolyn G. Heilbrun, "Bringing the Spirit Back to English Studies," *Hamlet's Mother,* 180.

53. Interview with Susan Fraiman, 26 Sept. 1996.

54. The phrase is from Heilbrun's "Bringing the Spirit Back to English Studies," 175–83.

55. Carolyn G. Heilbrun and Judith Resnik, "Convergences: Law, Literature, and Feminism," 99 *Yale Law Journal* 913, 1920, 1920–21 (1990).

56. Interview with Judith Resnik, 22 Apr. 1996.

57. Heilbrun, *An Imperfect Spy,* 187, 188.

58. Heilbrun and Resnik, "Convergences," 1921, 1922, 1923.

59. Gail B. Griffin, *Calling: Essays on Teaching in the Mother Tongue* (Pasadena CA: Trilogy, 1992), 35–36.

60. Heilbrun and Resnik, "Convergences," 1923.

61. Trisha Yarbrough, "The Achievement of Amanda Cross," makes the valuable point that in Cross's novels, "the woman victim has become more powerful and independent, as Cross explores the nature of the threat to men posed by women, first by their biological identity, later by their identity as rival workers" (102).

62. Interviews with Sandra M. Gilbert, 20 Sept. 1996; Susan Gubar, 5 Sept. 1996.

63. Letter, Rachel Blau DuPlessis to the author, 24 Sept. 1996.

64. Interview with Catharine Stimpson, 27 Mar. 1996.

65. Cathy N. Davidson, "Androgyny," in *The Oxford Companion to Women's Writing in the United States,* ed. Cathy N. Davidson and Linda Wagner-Martin (Oxford: Oxford Univ. Press, 1995), 50–51.

66. See Phyllis Rose, "Shall We Dance? Confessions of a Fag Hag," in *Between Friends,* ed. Mickey Pearlman (Boston: Houghton Mifflin, 1994), where Rose recalls dismissing Heilbrun's androgyny theory at first, but then reconsidering the notion in the light of her friendship with a man who "represented something new—not just in my life, but within the range of possibilities for masculine life in America" (208).

67. Interviews with Nancy K. Miller, 2 Aug. 1996; Sandra M. Gilbert, 23 Sept. 1996.

68. Maureen T. Reddy, "The Feminist Counter-Tradition in Crime: Cross, Grafton, Paretsky, and Wilson," *The Cunning Craft: Original Essays on Detective Fiction and Contemporary Literary Theory,* ed. Ronald G. Walker and June M. Frazer (Macomb IL: Yeast Printing, 1990). Reddy argues that "feminist crime novels are best understood as constituting a new genre, less part of an existing tradition than a distinct counter-tradition" (174).

69. Carolyn G. Heilbrun, "Keynote Address: Gender and Detective Fiction," in *The Sleuth and the Scholar: Origins, Evolution, and Current Trends in Detective Fiction,* ed. Barbara A. Rader and Howard G. Zettler (New York: Greenwood, 1988), 7.

70. Heilbrun, *Writing a Woman's Life,* 12–13.

71. Heilbrun and Stimpson, "Theories of Feminist Criticism," 72.

72. Carolyn G. Heilbrun, "Men over Forty, Women under Forty," *Chronicle of Higher Education,* 15 Nov. 1976, 32.

73. Ibid., 32.

74. Heilbrun, *Writing a Woman's Life,* 130; Heilbrun, *James Joyce Murder,* 160. Heilbrun herself "keep[s] going"; she is presently completing a book to be titled *The Last Gift of Time.* I have not seen this manuscript, but it promises to offer new insights into women and aging.

Epilogue

1. See Carolyn G. Heilbrun, "Guest Column: From Rereading to Reading," *PMLA* 119 (2004): 211–17.

2. For an account of this last walk with Mary Ann Caws, see Vanessa Grigoriadis, "A Death of One's Own," *New York Magazine*, 8 Dec. 2003, 40–42.

3. Carolyn G. Heilbrun, "My Isherwood, My Bachardy," in *The Isherwood Century: Essays on the Life and Work of Christopher Isherwood*, ed. James J. Berg and Chris Freeman (Madison: Univ. of Wisconsin Press, 2000), 74.

4. Carolyn G. Heilbrun, *The Last Gift of Time: Life Beyond Sixty* (New York: Dial Press, 1997), 7, 210.

5. Ibid., 10.

6. The autopsy recorded the official date of death as 9 October 2003, but it is possible that Carolyn died on 8 October .

7. Heilbrun, *Reinventing Womanhood*, 57, 58, 53.

8. Heilbrun, *The Last Gift of Time*, 201.

9. In *The Last Gift of Time*, Carolyn explains, "My avoidance of therapy is . . . a generational one: in my young adult days, had there been therapists sympathetic to feminism and with genuine, post-Freudian understanding of the conflicts in women's lives, I could certainly have consulted one" (121–22). However, in conversation with me, she always dismissed psychoanalysis.

10. Ibid., 184, 187.

11. Heilbrun, "My Isherwood, My Bachardy," 71, 72, 74.

12. Heilbrun, *Reinventing Womanhood*, 55, 57.

13. Heilbrun, "My Isherwood, My Bachardy," 73.

14. Heilbrun, *Reinventing Womanhood*, 126.

15. Heilbrun, "My Isherwood, My Bachardy," 74.

16. Ibid., 75. See also my earlier discussion of the angst revealed in Carolyn's "Hers" column published in 1981, 119–20, 121, 147.

17. Heilbrun, *Sweet Death, Kind Death*, 16, 23, 41, 4–5, 8.

18. Carolyn G. Heilbrun [Amanda Cross, pseud.], *The Puzzled Heart* (New York: Ballantine, 1998), 175.

19. Carolyn G. Heilbrun, "Taking a U-turn: The Aging Woman as Explorer of New Territory," *Women's Review of Books*, July 2003, 18, 19.

20. Carolyn had written often of men as models for women; see especially *Reinventing Womanhood* and *When Men Were the Only Models We Had: My Teachers Barzun, Fadiman, Trilling* (Philadelphia: Univ. of Pennsylvania Press, 2002).

21. Heilbrun, "Taking a U-turn," 19, 18.

22. Susan Kress, in "Forum Responses to Carolyn G. Heilbrun's Guest Column," *PMLA* 119 (2004): 331–32. Eighteen other colleagues, former students, and literary critics also wrote responses to this column.

23. For more on the *Rubáiyát*, see ibid., 331–32.

24. See the epigraph to Carolyn G. Heilbrun [Amanda Cross, pseud.], *Honest Doubt* (New York: Ballantine, 2000).

25. Heilbrun, "Taking a U-turn," 19.

26. Heilbrun, *A Trap for Fools*, 152.

27. Heilbrun, *Writing a Woman's Life*, 122.

28. Ibid., 11.

29. Ibid., 120.

30. Carolyn G. Heilbrun [Amanda Cross, pseud.], *The Collected Stories* (New York: Ballantine, 1997), 1. It is worth noting that when the story was originally published in *Ellery Queen's Mystery Magazine* and then reprinted in *Women of Mystery*, ed. Cynthia Manson (New York: Carroll & Graf, 1992), the title was "Tania's No Where." In *The Collected Stories*, from which I quote in this chapter, the title has been collapsed to two words.

31. "The Mysterious Life of Kate Fansler," an earlier version of this meditation on "Tania's Nowhere," can be found in *Tulsa Studies in Women's Literature* 24, no. 2 (fall 2005). I am grateful for permission to reprint here.

32. See as well the earlier discussion of this story, 170–72.

33. Heilbrun, *The Collected Stories*, 1.

34. Heilbrun, "Tania's Nowhere" (1987; reprinted in *The Collected Stories*), 15, 24 (citations are to the reprint edition).

35. See 180, 194.

36. Heilbrun, "Tania's Nowhere," 23, 24.

37. Ibid., 6–7, 24.

38. Heilbrun, *Writing a Woman's Life*, 120–21.

39. Nathaniel Hawthorne, "Wakefield" (1835; reprinted in *Twice-Told Tales*, London: Dent, 1961), 96, 99 (citations are to the reprint edition).

40. Ibid., 99.

41. Quoted in Daniel Mendelsohn, "Not Afraid of Virginia Woolf," review of *The Hours*, a film directed by Stephen Daldry based on the novel by Michael Cunningham, with a screenplay by David Hare, *New York Review of Books*, 13 Mar. 2003, 18.

42. Heilbrun, "Tania's Nowhere," 23, 11.

43. Ibid., 22–23.

44. Bill Peschel, "Annotating Wimsey," *Unnatural Death:* www.planet peschel.com/Sayers/Unnatural/unnatural1.htm, accessed Nov. 2004.

45. Dorothy L. Sayers, *Unnatural Death* (1927; reprint, New York: HarperPaperbacks, 1995), 3. The quotation is from the epigraph to chapter 1 (citation is to the reprint edition).

46. Heilbrun, *The Last Gift of Time*, 207.

47. Emily Dickinson, Poem #712 (1890; reprinted in *The Complete Poems of Emily Dickinson,* ed. Thomas H. Johnson, Boston: Little, Brown, 1960), 350 (this and subsequent citations are to the reprint edition).

48. I refer, of course, to Doris Lessing's "To Room Nineteen," in which the protagonist, Susan Rawlings, slowly withdraws from the life of her family and eventually commits suicide—and to Virginia Woolf's *A Room of One's Own.*

49. Sylvia Plath, "Tulips" (1961; reprinted in *The Collected Poems,* ed. Ted Hughes, New York: HarperPerennial, 1992), 160 (citation is to the reprint edition).

50. Quoted in Heilbrun, *The Last Gift of Time*, 210–11.

51. Heilbrun, "Tania's Nowhere," 24.

52. Heilbrun, *The Last Gift of Time*, 14, 16–17.

53. Heilbrun, *No Word from Winifred*, 33.

54. Ibid., 34.

55. Heilbrun, *The Last Gift of Time*, 19.

56. See Heilbrun's *Honest Doubt*, 113–22.

57. Ibid., 116, 115.

58. Heilbrun, *The Last Gift of Time*, 22, 23.

59. See also Katha Pollitt, "Choosing Death," *NYT Magazine,* 28 Dec. 2003, 30. Pollitt observes that perhaps "[the paring down of Heilbrun's life] led to a room that was too empty."

60. Heilbrun, *The Last Gift of Time*, 16, 17.

61. Quoted in ibid., 11.

62. Heilbrun, *Sweet Death, Kind Death*, 87.

63. Earlier in this book (208), I noted that Carolyn had indicated that her decision to live more deliberately had dated from her fifties. Later, it became clear that her earlier experience with cancer had precipitated that decision.

64. Heilbrun, *Sweet Death, Kind Death*, 12.

65. Heilbrun, *The Last Gift of Time*, 34–35.

66. Heilbrun, *Sweet Death, Kind Death*, 171.

67. Heilbrun, "Tania's Nowhere," 23.

68. Heilbrun, *Sweet Death, Kind Death*, 95.

69. See Jeffrey Berman's insightful account of "suicide's shattering aftermath," especially in his discussion of Anne Sexton's "Sylvia's Death," in *Surviving Literary Suicide* (Amherst: Univ. of Massachusetts Press, 1999), 191.

70. Heilbrun, *Sweet Death, Kind Death,* 25.

71. Heilbrun, *The Last Gift of Time,* 10.

72. Carol Lee Flinders, *At the Root of This Longing: Reconciling a Spiritual Hunger and a Feminist Thirst* (New York: HarperSanFrancisco, 1998), 146.

Books by Carolyn G. Heilbrun

The Garnett Family. New York: Macmillan, 1961.

Christopher Isherwood. New York: Columbia Univ. Press, 1970.

Toward a Recognition of Androgyny. New York: Knopf, 1973.

Lady Ottoline's Album. Ed. Carolyn G. Heilbrun. New York: Knopf, 1976.

Reinventing Womanhood. New York: Norton, 1979.

The Representation of Women in Fiction: Selected Papers from the English Institute, 1981. Ed. Carolyn G. Heilbrun and Margaret R. Higgonet. Baltimore: Johns Hopkins Univ. Press, 1983.

Writing a Woman's Life. New York: Norton, 1988.

Hamlet's Mother and Other Women. New York: Columbia Univ. Press, 1990.

The Education of a Woman: The Life of Gloria Steinem. New York: Dial, 1995.

The Last Gift of Time: Life beyond Sixty. New York: Dial, 1997.

Women's Lives: The View from the Threshold. Toronto: Univ. of Toronto Press, 1999.

When Men Were the Only Models We Had: My Teachers Barzun, Fadiman, Trilling. Philadelphia: Univ. of Pennsylvania Press, 2002.

As Amanda Cross

In the Last Analysis. New York: Macmillan, 1964.

The James Joyce Murder. New York: Macmillan, 1967.

Poetic Justice. New York: Knopf, 1970.

The Theban Mysteries. New York: Knopf, 1971.

The Question of Max. New York: Knopf, 1976.

Death in a Tenured Position. New York: Dutton, 1981.

Sweet Death, Kind Death. New York: Dutton, 1984.

No Word from Winifred. New York: Dutton, 1986.

A Trap for Fools. New York: Dutton, 1989.

The Players Come Again. New York: Random House, 1990.

An Imperfect Spy. New York: Ballantine, 1995.

The Collected Stories. New York: Ballantine, 1997.

The Puzzled Heart. New York: Ballantine, 1998.

Honest Doubt. New York: Ballantine, 2000.

The Edge of Doom. New York: Ballantine, 2002.

Index

Page numbers in italics refer to illustrations.

Index

Bennett, William, 156, 161
Berman, Jeffrey, 274 n.68
biography, and Heilbrun, 1–2, 4–5, 36, 154, 165, 166, 192
biography, intellectual. *See* intellectual biography
Birch Wathen School, 13
Bird's Nest, The (Jackson), 79
Birkle, Carmen, 252 n.30, 260 n.89
blacks. *See* African Americans
Bloom, Alexander, 245 n.64
Bloom, Allan, 41–42
"Bloomsbury Group, The" (Heilbrun), 70
"Body Politic, The" (junior show), 19–20
Bok, Sissela, 188–89
Bork, Robert, 151
Boston, Massachusetts, anti-Semitism in, 33
Brabazon, James, 111, 166
Brando, Marlon, 41
Brée, Germaine, 88
"Brief Encounter" (Emerson), 30
Brightman, Carol, 188
Brittain, Vera, 169
Brooklyn College, 45, 48
Brown, Laura Hotchkiss, 160
Brownmiller, Susan, 127–28, 152
Brown v. Board of Education (legal case), 41
Buckley, Jerome, 48
Bunting, Mary, 66
Burroughs, William, 42

"Cacky." *See* Heilbrun, Carolyn G.
Campbell, Joseph, 183
Cantwell, Mary, 259 n.76
Carter, Steven, 253 n.39, 255 n.8, 263 n.43, 263 n.45
Caws, Mary Ann, 216, 272 n.2
Cerf, Bennett, 183
Changing Subjects (G. Greene and Kahn, eds.), 195
"Changing Years, The" (Batchelder), 30
"Character of Hamlet's Mother, The" (Heilbrun): feminism in, 62–63; Gertrude in, 62–63, 64, 76; publication of, 59–60
Cheney, Lynne, 189

Chesler, Phyllis, 86–87
Chodorow, Nancy, 130
Christian, Barbara, 198
Christopher Isherwood (Heilbrun), 93
Church and the Second Sex, The (Daly), 86
Civil Rights Act of 1964, 68
Clark, Susan L., 175
Closing of the American Mind, The (Allan Bloom), 41–42
Cold War, 44
Collected Stories, The (Cross), 226
Color Purple, The (Walker), 169
Columbia College, 45–46. *See also* Columbia University
Columbia University: African Americans at, 44, 198; anti-Semitism at, 33; bureaucracy of, 198; and communism, 44; discrimination at, 44; and Dulles, 46; and DuPlessis, 198; Eisenhower at, 44; exclusion and inclusion at, 44–45; and Fast, 44; and feminists and feminism, 198, 199, 200; and Heilbrun, 4, 7, 43–44, 45, 82–83, 146, 181, 194, 196–202, 236; and HEW, 91–92; Kirk at, 44; Klingenstein on, 44; Magid on, 49–50; Marcus on, 45; Miller on, 112; Mills at, 44; organization of, 44–45; secrecy at, 198; student concerns at, 44; student uprising at, 81, 82; suspicion and distrust at, 198; tenure at, 198, 199; and L. Trilling, 44, 50–51; Van Doren at, 44; and women, 45–46, 50, 153, 198. *See also* Commission on the Status of Women; School of General Studies
Columbia Women's Liberation, 91
comedies of manners, defined, 72
Commission on the Status of Women: formation of, 91–92, 199; and Heilbrun, 93. *See also* Columbia University
Commission on the Status of Women in the Profession, 89–90. *See also* Modern Language Association (MLA)
Common Sense (magazine), 24
communism, and Columbia University, 44

Index

Education of a Woman, The (cont.)
to, 189; purposes of, 191–92; risks
in, 191; women's work in, 190
EEOC, 151–52
Eisenhower, Dwight D., 44
Eisenstein, Hester, 258 n.70
Ellmann, Mary, 104, 211
"Emma and the Legend of Jane
Austen" (L. Trilling), 99–100
Ephron, Nora, 23–24
Equal Employment Opportunity
Commission (EEOC), 151–52
Equal Rights Amendment (ERA),
150–51
Evans, Sir Arthur, 183

Faludi, Susan, 151, 260 n.1, 261 n.18,
264 n.9
Fansler, Kate: affairs of, 139, 208;
and Amhearst, 74, 84, 85,
208, 253 n.38; anger of, 139;
characteristics of, 5, 73–74, 75,
107–8; childlessness of, 62, 79;
and civilization, 107–8; and civil
rights march, 163; class status of,
73; on Columbia University student
uprising, 254 n.2; conventionality
of, 75, 76–77, 83–84, 111, 144;
on English novel, 184; as fantasy
figure, 73–74; and feminists and
feminism, 74, 75, 77, 112; and
Heilbrun, 5, 73, 223, 253 n.33;
heterosexuality of, 137, 138–39,
140; on the hidden story, 224;
and historical movements, 5;
as interstitial person, 139, 140;
isolation and loneliness of, 74, 138,
140, 141, 253 n.36; on lesbianism,
137, 138–39; as mediator, 140–41,
143–44; Munt on, 262 n.38; on
nostalgia, 180; and purposelessness,
223; as outsider, 137, 144; physical
appearance of, 208; radicalization
of, 135, 163, 266 n.47; and
relationship to Heilbrun, 224, 226;
self-definition of, 137; as WASP,
31, 73; on women's colleges, 162.
See also Cross, Amanda; Death in a
Tenured Position (Cross); Heilbrun,
Carolyn G.; Imperfect Spy, An
(Cross); In the Last Analysis
(Cross); James Joyce Murder, The

(Cross); No Word from Winifred
(Cross); Players Come Again, The
(Cross); Poetic Justice (Cross);
Puzzled Heart, The (Cross);
Question of Max, The (Cross);
Sweet Death, Kind Death (Cross);
Theban Mysteries, The (Cross);
Trap for Fools, A (Cross)
Fansler, Leighton, 225, 226, 227, 228,
231
Fast, Howard, 44
Female Imagination, The (Spacks), 127
feminazis, 188
Feminine Mystique, The (Friedan):
discontent in, 64; discrimination in,
68; feminism in, 43; forfeited selves
in, 4; motherhood in, 61
"Feminism Meets the Detective Novel"
(Wilt), 263 n.45
"Feminist Counter-Tradition in Crime,
The" (Reddy), 271 n.68
"Feminist Criticism in the Wilderness"
(Elaine Showalter), 126–27
"Feminist Murder" (Roberts), 97, 257
n.45
Feminist Press, 89, 91
Feminists, 85
feminists and feminism: and academy,
4, 153; achievements of, 87, 149–
50; and assimilation, 37; backlash
against, 173–74, 187–88, 200; and
Columbia University, 198, 199, 200;
and consciousness-raising groups,
85; directionlessness of, 87, 148–49,
150, 151–52, 173; and Heilbrun, 7,
20, 37, 38, 95, 105, 106, 111–12,
145, 154, 157–59, 166, 189,
209–10, 214; history of, 63–64,
123–26; and Jewishness, 37; Miller
on, 200; negative images of, 23;
and Radcliffe College, 20; radical
groups of, 85–86; retrospective view
of, 3–4; Rich on, 43; and Smith
College, 20; and Steinem, 153;
and theory, 126–27; and Wellesley
College, 17–18, 19–20, 23–24; in
Wellesley College News, 15; in WE
of Wellesley, 15. See also marriage;
"schizophrenia"
Feminist Studies (journal), 91
Ferguson, Ann, 260 n.6
Ferrante, Joan, 93, 199, 201, 250 n.47